The
Young Oxford Companion
to the

CONGRESS

OF THE UNITED STATES

SECTION THROUGH DOME OF U.S. CAPITOL

The
Young Oxford Companion
to the
CONGRESS
OF THE UNITED STATES

Donald A. Ritchie

Oxford University Press
New York

Oxford University Press

Oxford New York Toronto
Delhi Bombay Calcutta Madras Karachi
Kuala Lumpur Singapore Hong Kong Tokyo
Nairobi Dar es Salaam Cape Town
Melbourne Auckland Madrid

and associated companies in

Berlin Ibadan

Published by Oxford University Press, Inc.,
200 Madison Avenue, New York, New York 10016

Oxford is a registered trademark of Oxford University Press

Library of Congress Cataloging-in-Publication Data

Ritchie, Donald A.
The young Oxford companion to the Congress of the United States / Donald A. Ritchie.
p. cm.
Includes bibliographical references and index.
Summary: An encyclopedic guide to the United States Congress, with articles focusing on key
concepts, personalities, and events.
 ISBN 0-19-507777-6
 1. United States. Congress—Encyclopedias, Juvenile. [1. United States. Congress-Encyclope-
dias.] I. Title.
JK1067.R58   1993
328.73'003—dc20
93-6466
CIP
AC

9 8 7 6 5 4 3 2 1

Printed in the United States of America
on acid-free paper

On the cover: *(top left) Henry Clay addressing the Senate, 1850; (top right) Senators Howard Baker and Sam Ervin at the Watergate hearings, 1973; (bottom) the U.S. Capitol, 1866*

Frontispiece: *Design for the Capitol dome, 1859. It took almost 9 million pounds of cast iron to build the dome.*

CONTENTS

PREFACE

Like countless others, I first visited Capitol Hill while a junior high school student, during a spring vacation in 1958. Because Congress was in recess then, I did not see it in session until I returned as a graduate student 10 years later. My most vivid memory of that occasion was the empty desk of Senator Robert F. Kennedy (Democrat–New York), who had been assassinated just days earlier. Pages had stacked every other desk with copies of the bills being debated that day. On Kennedy's desk lay a single red rose that Senator Margaret Chase Smith (Republican–Maine) had placed there in his memory. A few years after that, I stood in the long lines waiting for a chance to hear John Dean testify before the Senate select committee investigating the Watergate scandal and later to watch the House Judiciary Committee deliberate whether to recommend the impeachment of President Richard Nixon.

In 1976 I joined the staff of the Senate Historical Office, where I have been privileged to witness Congress firsthand, once even testifying before a Senate committee. From this vantage, I have watched a procession of senators and representatives appear on the legislative stage to debate critical issues, enact legislation, confirm nominations, and consent to treaties of great consequence to every citizen. I have found Congress a fascinating, ever-changing institution. At the same time, Congress has been the subject of much public criticism, perhaps never more negatively than during the 102nd Congress, while I compiled this book. Senate majority leader George J. Mitchell (Democrat–Maine) sought to explain this public dissatisfaction when he commented: "Congress is not now, has never been, and will never be a beloved institution in American life. It does not speak with a single voice. Like our democracy itself, it reflects a diversity of demands, ambitions, hopes, fears, and frustrations." Similarly, House minority leader Bob Michel (Republican–Illinois) called Congress "a story of fallible human beings freely chosen by free people, trying to make representative government work. Sometimes we are up to the task, and sometimes we fall short, but we at least know we are part of something that is much greater than we are, this institution. Such a thought gives us hope and a sense of renewal."

In that spirit, the entries in this book seek to examine Congress objectively, offering critical analysis and observations laced with humor rather than cynicism. These entries will introduce the reader to the people, events, procedures, and peculiar language of Congress and explain some of the behavior you may see in the televised debates of the Senate and House of Representatives. These brief entries may answer your questions or lead you on to further study through the suggested additional readings. In addition to the references to books and articles that follow many of the entries, a general bibliography at the end of the book will provide tips on conducting research on the legislative branch. I hope that this book will stimulate interest among readers who will be future congressional visitors and voters—and perhaps future senators and representatives as well.

HOW TO USE THIS BOOK

The articles in this *Companion* are arranged alphabetically, so you can look up words, concepts, or names as you come across them in other readings. You can then use the SEE ALSO listings at the end of an article to find entries about related subjects. Sometimes you may find that the *Companion* deals with information under a different article name than what you looked up. The book will then refer you to the proper article. For example, if you look up Appointments, you will find the notation "SEE Nominations, confirmation of." If you cannot find an article on a particular subject, look in the index, which will guide you to the relevant articles. All people are listed alphabetically by last name; for example, the entry for Shirley Chisholm is listed as Chisholm, Shirley under C.

You can also use this *Companion* topically, by reading all the articles about a particular aspect of the Congress. Below are several groupings of topics around common themes.

Notable members of Congress: If you want to know about a particular senator or representative, look the person up by his or her surname. Huey Long is listed alphabetically as Long, Huey P. This book contains 62 articles about specific members of Congress, past and present. Many of the leaders of both houses and others who personified important eras in congressional history are included. There are also topical articles on particular groups of members in Congress, such as African Americans, Asian Americans, Hispanic Americans, Native Americans, and women. Brief biographies of the nearly 12,000 people who have served over the past 200 years can be found in the *Biographical Directory of the United States Congress, 1774–1989* (Washington, D.C.: Government Printing Office, 1989).

Powers: To learn about the constitutional powers of Congress, you can look up Advice and consent, Investigations, or Treaties, for example.

Elections and succession: A number of articles deal with congressional elections, including Campaign financing, Incumbents, and Term limits.

Congressional agencies and staff: If you want to know about the staff agencies and officials who help the Congress perform its functions, you might look up Bill clerks, Congressional Budget Office, or Parliamentarian.

Leadership of Congress: Information about House and Senate leaders can be found, for example, in the entries on Floor managers, Leadership, or Whip.

Procedures: You can read about the process by which legislation is drafted, debated, and voted on in entries on Acts, Committees, Hearings, and Resolutions, among others.

Traditions: Congress is home to many long-standing traditions. You can look up Bean soup, Senatorial courtesy, or Snuff, for example.

Capitol Building: If you visit the Capitol or want to learn more about the place where members of Congress work, you could look up Architect of the Capitol, Cloakrooms, or Subways.

Relations with the President: The fascinating relationship between Congress and the executive branch is discussed under Bipartisan foreign policy, Executive privilege, and Separation of powers, for example.

Notable events and legislation: To read about important events in congressional history and about particular laws enacted by Congress, you might consult Impeachment of Andrew Johnson (1868), Treaty of Versailles, or Watergate investigation (1973).

Information about Congress: Congressional publications as well as members of the news media provide regular sources of information about Congress. Some of the entries discussing these sources are Congressional Record, C-SPAN, and Media coverage of Congress.

Further Reading: If you want to know more about a specific topic, you can use the FURTHER READING entries at the end of each article as well as the Further Reading guide at the end of the book, which lists more general sources.

Acts

AN ACT of Congress is a bill that has passed both the House and Senate and has been signed by the President or passed by a two-thirds vote of both houses over the President's veto. Each act of Congress is numbered as a public law or private law. PL 103-35 would be the 35th public law enacted by the 103rd Congress. Private laws are numbered separately, from Private Law 103-1 on up.

SEE ALSO
Bills; Private laws

The Kansas-Nebraska Act as submitted to Congress on December 5, 1853.

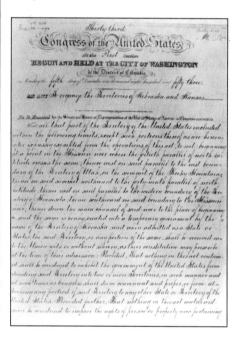

Adams, John Quincy

☆ *Born: July 11, 1767, Braintree, Mass.*
☆ *Political party: Federalist, Whig*
☆ *Senator from Massachusetts: 1803–08*
☆ *President: 1825–29*
☆ *Representative from Massachusetts: 1831–48*
☆ *Died: Feb. 23, 1848, Washington, D.C.*

HE HAD already been a senator, secretary of state, and President of the United States, but John Quincy Adams said of his election to the House of Representatives in 1830, "No election or appointment conferred upon me ever gave me so much pleasure." After Adams was defeated for reelection as President, people wondered why he did not retire from public life. Instead, at age 63 Adams reentered politics as a member of the House, to which he devoted the last 18 years of his life. He felt satisfaction and vindication that the voters of his district wanted him to be their representative. In the House he won the name Old Man Eloquent for speaking out vigorously against slavery and for defeating a "gag rule" that Southern representatives had imposed against antislavery petitions. In 1848, John Quincy Adams suffered a stroke at his desk in the House chamber and died in a nearby room. A bronze marker on the floor indicates where Adams's desk once stood. Visitors to the Capitol know it as the "whispering spot" in Statuary Hall.

FURTHER READING
Richards, Leonard L. *The Life and Times of Congressman John Quincy Adams.* New York: Oxford, 1986.

Adjournment

ADJOURNMENT IS the way in which Congress goes *out* of session. Whenever the House or Senate adjourns, it formally ends a legislative day. The next time that chamber reconvenes, it must go through the general order of business, including the reading of the journals (the minutes of previous sessions, which provide information such as bills and resolutions introduced, committee referrals, and votes) and other morning business. The House usually adjourns each day, but because routine morning business can be prolonged as part of a Senate filibuster, a delaying tactic, the Senate may recess rather than adjourn. A recess keeps the chamber in the same legislative day. A single legislative day of the Senate once ran for 162 calendar days, from January 3 to June 12, 1980.

The Constitution forbids either house to adjourn for more than three days without the other's permission. During an annual session of Congress, the Senate and House from time to time will adjourn for a week to allow members to return to their districts and states, often in connection with a holiday. In nonelection years, Congress usually adjourns for the month of August. An adjournment resolution will set a specific date when the Senate and House plan to return. At the end of the session, the leadership will make a motion to adjourn *sine die*. This Latin phrase means "without a day," since the resolution sets no time for Congress to return before the beginning of the next session on January 3. If a national emergency or some other unexpected business develops after an adjournment, the President can call Congress back into special, or extraordinary, session. In recent years, adjournment resolutions have also authorized the House and Senate majority leaders jointly to call Congress back from a *sine die* adjournment.

SEE ALSO
Recess

Administrative assistants

ADMINISTRATIVE ASSISTANTS (AAs) serve as office managers and often as chief advisers for their senator or representative. Although responsibilities vary in different offices, AAs generally supervise the rest of the office staff, schedule appointments, and oversee correspondence and case files, such as military academy appointments. They also handle constituents' problems with Social Security payments, veterans' benefits, and dealings with federal government agencies.

SEE ALSO
Legislative assistants; Staff

Advice and consent

PRESIDENTS NOMINATE people to federal office and negotiate treaties with other nations, but these actions become official only after the Senate gives its "advice and consent." Such sharing of power between the executive and legislative branches of the federal government is a critical part of the system of checks and balances. The Constitution (Article 2, Section 2) explains how the Senate can grant its consent: a majority vote confirms a nomination, and a two-thirds vote is necessary to ratify a treaty. Giving advice, however, is much less clear.

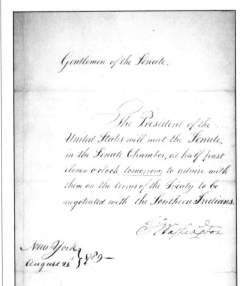

President George Washington sought the Senate's advice as well as its consent.

Washington seeks advice

During the 1st Congress, senators wanted the President to appear in their chamber to present all nominations and treaties in person. President George Washington believed nominations would be too numerous to make appearing in person practical, and he preferred to submit them to the Senate in writing. But he agreed to consult with the Senate personally about treaties. On August 24, 1789, Washington came to the Senate chamber seeking advice on a series of proposed treaties with Indian nations. He presented a list of questions for debate and response. But because the senators felt uncomfortable discussing these matters in the imposing presence of George Washington, they decided instead to refer the questions to a committee for further study. "This defeats every purpose of my coming here!" Washington exclaimed. Unhappily, he agreed to return to the Senate at a later date to receive their answers. This marked the last time that Washington, or any President, came to the chamber personally in search of advice as well as consent.

Over the years, however, both legislators and the President have devised various other means of involving the Senate in nominations and treaties prior to granting its consent. For instance, Presidents may invite senators to help negotiate treaties or to attend the negotiations as observers. The attorney general and other cabinet officers are careful to consult with key senators before the President nominates federal judges, U.S. attorneys, and other appointed officials. Modern Presidents regularly telephone or meet privately with senators to win their support for pending treaties and nominations.

SEE ALSO
Checks and balances; Nominations, confirmation of; Treaties

African Americans in Congress

AFTER THE Civil War and the abolition of slavery, the 14th Amendment (1868) granted African Americans citizenship, and the 15th Amendment (1870) gave black men (but not women) the right to vote. In February 1870, Hiram Revels (Republican–Mississippi) became the first black senator, taking the seat once occupied by Jefferson Davis, President of the Confederacy. In December 1870, Joseph Rainey (Republican–South Carolina) became the first black representative.

Several Southern states sent African Americans to Congress during Reconstruction. But later efforts by white Southerners to restrict black voting, often through violence and intimidation, resulted in the defeat of most black incumbents. After 1901 no blacks served in Congress until the election of Oscar DePriest (Republican–Illinois) in 1928. By then, Washington had become a segregated city, and DePriest had to struggle even for his staff members to eat in the Capitol restaurants. In 1934, Arthur Mitchell (Democrat–Illinois), also an African American, defeated DePriest, signifying a dramatic shift in African-American voters from the party of Lincoln to the party of Franklin D. Roosevelt. William Dawson (Democrat–Illinois) succeeded Mitchell and later became the first black member of Congress to chair a major committee. During the 1940s, Dawson and Adam Clayton Powell, Jr. (Democrat–New York) were the only black members of Congress. But beginning in the 1950s, the number of blacks winning election to the House slowly grew, first from Northern cities and then from Southern rural districts. In 1968,

Barbara Jordan represented Houston, Texas, in the House of Representatives.

African-American members of Congress during the Reconstruction era, from 1869 to 1873. Seated from left to right are Senator Hiram R. Revels of Mississippi and Representatives Benjamin S. Turner of Alabama, Josiah T. Walls of Florida, Joseph H. Rainey of South Carolina, and Robert Brown Elliott of South Carolina. Standing are Representatives Robert C. De Large of South Carolina and Jefferson F. Long of Georgia.

Shirley Chisholm (Democrat–New York) became the first black woman elected to Congress. By contrast to the growing number of black representatives, Edward Brooke (Republican–Massachusetts) and Carol Moseley-Braun (Democrat–Illinois) have been the only black senators to serve during the 20th century.

As their ranks increased, African-American representatives formed the Congressional Black Caucus. Begun in 1971, the Black Caucus has sought a leadership role among African Americans, speaking for their concerns and promoting their legislative interests. The Black Caucus has worked for civil rights and for equal opportunity in education, employment, and housing but also has taken stands on Presidential nominations and matters of foreign policy.

SEE ALSO

Chisholm, Shirley; Civil rights legislation; Powell, Adam Clayton, Jr.; Reconstruction, congressional; Revels, Hiram R.

FURTHER READING

Clay, William L. *Just Permanent Interests: Black Americans in Congress, 1870–1991.* New York: Penguin, 1992.
Ragsdale, Bruce A., and Joel D. Treese, eds. *Black Americans in Congress, 1870–1989.* Washington, D.C.: Government Printing Office, 1990.

Aldrich, Nelson W.

☆ Born: Nov. 6, 1841, Foster, R.I.
☆ Political party: Republican
☆ Senator from Rhode Island: 1881–1911
☆ Died: Apr. 16, 1915, New York, N.Y.

AT THE beginning of the 20th century, a powerful group of conservative Republicans known as the Senate Four held enormous influence over federal policy. "The four bosses of the Senate can and do control that body," one journalist wrote of senators Nelson Aldrich, Wil-

This cartoon portrays Senator Aldrich as the spider who trapped reform legislation in the web of his committee.

liam Allison, Orville Platt, and John C. Spooner. "This means that these four men can block and defeat anything that the president or the House may desire."

Of the four, Nelson Aldrich wielded the greatest power because he was chairman of the Finance Committee, which determined all tariff legislation (tariffs are taxes placed on imported goods and materials). American industry sought protection from foreign competition through high tariffs, and business leaders looked to Aldrich to protect their interests. Aldrich strongly opposed President Theodore Roosevelt's proposals to regulate big business and fought the attempts of progressive reformers to lower tariff rates. The press called Aldrich a "dictator," "tyrant," and "boss of the Senate," making him a symbol of the need for reform through direct election of senators.

FURTHER READING

Merrill, Horace Samuel, and Marion Galbraith Merrill. *The Republican Command, 1897–1913.* Lexington: University Press of Kentucky, 1971.

Alien and Sedition Acts (1798)

CONGRESS HAS not always been able to tolerate criticism from the press. In 1798, there was a distinct threat of war between the United States and France because of the French navy's interference with American shipping. The majority Federalist party in Congress reacted angrily to attacks from the minority Democratic-Republican party press by enacting the Alien and Sedition Acts.

The Alien Act allowed the President to deport any noncitizen he considered "dangerous to the peace and safety of the United States." This provision was aimed at the many Democratic-Republican editors who were born abroad. The Sedition Act made it a crime to publish anything false or malicious about either house of Congress or about the executive branch. Benjamin Franklin Bache, editor of the *Philadelphia Aurora*, predicted that "to laugh at the cut of a coat of a member of Congress will soon be treason." In fact, many editors went to prison for writing critically about Congress and the President. Even Representative Matthew Lyon (Democratic-Republican–Vermont) spent time in jail for condemning the government in his newspaper. Democratic-Republicans considered these laws unconstitutional. "Men who engage in public life, or are members of legislative bodies, must expect to be exposed to . . . attacks on their principles and opinions," said Senator Charles Pinckney (Democratic-Republican–South Carolina). When they gained the majority in the election of 1800, Democratic-Republicans allowed the Alien and Sedition Acts to expire.

SEE ALSO
Media coverage of Congress

Representative Matthew Lyon of Vermont, jailed under the Sedition Act, is shown fighting with another member in the House chamber. Lyon was imprisoned because he criticized the government in his newspaper.

FURTHER READING

Smith, James Morton. *Freedom's Fetters: The Alien and Sedition Laws and American Civil Liberties.* Ithaca, N.Y.: Cornell University Press, 1956.

Amendments, constitutional

CONGRESS CAN propose amendments to the Constitution. According to the Constitution (Article 5), it takes a two-thirds vote of both houses of Congress to propose new amendments, which must then be ratified by three-fourths of the states. The only other way to amend the Constitution is for two-thirds of the state legislatures to call for a constitutional convention.

Many of the constitutional amendments passed to date have altered the powers and functions of Congress. The first 10 amendments, known as the Bill of Rights and adopted in 1791, prohibited Congress from passing legislation that might limit such rights as freedom of the press, speech, and religion. The 14th Amendment (1868) gave Congress authority to enact laws to protect the civil rights of all citizens. The 16th Amendment (1913) gave Congress the power to collect a federal income tax.

The 17th Amendment (1913) allowed for the direct election of U.S. senators. Previously, state legislatures had been responsible for this task. The 20th Amendment (1933) moved the opening of a new session of Congress up from the first Monday in December, at the end of the following year, to January 3, at the beginning of that year, ending the lame-duck sessions that took place after the election but before the new members could be sworn in. The 25th Amendment

A woman campaigned for repeal of the 18th Amendment, which would end Prohibition.

(1967) specified the role of Congress in case the office of Vice President becomes vacant. The President nominates a new Vice President, but a majority vote of both the House and Senate is necessary to confirm that nomination. In 1992, 202 years after Congress proposed it, three-quarters of the states ratified the 27th Amendment, which requires that no congressional salary increase go into effect until after the next election.

SEE ALSO

Bill of Rights; Constitution; Lame-duck sessions

FURTHER READING

Ritchie, Donald A. *The Constitution.* New York: Chelsea House, 1989.

Amendments, legislative

Amendments modify legislation in a variety of ways. Amendments can add new language, strike out certain provisions, or otherwise revise and improve a bill to gain enough votes to win its passage. After the sponsors have introduced a bill, other members will offer amendments to make it more acceptable to them. Lobbyists for private groups and the executive branch will also encourage amendments to make a bill more to their liking. Most amendments are added in committee, but others are added on the floor or later in the conference committee. All amendments must be voted on by the full Senate and House before becoming part of the bill.

Opponents use amendments to weaken a bill's initial purpose. They may offer amendments that would offend enough legislators to defeat the entire bill. Those seeking to filibuster against a bill, to delay it in debate, will pile on nu-

The scene on January 31, 1865, when the House passed the 13th Amendment, abolishing slavery.

merous technical amendments, changing a word or just the punctuation, in order to extend the debate and delay or defeat the bill's final passage. Even after a bill becomes law, future legislation may amend it. Many bills that Congress enacts are really amendments to previous legislation.

SEE ALSO
Committees; Germaneness

"American House of Lords"

THE PRESS has sometimes compared the U.S. Senate to the House of Lords, the upper chamber of the British Parliament. But senators actually have far greater power than the Lords and are much more involved in legislation. The term "House of Lords" has also been used to suggest the special privileges and "lordly" behavior of the Senate.

SEE ALSO
"Millionaires' club"

Appointments

SEE Nominations, confirmation of

Apportionment

SEE Gerrymandering; Reapportionment

Appropriations

CONGRESS HOLDS the "power of the purse," the power to control how the government spends money. Neither the military nor any civilian agency of the federal government can spend any federal money unless it receives an appropriation from Congress. Americans inherited this powerful check on the executive branch from the early struggles between the British Parliament and the king. The Constitution provided for the popularly elected House to originate all revenue and appropriations bills and for the Senate to vote on these bills and to amend them.

Control of federal spending carries great power and influence, so there is always much competition for assignment to the House and Senate Appropriations Committees. Every bill that authorizes federal spending to carry out its programs must go to the Appropriations Committees, which decide whether to fund the programs fully, partially, or not at all. During each session, the Appropriations Committees will also hear extensive testimony about the operations and costs of executive branch agencies. Appropriations bills are regularly the last major bills enacted each session. It is not unusual for Congress to debate an appropriations bill late at night or early in the morning, with the clock ticking toward adjournment.

Not until after the Civil War did Congress create separate Appropriations Committees, to relieve the burden of appropriations from committees charged with raising revenue and to give Congress better control over federal spending. In the House, the Ways and Means Committee handled appropriations until 1865. In the Senate, the Finance Committee oversaw appropriations until 1867. The Appropriations Committees are the largest in both bodies, with 59 members in the House and 29 in the Senate.

SEE ALSO
Recision bills

FURTHER READING
Fenno, Richard F., Jr. *The Power of the Purse: Appropriations Politics in Congress.* Boston: Little, Brown, 1966.

Architect of the Capitol

APPOINTED BY the President, the Architect of the Capitol is in charge of any construction and maintenance of the Capitol building, House and Senate office buildings, Library of Congress, Supreme Court, and other sites and landscaping on Capitol Hill.

The original designer of the Capitol, William Thornton, was a physician rather than an architect. Thornton frequently argued with the professionally trained architects and engineers during the initial construction of the Capitol. A British architect, Benjamin Henry Latrobe, took over the project in 1803 and added his own influence to the designs, especially to the Capitol's interior. An American-born architect, Charles Bulfinch, oversaw completion of the original Capitol. From 1830 to 1851 there was no position of official architect. To supervise the building of the massive wings to house the new Senate and House chambers, Thomas U. Walter was appointed Architect of the Capitol in 1851. Walter was also in charge of building the massive cast-iron dome over the rotunda.

In the 20th century, Architects of the Capitol planned the extension of the East Front, the renovation of the West Front, and the construction of the office buildings. The architect is a member of the U.S. Capitol police board and supervises a large staff that handles all the necessary engineering, electrical work, air-conditioning, and landscaping around the Capitol.

FURTHER READING

Aikman, Lonnelle M. *We, the People: The Story of the United States Capitol, Its Past and Its Promise.* Washington, D.C.: U.S. Capitol Historical Society, 1991.

Armed Services Committees

AFTER THE immense expansion of American military forces during World War II, Congress reorganized its many separate committees on military affairs, naval affairs, and militia into the House and Senate Armed Services Committees. These committees hold hearings and report legislation on all aspects of national

In the 1850s, workers under the supervision of the Architect of the Capitol hauled columns for the expansion of the Capitol building.

Counsel for the army Joseph Welch (seated, left) listens to Senator Joseph McCarthy during the Army-McCarthy hearings.

defense, including military spending, weapons systems, strategies, bases, military academies, and the promotion of military officers. The influence of the Armed Services Committees grew in direct proportion to the billion-dollar increases in the defense budget during the cold war. Three Georgians, Representative Carl Vinson and Senators Richard Russell and Sam Nunn, established strong national reputations and earned respect within Congress as chairmen of the Armed Services Committees.

SEE ALSO
Committees

Army-McCarthy hearings (1954)

THE TELEVISED hearings that investigated alleged communist infiltration of the U.S. Army diminished public support for Senator Joseph R. McCarthy (Republican–Wisconsin) and led to his censure (rebuke) by the Senate. McCarthy was at the height of his influence when, as chairman of the Permanent Subcommittee on Investigations, he launched an investigation of espionage and subversion in the army. During the inquiry, McCarthy verbally assaulted an army general, calling him "not fit to wear that uniform." The army responded that McCarthy was browbeating and humiliating its officers. It accused the senator of seeking preferential treatment for one of his staff members who had recently been drafted into the army. McCarthy stepped down temporarily as chairman to let the subcommittee investigate these charges.

Television covered the 35 days of hearings, from April to June 1954, and gave many Americans the opportunity to observe closely McCarthy's bullying tactics and irresponsible charges. "Have you no sense of decency, sir?" demanded the army's counsel, Joseph Welch. The public and the Senate had seen enough. In December, the Senate censured McCarthy for conduct unbecoming a senator.

SEE ALSO

Censure; Investigations; McCarthy, Joseph R.

FURTHER READING

Wallace, H. Lew. "The McCarthy Era, 1954." In *Congress Investigates: A Documented History, 1792–1974*, edited by Arthur M. Schlesinger, Jr., and Roger Bruns. New York: Bowker, 1975.

Articles of Confederation

BEFORE THE current federal government existed, the government of the newly independent American states consisted of a Congress that operated under the Articles of Confederation. Adopted in 1781, the Articles set up a national legislature that could raise an army and navy, declare war and negotiate treaties, borrow and coin money, run a postal system, and handle relations with Native Americans. Each state could send two delegates to Congress but had only one vote. Delegates from 7 of the 13 states had to be present to establish a quorum and conduct business. Delegates were elected for one-year terms and could not serve for more than three years in any six-year period.

The single-body Congress under the Articles of Confederation comprised the entire national government. There was neither an executive nor a judicial branch. Congress elected a President as its presiding officer. Committees of Congress served as a cabinet and handled all government business. But Congress had no control over foreign or interstate commerce and no power to collect taxes. These powers belonged to the states. Revolutionary war leaders such as Alexander Hamilton called the government under the Articles of Confederation merely the "appearance" of a Union. General George Washington worried about the consequences of having a "half-starved, limping government, always moving upon crutches and tottering at every step." Hamilton and Washington took the initiative in calling for a Constitutional Convention in 1787 in order to establish a stronger national government.

SEE ALSO
Continental Congress

FURTHER READING
Morris, Richard B. *The Forging of the Union, 1781–1789.* New York: Harper & Row, 1987.

Asian Americans in Congress

BEFORE 1965, American immigration laws restricted Asians from coming to the United States. Asian-American communities existed in the larger cities, but their populations generally were not large enough to elect members to Congress. The territory of Hawaii contained a high proportion of Chinese-, Japanese-, and Polynesian-American citizens. Much of the opposition to making Hawaii a state came from racially biased members who feared that Hawaii would send to Congress Asian Americans sympathetic to civil rights legislation. Indeed, when Hawaii became a state in 1959, it elected the first Chinese-American member of the Senate, Hiram Fong (Republican) and the first Japanese-American member of the House, Daniel Inouye (Democrat). In 1964, Patsy Mink (Democrat–Hawaii) was the first Japanese-American woman elected to the House. Daniel Akaka (Democrat–Hawaii) became the first Polynesian-American member of the House in 1977 and the first in the Senate in 1990.

California has also sent several Asian Americans to the House and Senate, including the first Asian American ever elected to Congress, Dalip

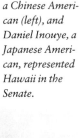

Hiram Fong, a Chinese American (left), and Daniel Inouye, a Japanese American, represented Hawaii in the Senate.

Singh Saund (Democrat). Born in India, Saund came to the United States to study at the University of California. He won a House seat in 1956 and served three terms. California sent Japanese American Norman Mineta (Democrat) to the House in 1974, and S. I. Hayakawa (Republican) to the Senate in 1976. In 1992 California voters elected Jay Kim (Republican) as the first Korean American to serve in the House.

FURTHER READING

Inouye, Daniel K. *Journey to Washington.* Englewood Cliffs, N.J.: Prentice-Hall, 1967.

Saund, Dalip Singh. *Congressman from India.* New York: Dutton, 1960.

Barkley, Alben W.

☆ *Born: Nov. 24, 1877, Lowes, Ky.*
☆ *Political party: Democrat*
☆ *Representative from Kentucky: 1913–27*
☆ *Senator from Kentucky: 1927–49, 1955–56*
☆ *Senate majority leader: 1937–46*
☆ *Senate minority leader: 1947–49*
☆ *Vice President: 1949–53*
☆ *Died: Apr. 30, 1956, Lexington, Va.*

ALBEN BARKLEY defined the role of majority leader as the President's man in the Senate. He devoted himself steadfastly to enacting the legislative programs of Presidents Franklin D. Roosevelt and Harry S. Truman. A liberal Democrat, Barkley had been assistant majority leader under Joseph Robinson. When Robinson died, President Roosevelt intervened in the leadership race to help Barkley win. As a result, many senators felt that Barkley spoke for the President to them, rather than for them to the President. This impression continued until 1944, when Barkley became angry about the President's veto of a tax bill against his advice. He urged Congress to override the veto—which it

did—and then resigned as majority leader. Barkley's independent stand elevated his stature among Senate Democrats, and they immediately and unanimously reelected Barkley as leader. In 1948, Truman chose Barkley to be his Vice Presidential running mate.

SEE ALSO

Majority leader; Robinson, Joseph T.

FURTHER READING

Ritchie, Donald A. "Alben W. Barkley: The President's Man." In *First among Equals: Outstanding Senate Leaders of the Twentieth Century,* edited by Richard A. Baker and Roger H. Davidson. Washington, D.C.: Congressional Quarterly, 1991.

Bean soup

BY TRADITION, bean soup is served daily in the House and Senate restaurants. One legend attributes this custom to the beginning of the twentieth century, when Senator Fred Thomas Dubois of Idaho chaired the committee that supervised the Senate restaurant. Others credit Senator Knute Nelson of Minnesota, who expressed fondness for the dish in 1903.

The House restaurant dates its practice back to 1904, when Speaker Joseph

Senate and House chefs prepare large quantities of bean soup to be served in congressional dining rooms.

G. Cannon found the soup missing from the menu. "Thunderation," roared the Speaker, "I had my mouth set for bean soup! From now on, hot or cold, rain, snow, or shine, I want it on the menu every day." The House and Senate recipes are similar, except that the House version omits the onions:

Take two pounds of small navy beans, wash, and run hot water through them until slightly whitened. Place beans in pot with four quarts of hot water. Add 1¹/₂ pounds of smoked ham hocks and simmer approximately three hours in a covered pot, stirring occasionally. Remove ham hocks and set aside to cool. Dice meat and return to soup. Lightly brown one chopped onion in two tablespoons of butter and add to the soup. Before serving, bring to a boil and then season with salt and pepper. Serves eight.

Bells

WHEN BELLS ring and the halls fill with hurrying people, the U.S. Capitol resembles a school between classes. Bells keep senators and representatives informed of the activities on the floor and summon them for votes and quorum calls.

Originally, pages and messengers rushed to alert absent members of votes in the chambers, but a more efficient system was needed as the Capitol complex grew larger. In 1893, after the Capitol was wired for electricity, one journalist noted, "The wires are connected with bells, and these notify the petted legislators of every urgent demand for their official service." Today members' offices, committee rooms, restaurants, and other locations around the Capitol and Senate and House office buildings are fitted with sets of lights. Whenever a bell rings,

a corresponding light comes on. One long bell and a single light indicate a vote. Members then have fifteen minutes to get to the chamber to cast their vote. When half the time has elapsed, five bells and five lights warn members to hurry. Other bells indicate quorum calls, the end of morning business, or adjournment.

Once, a new page escorted an elderly woman up to the galleries. "Why do these bells ring so constantly and stridently?" the woman asked. "I'm not quite sure," replied the page, "but I think maybe one of them has escaped."

Benton, Thomas Hart

☆ *Born: Mar. 14, 1782, Harts Mill, N.C.*
☆ *Political party: Democrat*
☆ *Senator from Missouri: 1821–51*
☆ *Representative from Missouri: 1853–55*
☆ *Died: Apr. 10, 1858, Washington, D.C.*

TWO GREAT compromises framed Thomas Hart Benton's 30 years in the U.S. Senate. In 1820, the Missouri Compromise drew a line across the country, above which slavery was not to spread. This compromise also made Missouri a state, and Thomas Hart Benton became one of its first senators. As a border state senator, he sided with neither the North nor the South on the issue of slavery. Benton saw Northern abolitionists and Southern sectionalists as two halves of the same pair of scissors, threatening to cut the nation in half. He thought that slavery would eventually become unprofitable and fade away. Benton fought his last Senate battles over the Compromise of 1850, to settle the issue of slavery in the new territories taken from Mexico. Emotions grew so heated that Senator Henry Foote (Whig–Mississippi) pulled a pistol on Benton during the debate. "Stand out of the way and let the assassin fire!" Benton shouted as other senators pulled them apart. Although he escaped without harm, Benton ultimately fell victim to sectional tensions and lost his race for reelection in 1850.

SEE ALSO
Compromise of 1850; Missouri Compromise (1821)

FURTHER READING
Benton, Thomas Hart. *Thirty Years' View; or, A History of the American Government for Thirty Years, from 1820–1850.* 2 vols. 1854–1856. Reprint. Westport, Conn.: Greenwood, 1968.
Smith, E. B. *Magnificent Missourian: Thomas Hart Benton.* Philadelphia: Lippincott, 1957.

Beveridge, Albert J.

☆ Born: Oct. 6, 1862, Sugar Tree Ridge, Ind.
☆ Political party: Republican
☆ Senator from Indiana: 1899–1911
☆ Died: Apr. 27, 1927, Indianapolis, Ind.

AS FRUITS of the Spanish-American War, the United States acquired control of the Philippines, Puerto Rico, and other overseas territories. Some members of Congress, including Speaker Thomas B. Reed, strongly opposed such an imperialist policy. But the cause of annexation—the acquisition of new territory—gained a dynamic champion in the young

Senator Albert Beveridge championed U.S. expansion overseas.

freshman senator Albert J. Beveridge. Making his first speech in the Senate, Beveridge declared that God "has made us the master organizers of the world to establish system where chaos reigns." He described the riches in raw materials that these colonies would provide for American industry and won thunderous applause from the galleries. Although Senator George F. Hoar (Republican–Massachusetts) objected that "the words Right, Justice, Duty, Freedom were absent" from the speech, Senator Beveridge successfully captured the spirit of American nationalism at the start of the 20th century.

FURTHER READING
Braeman, John. *Albert J. Beveridge: American Nationalist.* Chicago: University of Chicago Press, 1971.

Bicameral

UNLIKE THE single-body Congress under the Articles of Confederation, the U.S. Congress is bicameral (from the Latin *bi*, meaning "two," and *camera*, meaning "chamber"). Congress consists of two separate bodies that share legislative powers. Members of the House and Senate have different qualifications for holding office, and they serve terms of different lengths. A House member represents a district within a state, and a senator represents an entire state. The two houses have different presiding officers, make their own rules, and have different ways of conducting business. Yet both houses of Congress must pass bills in exactly the same form in order for them to become law.

James Madison, a major author of the Constitution, reasoned that a single, popularly elected legislature might respond too quickly to changes in public opinion and would enact "defective laws which do mischief before they can be mended." Madison believed that a second legislative body "consisting of fewer and riper members, deliberating separately & independently of the other, may be expected to correct many errors and inaccuracies" of the other.

In theory, the House would represent the common people, while the Senate would represent wealthier property owners and serve as a check against the pressures of public opinion. But those who wanted a more democratic government objected to creating an aristocratic "upper" house. Thomas Jefferson supposedly asked George Washington why a Senate was necessary. "Why did you pour that coffee into your saucer?" Washington responded. "To cool it," Jefferson replied. "Even so," said Washington, "we pour legislation into the senatorial saucer to cool it."

Two centuries later, senators, like representatives, are elected directly by the people (originally, they were elected by state legislatures), but the two bodies continue to balance each other. House rules favor majority rule, and the Senate rules give greater voice to minority objections. The House responds more quickly to public opinion, whereas the Senate prefers to take time to deliberate. As journalist William S. White observed, "The House marches; the Senate thinks, and sometimes overlong."

SEE ALSO

Articles of Confederation; Checks and balances; Constitution; House-Senate relations; Separation of powers

FURTHER READING

Baker, Ross K. *House and Senate*. New York: Norton, 1989.
Bowen, Catherine Drinker. *Miracle at Philadelphia: The Story of the Constitutional Convention, May to September 1787*. Boston: Little, Brown, 1966.
Ritchie, Donald A. *The U.S. Constitution*. New York: Chelsea House, 1989.

Bill clerks

BILL CLERKS assign numbers to all bills and resolutions, and they record in the journals any actions that the Senate and House take on that legislation. They also supervise the printing of all bills, resolutions, reports, and amendments through the Government Printing Office. Each day, the bill clerks enter all legislative activities into a computer system known as LEGIS so that members, staff, and others can have instant information on how far the bill has progressed through the legislative process and what amendments might have been added.

SEE ALSO
Bills; Journals; Legislative clerks; Resolutions

Bill of Rights

A MAJOR accomplishment of the 1st Congress was the drafting of the first 10 amendments to the Constitution, known as the Bill of Rights. During the campaign to ratify the Constitution, Anti-Federalists charged that the document failed to protect individual liberties from government encroachment. The Federalist supporters of the Constitution argued that state laws already safeguarded such rights. But in order to win ratification in such key states as Massachusetts and Virginia, Federalists promised to amend the Constitution as soon as possible.

In June 1789, Representative James Madison introduced a series of constitutional amendments in the House. Madison argued that critics of the Constitution were patriotic people who wanted to protect their liberties and who

The original handwritten copy of the Bill of Rights shows that Congress passed 12 amendments to the Constitution. The states approved 10 in 1791 and 1 more in 1992.

Bills

ANY MEMBER of Congress with an idea for a law can introduce it as a bill. But many hurdles must be overcome before that bill becomes law. In a two-year Congress, some 20,000 bills may be introduced, only 5 percent of which will become law. Representatives introduce bills by dropping them in a box called a hopper. Senators rise at their desk in the chamber and request permission to introduce a bill. Bill clerks assign the bill a number. H.R. 1 would be the first bill introduced in the House during that Congress; S. 256 would be the 256th bill introduced in the Senate. Members often reserve special numbers, such as 1776, to draw attention to their legislation. The names of the bill's sponsors are printed at the top of the bill, and bills are often known by their sponsors, such as the Wagner Bill or the Taft-Hartley Bill.

The parliamentarian refers the bill to the committee (or committees) with jurisdiction over its subject matter. A bill to reform the federal courts would go to the Judiciary Committee; a bill dealing with auto pollution might be divided between the energy and environmental committees.

Most bills die in committee because the committee fails to act on them. The successful few are usually considered first in a subcommittee, which may hold hearings to gather information and may amend, substitute, or combine the bill with other related bills. The full committee will "mark up" a bill, making final changes before reporting it back to the House or Senate.

The bill then goes on the calendar until it is called up for consideration. With the committee chairman or the bill's chief sponsor acting as floor manager, members will debate and amend the bill before passing or defeating it.

thought that the new Congress was "not sincere" if it did not act promptly. By September, the House passed 17 potential amendments. The Senate edited these down to 12, and by 1791 the states had ratified 10. These 10 amendments have provided the basic guarantee of American civil liberties.

Two hundred years later, in 1992, the states ratified one more of these original amendments, which requires that no increase in congressional salaries take effect until after the next election. Congress then enacted a joint resolution declaring the last unratified amendment—which would have set a formula for apportioning congressional districts—to have expired and therefore to be void.

SEE ALSO

Amendments, constitutional; Constitution; Madison, James

FURTHER READING

Ritchie, Donald A. *The Constitution.* New York: Chelsea House, 1989.
Rutland, Robert Allen. *The Birth of the Bill of Rights, 1776–1791.* New York: Collier, 1962.

Advancing toward passage, bills moved up from shelf to shelf on this "bill hopper," used by the Senate before the Civil War.

Once one house passes a bill, messengers carry the bill to the other body, and the entire process begins again. Invariably, the Senate and House pass bills in different forms. They will then appoint a conference committee to try to negotiate a common version. The House and Senate must vote "up or down" (yes or no, without amendment) on the conference report.

If Congress passes the bill, it goes to the President, who can sign the bill, allow it to become law without his signature after 10 days, or veto (reject) it. A two-thirds vote of both houses of Congress is necessary to override a veto.

SEE ALSO
Acts; Bill clerks; Resolutions; Veto

FURTHER READING
Reid, T. R. *Congressional Odyssey: The Saga of a Senate Bill.* New York: Freeman, 1980. Willett, Edward, Jr., ed. *How Our Laws Are Made.* Washington, D.C.: Government Printing Office, 1986.

Bipartisan foreign policy

BIPARTISANSHIP OCCURS when the two major parties put aside their political differences and work together. In 1947, when the United States entered the cold war of international tensions and competition with the Soviet Union and its allied communist bloc nations, both parties in Congress rallied behind a common, bipartisan foreign policy.

Bipartisanship developed during the 80th Congress (1947–48), with Republicans in the majority on Capitol Hill and Democratic President Harry S. Truman in the White House. Although opposed to Truman's domestic programs, Republicans such as Senator Arthur H. Vandenberg argued that "politics should

stop at the water's edge." Most congressional Republicans supported Truman's foreign policies to rebuild Europe and to contain the spread of communism.

Republican Dwight D. Eisenhower was elected President in 1952, and congressional Democrats continued the bipartisan foreign policy, believing that it allowed the United States to respond effectively to the communist nations. But bipartisanship also stifled debate and eroded the legislative role in foreign policy. Asserting "national security," the executive branch determined foreign policy on its own, with minimum consultation with Congress.

Decline of bipartisanship

Bipartisan policy contributed to the Vietnam War and came apart because of it. President Lyndon B. Johnson, a former Senate majority leader, expected Congress to support his Vietnam initiatives. In 1964, with little debate, Congress almost unanimously passed the Gulf of Tonkin Resolution, which supported the use of American military force

Secretary of State John Foster Dulles (seated at rear, on the left) met with senators to seek bipartisan support for U.S. foreign policy in the 1950s.

in Vietnam. But as the war escalated, many members—especially in Johnson's own Democratic party—grew disillusioned and dismayed. When Republican Richard Nixon continued the war after 1969, Democrats increasingly opposed his policies. Congress asserted a much stronger voice and began to challenge Presidential foreign policies. Enactment of the War Powers Resolution in 1973, over President Nixon's veto, set specific limits on the President's power to deploy military forces and marked the end of bipartisanship. Congress placed a renewed emphasis on the separation of powers and checks and balances in foreign policy.

SEE ALSO

Gulf of Tonkin Resolution (1964); Johnson, Lyndon B.; Vandenberg, Arthur H.; War powers

FURTHER READING

Schlesinger, Arthur M., Jr. *The Imperial Presidency*. Boston: Houghton Mifflin, 1973.

Black caucus

SEE African Americans in Congress

Blaine, James G.

☆ *Born: Jan. 31, 1830, West Brownsville, Pa.*
☆ *Political party: Republican*
☆ *Representative from Maine: 1863–76*
☆ *Speaker of the House: 1869–76*
☆ *Senator from Maine: 1876–81*
☆ *Died: Jan. 27, 1893, Washington, D.C.*

AGGRESSIVE IN debate, bold in behavior, and greedy for wealth and power, James G. Blaine dominated American politics during the decades after the Civil War. "Other leaders were admired, loved, honored, revered, respected," one

senator observed, "but the sentiment for Blaine was delirium." As presiding officer, Blaine used his power to recognize speakers in order to bring more order to the House by controlling floor scheduling. Blaine's forceful leadership made him a front-runner for the Republican Presidential nomination in 1876, until he was accused of having taken railroad stocks as a bribe. A brokerage firm bookkeeper, James Mulligan, produced some incriminating letters that Blaine had written. Blaine went to Mulligan's room, seized the letters, and selectively read them to the House to vindicate himself. Although he lost the Presidential nomination, Blaine went on to serve as senator and secretary of state. At last, in 1884, he became the Republican candidate for President, but suspicions about his financial dealings still haunted him, and Blaine lost what was then considered the "dirtiest campaign in history" to the Democratic candidate, Grover Cleveland.

FURTHER READING

Muzzey, David S. *James G. Blaine: A Political Idol of Other Days*. 1934. Reprint. Port Washington, N.Y.: Kennikat Press, 1963.

Bolling, Richard W.

☆ *Born: May 17, 1916, New York, N.Y.*
☆ *Political party: Democrat*
☆ *Representative from Missouri: 1949–83*
☆ *Died: Apr. 21, 1991, Washington, D.C.*

ARGUING THAT foreign and domestic problems had mushroomed after World War II, Representative Richard Bolling called for institutional reform to make the House of Representatives function "effectively and responsibly." Bolling wanted greater party discipline, stronger leadership from the Speaker, reduced powers of seniority, and general reform of the committee structure. As Speaker

Sam Rayburn's "lieutenant and leg man" on the Rules Committee, Bolling led the opposition to the conservative faction under chairman Howard Smith, which was blocking debate on civil rights and other liberal legislation. In 1961, Bolling helped Rayburn win expansion of the membership of the Rules Committee to break the conservatives' majority. Later, when he became chairman of the Rules Committee himself, Bolling helped carry out many of the reforms he had proposed.

SEE ALSO

Rayburn, Sam; Rules committees; Rules, House and Senate; Smith, Howard W.

FURTHER READING

Bolling, Richard. *House Out of Order.* New York: Dutton, 1965.
Bolling, Richard. *Power in the House: A History of the Leadership of the House of Representatives.* New York: Capricorn Press, 1974.

Boll Weevils

WHEN RONALD REAGAN won the Presidency in 1980, he carried with him the first Republican majority in the Senate in 26 years. Democrats retained their majority in the House, but the margin between the parties was narrowed. The balance of power in the House was held by a group of conservative Democratic representatives from the South and West. They organized themselves as the Conservative Democratic Forum but were more popularly known as the Boll Weevils, after the beetle that infests Southern cotton.

Led by Representative Phil Gramm (Democrat–Texas), the Boll Weevils voted with Republicans to enact Reagan's economic program, which involved cuts in federal spending and a plan to stimulate the economy by cutting

taxes. Democrats responded by removing Gramm from his seat on the Budget Committee. Gramm resigned and won reelection as a Republican and soon after was elected to the Senate. Several other Boll Weevils also changed their party affiliation, but with less electoral success.

Bonus Marchers

TWELVE THOUSAND American veterans of World War I stood on the Capitol lawn on June 17, 1932, while the Senate debated the "Bonus Bill." Already passed by the House, the bill would have authorized immediate payment of a bonus that the veterans were due to receive in 1945. The veterans demanded their bonus right away, to help them and their families survive the economic hardships of the Great Depression. Bonus Marchers came from all over the country, set up tents on vacant land around Washington, and then gathered at the Capitol to await the final vote. Some senators feared mob violence, but when the Senate defeated the Bonus Bill, the marchers vowed to continue their fight, sang "America," and returned to their camps. Yet the Bonus March ended tragically. U.S. Army troops under the command of General Douglas MacArthur drove the

The Capitol formed the backdrop for a Bonus Marchers' camp in 1932.

marchers from the city and burned their camps. There were 100 casualties, and two children died in tear-gas attacks. Still, the Bonus Marchers had demonstrated the seriousness of their plight and the need for federal action to end the depression.

FURTHER READING

Manchester, William. *The Glory and the Dream: A Narrative History of America, 1932–1972.* Boston: Little, Brown, 1974.

Borah, William E.

☆ *Born: June 29, 1865, Fairfield, Ill.*
☆ *Political party: Republican*
☆ *Senator from Idaho: 1907–40*
☆ *Died: Jan. 19, 1940, Washington, D.C.*

THE CRY "Borah's got the floor!" sent newspaper reporters rushing to the press gallery, and senators to their seats, to hear him speak. William E. Borah was an independent maverick whose position  was often unpredictable but whose speeches were always well reasoned and magnificently delivered. Thoughtful and deliberate, he was never swayed by the prevailing passions but sought to influence and change public opinion. Borah came to the Senate during the Progressive Era, and his efforts led to the direct election of senators, lower tariffs, the graduated income tax, and other progressive reforms.

After World War I, Borah's attention shifted to foreign policy, and he spoke out strongly against the Treaty of Versailles, which ended the war. During the 1920s, as chairman of the Foreign Relations Committee, he promoted isolationist policies designed to keep the United States out of foreign wars. One observer found Borah "so thoroughly in-dependent that there was hardly a person with whom he did not differ at one time or another." But even if they disagreed with him, liberals and conservatives alike found that Borah's independence helped give them sharper perspectives on the issues.

SEE ALSO

Elections; Treaty of Versailles

FURTHER READING

Ashby, LeRoy. *The Spearless Leader, Senator Borah and the Progressive Movement in the 1920s.* Urbana: University of Illinois Press, 1972.

Bricker Amendment (1954)

CONGRESS CAME close to passing a constitutional amendment to limit the President's ability to enter into executive agreements with other nations. During World War II, President Franklin D. Roosevelt conducted extensive personal diplomacy with Allied leaders, involving many executive agreements. Unlike treaties, executive agreements do not require the Senate's advice and consent. Republicans in Congress objected to these secret agreements and sought to reverse the trend. In the 1950s, Senator John Bricker (Republican–Ohio) proposed a constitutional amendment to give Congress "power to regulate all executive and other agreements with any foreign power or international organization." Republican President Dwight Eisenhower opposed the Bricker Amendment, believing it would diminish a President's ability to conduct foreign policy. "If it's true that when you die the things that bothered you most are engraved on your skull," Eisenhower once remarked, "I am sure I'll have there . . . the name of Senator Bricker." In 1954, Eisenhower convinced enough senators to reject both the Bricker Amendment and a Democratic substitute amendment, which came within one vote of passing.

SEE ALSO

Advice and consent; Treaties

FURTHER READING

Tanenbaum, Duane. *The Bricker Amendment Controversy: A Test of Eisenhower's Political Leadership.* Ithaca, N.Y.: Cornell University Press, 1988.

Budget and Impoundment Control Act, Congressional (1974)

EACH YEAR the President submits a budget for the federal government, only to have Congress alter that budget to meet its own goals. "I've been around here a long time," said Senate Appropriations Committee chairman Robert C. Byrd in 1992, "and I can't remember when the President's budget passed the Congress." President Richard Nixon considered such congressional tinkering with his budget "undisciplined" and "fiscally irresponsible." Nixon took it upon himself to impound (not spend) funds that Congress appropriated for programs that he thought unnecessary. Members of Congress angrily accused Nixon of encroaching on the separation of powers and dangerously expanding the "imperial Presidency."

Not until Nixon stumbled in the Watergate scandal was Congress able to pass the Congressional Budget and Impoundment Control Act of 1974, over Nixon's veto. In addition to prohibiting Presidential impoundment of funds, the act established the House and Senate Budget Committees. These committees hold hearings and submit a concurrent resolution to the House and the Senate with their estimates of the next year's expected revenues and expenditures. The Appropriations Committees must limit appropriations to the amount that the concurrent resolution sets, or else the House and Senate must "reconcile" the difference by amendment. In the 1980s, reconciliation combined the numerous budget decisions into an omnibus measure that could be enacted by a single vote. This consolidation helped President Ronald Reagan regain greater influence over the budget in Congress.

Although impounding funds is now prohibited, under the Budget Act the President can ask Congress for a recision—or cutback—of appropriated funds for projects no longer considered necessary.

SEE ALSO

Appropriations; Concurrent resolution; Nixon, Richard M.; Recision bills; Watergate investigation (1973)

FURTHER READING

Polsby, Nelson W. *Congress and the Presidency.* Englewood Cliffs, N.J.: Prentice-Hall, 1986.

Bunk

SPEECHES DESIGNED for home consumption, to promote a member's chances of reelection, got the name "bunk" from Representative Felix Walker of Buncombe County, North Carolina. In 1820, Walker interrupted debate over the Missouri Compromise to make a speech directed chiefly to his constituents. Other representatives need not bother to stay to listen, he advised them, because "this is for Buncombe."

Burr, Aaron

☆ *Born: Feb. 6, 1756, Newark, N.J.*
☆ *Political party: Democratic-Republican*
☆ *Senator from New York: 1791–97*
☆ *Vice President: 1801–05*
☆ *Died: Sept. 14, 1836, Staten Island, N.Y.*

CLEVER AND ambitious, Aaron Burr twisted and broke the rules of behavior that bound other politicians. Elected to the Senate in 1790, he led the opposition to Treasury Secretary Alexander Hamilton's financial programs. "As a public man he is one of the worst sort," Hamilton complained, "a friend of nothing but as it suits his interest and ambition." In 1800, Burr ran as Thomas Jefferson's Vice President. Their ticket won, but Jefferson and Burr tied in electoral ballots, and the Federalist-dominated House of Representatives had to decide the election. Disliking Jefferson, many Federalists voted for Burr for President, and he did not dissuade them. After more than 30 ballots, Hamilton intervened with the Federalists and Jefferson was elected.

The rivalry ended tragically in 1804, when Vice President Burr shot and killed Hamilton in a duel. Burr returned to the Senate, one step ahead of the law, and in his farewell speech recognized the Senate as "a sanctuary; a citadel of law, of order, and of liberty; and it is here . . . in this exalted refuge; here, if anywhere, will resistance be made to the storms of political frenzy." He left the Senate chamber with his once-brilliant career in ruins.

FURTHER READING

Parmet, Herbert S., and Marie Hecht. *Aaron Burr: Portrait of an Ambitious Man.* New York: Macmillan, 1967.

Vice President Aaron Burr (right) destroyed his political career by killing Alexander Hamilton in a duel.

Byrd, Robert C.

☆ *Born: Nov. 20, 1917, North Wilkesboro, N.C.*
☆ *Political party: Democrat*
☆ *Representative from West Virginia: 1953–59*
☆ *Senator from West Virginia: 1959–*
☆ *Senate majority whip: 1971–77*
☆ *Senate majority leader: 1977–81, 1987–89*
☆ *Senate minority leader: 1981–87*
☆ *President pro tempore: 1989–*

A COAL MINER'S son who worked as a meat cutter and ship welder before entering politics, Robert C. Byrd advanced as a legislator through diligent study. Not until after his election to the House in 1952 did he begin law school at night, and not until after his election to the Senate did he receive his law degree in 1963. Byrd showed the same persistence in mastering the Senate's rules of procedure, which led to his election as Democratic whip and, in 1977, as majority leader. Byrd explained his ability to move the Senate and enact his party's programs by noting that "to be an effective leader, one ought to know the rules and precedents and understand how to use them." In 1989, Byrd stepped aside as majority leader in order to chair the powerful Senate Appropriations Committee. He pledged to use his chairmanship to channel a billion dollars' worth of federal funds into his relatively poor home state of West Virginia.

SEE ALSO

Leadership; Majority leader

FURTHER READING

Byrd, Robert C. "Reflections of a Party Leader." In *The Senate, 1789–1989: Addresses on the History of the United States Senate.* Vol. 2. Washington, D.C.: Government Printing Office, 1991.

Calendars

PUBLISHED DAILY whenever Congress is in session, calendars list all pending bills, resolutions, motions, and House-Senate conference committee actions. Only after a committee reports out a bill and the bill is placed on the calendar can it be called up for the full House or Senate to debate and vote on it. The House Rules Committee and the Senate majority leader decide the order in which bills will be called from the calendar for action. The Senate publishes two calendars, one for legislative and one for executive business (treaties and nominations). The House publishes five calendars for different types of legislation: revenue and appropriations bills, nonrevenue bills, noncontroversial bills that need not be debated, private claims and individual immigration bills, and—in very rare cases—motions to discharge (remove) bills from committees that were slow to act.

Calhoun, John C.

☆ *Born: Mar. 18, 1782, Mount Carmel, S.C.*
☆ *Political party: Democrat*
☆ *Representative from South Carolina: 1811–17*
☆ *Vice President: 1825–32*
☆ *Senator from South Carolina: 1832–43, 1845–50*
☆ *Died: Mar. 31, 1850, Washington, D.C.*

HE SEEMED a man with rock solid, immovable beliefs, but John C. Calhoun changed his position completely during his many years in Congress. Calhoun entered the House of Representatives as a nationalist, supporting a national bank, protective tariffs, and internal improve-

ments to build the nation as a whole. Forty years later, Calhoun died as a defender of states' rights, a man who had sacrificed his Presidential ambitions in his devotion to the slave-owning South.

Calhoun was Vice President under Andrew Jackson in 1828 when Congress enacted the "Tariff of Abominations," which levied high duties on imported goods. Outraged people in South Carolina talked about withdrawing from the Union. In danger of losing his political base, Calhoun secretly drafted a "nullification" plan by which a state could nullify a federal law. When President Jackson denounced nullification as treason, Calhoun resigned as Vice President and was elected to the Senate. With increasing passion he spoke for his state and his section. "If we do not defend ourselves none will defend," he declared; "if we yield we will be more and more pressed as we recede; and if we submit we will be trampled under foot." He died fighting against the Compromise of 1850, which was intended to defuse the slavery issue in new western territories but which Calhoun feared would restrict the spread of slavery and weaken the South. On his deathbed Calhoun's only wish was for one more hour to speak in the Senate for his cause.

S E E   A L S O

Compromise of 1850; Tariff of Abominations (1828)

F U R T H E R   R E A D I N G

Niven, John. *John C. Calhoun and the Price of Union: A Biography.* Baton Rouge: Louisiana State University Press, 1988.

Campaign committees

DEMOCRATS AND Republicans in the House and Senate appoint their own campaign committees to raise funds for their party's congressional campaigns. Senators and representatives chair these committees and direct money to promising candidates, especially those in close races. Individual candidates also establish their own campaign committees and raise their own funds. The success of these individual efforts has increasingly helped elect to Congress members who are independent of their state and national party organizations. These members are less subject to party discipline in Congress.

Campaign financing

THE ESCALATING cost of campaigning for Congress, especially the cost of political advertisements on television, has turned many senators and representatives into part-time legislators and full-time fund-raisers. The "money chase" continues even in nonelection years, as members build up large campaign chests. Although the quest for campaign financing places a wearisome burden on members of Congress, they still have great advantage over rival candidates who try to unseat them. Organized interest groups traditionally donated more money to incumbents (those already holding office), in recognition of the power of their office and the likelihood of their reelection. Incumbents also have the advantage of greater visibil-

Democrat Lynn Yeakel campaigns for a Pennsylvania senate seat in 1992.

ity in the news media, a paid staff to assist them, and the franking privilege to keep their names before their constituents. The growing imbalance in fund-raising between incumbents and challengers has been a major reason for the high rate of reelection to Congress and has provoked demands for reform in campaign fund-raising and even for limiting the number of terms that members of Congress may serve.

The Federal Election Commission requires all congressional candidates to file statements showing all the funds they raised and spent. Federal election laws also limit individual contributions to campaigns, but in the 1976 case of *Buckley v. Valeo* the Supreme Court ruled that it was an unconstitutional violation of free speech to set any restriction on the amount of money that wealthy people could spend on their own campaigns. Many members of Congress complain that this ruling gives unfair advantage to wealthy candidates.

The largest share of money for congressional campaigns comes from political action committees (PACs) representing various special interest groups. The predominance of PACs has raised concern that these contributors are attempting to "buy" special influence over legislation. In 1991, the Senate ethics committee investigated five senators who received campaign contributions from wealthy savings and loan banker Charles Keating. The Keating Five investigation questioned whether the senators had intervened with a government agency on behalf of Keating's bank because he was a constituent or because he had contributed financially to their campaigns. The ethics committee found that four of the senators had used poor judgment but had not violated Senate rules. A fifth senator, Alan Cranston (Democrat–California)—who had raised nearly a million dollars in campaign funds from

Keating—was reprimanded by the full Senate for engaging in "an impermissible pattern of conduct."

SEE ALSO
Incumbents

FURTHER READING
Magleby, David B., and Candice J. Nelson. *The Money Chase: Congressional Campaign Finance Reform.* Washington, D.C.: Brookings Institution, 1990.

Cannon, Joseph G.

☆ *Born: May 7, 1836, Guilford, N.C.*
☆ *Political party: Republican*
☆ *Representative from Illinois: 1873–91, 1893–1913, 1915–23*
☆ *Speaker of the House: 1903–13*
☆ *Died: Nov. 12, 1926, Danville, Ill.*

THE MOST powerful Speaker of the House of Representatives, Joseph G. Cannon represented the Republican conservative Old Guard during the Progressive Era. Uncle Joe looked like a crusty old farmer, but he ruled the House with an iron fist. The growth of big business did not worry Cannon, and he used his control of the House rules to suppress debate on government regulation of the

Joseph G. Cannon (center) addressed the House of Representatives in 1921.

railroads and other industries. "The country don't need any legislation," he insisted in typically earthy style.

On March 19, 1910, 149 Democrats and 42 progressive Republicans banded together to overthrow Cannon's power. Representative George Norris (Republican–Nebraska) made a motion for the House to elect members of the Rules Committee, rather than let the Speaker appoint them, and to bar the Speaker from being a member of the committee. Cannon offered to resign, but the House voted to keep him as Speaker, now that his powers had been trimmed. Despised by progressives (especially those outside of Congress), Cannon remained personally popular with members of the House. Despite the "revolt" against him, the House named its first office building in his memory.

SEE ALSO

Norris, George W.; Rules committees; Speaker of the House

FURTHER READING

Cheney, Richard B., and Lynne V. Cheney. *Kings of the Hill: Power and Personality in the House of Representatives.* New York: Continuum, 1983.

Capitol building

THE MOST widely recognized symbol of American democracy, the U.S. Capitol building houses the Congress. The Capitol contains more than 500 rooms in addition to the massive House and Senate chambers. Outside, in the shadow of its magnificent dome, Presidents of the United States take their inaugural oath, and they return to the Capitol to deliver their annual State of the Union message. State funerals and other ceremonies take place within the Rotunda, and foreign

leaders frequently visit the Capitol to address joint sessions of Congress.

Expansion of the Capitol

The Capitol expanded along with the nation. President George Washington selected the original building design by Dr. William Thornton, and Washington laid the cornerstone in 1793. When Congress arrived in November 1800, only the Senate wing of the Capitol was completed. Within this small, boxlike structure operated the Senate, House, Supreme Court, and Library of Congress. When the House wing opened in 1810, a wooden walkway connected the two structures. This was how the building looked in August 1814, when British troops invaded Washington. Piling up furniture and books, the British set fire to the Capitol and destroyed its interior. A heavy rain saved the exterior walls. Congress reconvened in the restored Capitol in 1819, and the oldest desks in the current Senate chamber date back to that year. Congress also purchased Thomas Jefferson's private library to replace the Library of Congress volumes consumed in the flames.

In the 1820s, construction of the central Rotunda, topped by a low copper dome, completed the original plans for the building. But the constant addition of new states—which resulted in more members of Congress—caused the Senate and House to outgrow their cham-

John Plumbe, Jr., took the first photograph of the Capitol building in 1846, before the new dome and wings were added.

A plaster model of the Statue of Freedom, which stands atop the Capitol dome.

bers. Massive wings were added to the north and south ends of the Capitol. The House moved into its new chamber in 1857 and the Senate in 1859. The Architect of the Capitol proposed that a higher cast-iron dome would better fit the newly enlarged building. Outbreak of the Civil War in 1861 temporarily halted work on this dome, but President Lincoln urged its completion as a symbol of the Union. In December 1863 the dome was completed and capped with a bronze statue of Freedom. The top of the statue reaches 287 feet and 5 inches above the base of the Capitol's East Front.

Beginning in 1874, Frederick Law Olmsted (designer of New York's Central Park) oversaw the landscaping and constructed terraces along the West Front to give the Capitol grounds a more formal appearance and add new office space. The West Front is the only portion of the original sandstone exterior still visible from outside the Capitol. The East Front was extended out some 30

feet and rebuilt in marble during renovation in 1958.

A colorful interior

In contrast to its austere white exterior, the Capitol's interior is colorfully decorated. Much of this embellishment was the work of the Italian painter Constantino Brumidi, known as the "Michelangelo of the Capitol." Trained in the art of fresco (the technique of applying paint to wet plaster so that it retains its colors), Brumidi began his work in the 1850s. In 1865 he painted a huge fresco under the dome, 180 feet above the Rotunda floor, depicting the "Apotheosis [glorification] of George Washington." Brumidi devoted the rest of his life to painting halls and committee rooms on the Senate side of the Capitol. He died in 1880 after falling from the scaffold while painting the frieze that rings the inside of the Rotunda. The House had declined Brumidi's services, but a century later, during the 1970s, artist Allyn Cox enlivened the House

The plan of the second floor of the Capitol, where the House and Senate chambers are located.

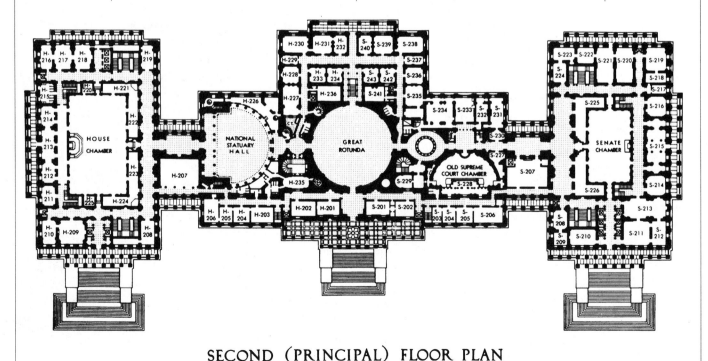

SECOND (PRINCIPAL) FLOOR PLAN

scale: 0 16 32 48 64 feet
© I P 1971 NORTH

Statuary Hall in the Capitol

corridors with similar historical scenes.

Enormous paintings of historical events decorate the public areas of the Capitol, and the corridors are lined with marble and bronze statues. In 1864 the House declared its old chamber to be National Statuary Hall and invited each state to send statues of two of its most illustrious citizens. Additional statues and busts honor many Presidents, Vice Presidents, foreign dignitaries, American Indian chiefs, and national heroes.

Congressional office buildings

Because of limited working space within the Capitol, the House and Senate have had additional office buildings constructed. In 1908, the House occupied its first permanent office building, now known as the Cannon building, and the Senate moved into the matching Richard Brevard Russell building the following year. Linked to the Capitol by underground tunnels and subways, these office buildings provide offices for committees, members, and their staffs. As its staff grew, the House built two additional office buildings, the Longworth (1933) and Rayburn (1965) buildings, and the Senate added the Everett McKinley Dirksen (1958) and Philip A. Hart (1982) buildings.

The Library of Congress operated out of the Capitol until 1897, when it transported its growing collection to a separate building across the street. Similarly, the Supreme Court met within the Capitol until 1935, when its own building was constructed. Today, the complex of massive structures surrounding the Capitol represents functions that once all took place within the small sandstone building that greeted Congress in 1800.

The U.S. Capitol remains the most open of federal buildings. Visitors on guided tours, senators, representatives, journalists, lobbyists, staff, and constituents all mingle in its corridors. The galleries stay open to the public whenever the Senate and House convene, except for those rare closed sessions dealing with highly classified information. Flags flying above the chambers indicate which house is meeting, and at night a beacon high up in the Capitol dome signifies that a night session of the Senate or House is in progress.

SEE ALSO

Architect of the Capitol; Library of Congress

FURTHER READING

Aikman, Lonnelle M. *We, the People: The Story of the United States Capitol, Its Past and Its Promise.* Washington, D.C.: U.S. Capitol Historical Society, 1991.
Brown, Glenn. *History of the United States Capitol.* 2 vols. 1903. Reprint. New York: Da Capo Press, 1970.

Capitol Hill

WHILE DRAWING up plans for the city of Washington, the French architect Pierre L'Enfant called Capitol Hill a "pedestal waiting for a monument." He chose the hill as the site of the U.S. Capitol building. Formerly known as Jenkins Hill, the plateau rises 88 feet above the nearby Potomac River. This high ground overlooking the city was renamed Capitol Hill after the Capitoline Hill of the ancient Roman Republic.

Construction of the Capitol began in 1793. During the next two centuries, as Congress grew, its functions spread to many other buildings clustered around the Capitol. *Capitol Hill* became a collective term for the entire complex of buildings that house and serve Congress, as well as for the neighborhood of shops and homes within sight of the Capitol. Capitol Hill (or just the Hill) also came to mean Congress itself, just as the White House has become synonymous with the President who occupies it.

Capitol Historical Society

IN 1962 Representative Fred Schwengel (Republican–Iowa) founded the U.S. Capitol Historical Society to promote greater public awareness of the history of Congress and the Capitol building. This not-for-profit membership organization raises funds largely through the sales of its guidebook, *We, the People,* and other Congress-related publications and memorabilia at a gift stand in the Capitol.

Capitol Police

SEPARATE FROM the Washington metropolitan police, the Capitol Police protect Congress and its visitors. In 1800, Congress needed only a single guard to patrol the Capitol. By 1828, the official date of the founding of the Capitol Police, the staff had increased to three non-

uniformed watchmen. By the Civil War, Capitol Police wore uniforms and badges and carried heavy canes as weapons.

As the Capitol grounds expanded, so did the Capitol police force. Officers guarded entrances, patrolled the grounds, directed traffic, and controlled crowds. At first, most police officers were appointed through patronage— they were war veterans or college students sponsored by members of Congress. In 1968, faced with a growing number of political demonstrations and civil disturbances in Washington, Congress moved to end the patronage system and create a professional police force. By the 1990s, more than 1,300 professionally trained men and women were serving in uniform as Capitol Police. At the same time, security devices such as electronic metal detectors were installed at the entrances to all buildings and at the House and Senate galleries.

FURTHER READING

Byrd, Robert C. "The Capitol Police." In *The Senate, 1789–1989: Addresses on the History of the United States Senate.* Vol. 2. Washington, D.C.: Government Printing Office, 1991.

The Capitol Police in the 1860s.

Carpetbaggers

DURING RECONSTRUCTION of the South after the Civil War, federal troops protected the right of freedmen to vote. Black voters helped elect Republican state governments and sent Republican candidates—both white and black—to the House and Senate from the Southern states. Many of these Southern Republicans were Northerners who had moved to the South after the war. Southern Democrats denounced them as "carpetbaggers," after the carpet-fabric bags in which many of these newcomers brought their belongings to the South. Among the carpetbaggers were some corrupt opportunists, but others wanted to rebuild the South and to help the freedmen during the transition from slavery to freedom.

Eventually, in state after state, Democrats overthrew the Republican Reconstruction governments. The last of the federal troops withdrew from the Southern states after the election of 1876. Violence and restrictive election laws took the vote away from the freedmen. After Reconstruction the "solid South" sent almost no Republicans to Congress again until the 1960s.

SEE ALSO
Reconstruction, congressional; "Solid South"

FURTHER READING
Current, Richard N. *Those Terrible Carpetbaggers*. New York: Oxford, 1988.

Caucuses

BORROWING THE word from the Algonquian Indians, members of the same political party *caucus*—or meet together—in closed session. Congressional

Federalists held the first party caucus in 1800, to endorse the reelection of President John Adams. The Democratic-Republicans held their own caucus to nominate Thomas Jefferson for President. Party caucuses nominated candidates until 1828, when Andrew Jackson campaigned against "King Caucus," calling it undemocratic. Later, party conventions assumed the role of nominating Presidential candidates.

After the end of the single-party Era of Good Feelings, which lasted from the War of 1812 until 1828, caucuses took on new importance as the lines in Congress once again became drawn between political parties. Beginning in 1845, the Senate party caucuses began preparing lists of majority and minority party members of the Senate committees. By the late 19th century, the chairman of the Senate's majority caucus (who was elected by the majority party senators) had taken on the duties of opening and closing the session and scheduling legislation, duties that would later be the responsibility of the majority leader.

In the House, strong Speakers such as Thomas B. Reed and Joseph G. Cannon effectively used the caucuses to exert leadership in passing legislation and to discipline political renegades. Republicans adopted "binding caucus" rules—meaning that whatever a majority of members voted for in caucus, *all* members of the caucus would vote for in the full House—to marshal the maximum strength of their forces behind their legislative programs. When Democrats won the majority in Congress in 1912, they adopted a similar rule to unify behind President Woodrow Wilson's progressive agenda. They agreed to debate the issues within the caucus and then to vote together as much as possible on the floor.

During the 1920s, the caucus declined as a vehicle of party unity and discipline. As caucuses developed a negative clined as a vehicle of party unity and discipline. As caucuses developed a negative public image, Republicans in both houses and Democrats in the Senate began calling the caucuses party conferences; only the House Democratic Caucus retained the name. Whether caucus or conference, the groups devoted themselves to electing floor leaders and performing organizational duties rather than to setting legislative agendas. Party leaders became reluctant to call many conference meetings because they did not want to expose the divisions within their party.

Numerous smaller caucuses also operate on Capitol Hill. The first such organization was the Democratic Study Group, begun in 1958. Others include the Congressional Black Caucus, the Congressional Caucus on Women's Issues, the Dairy Caucus, and other like-minded or single-issue groups that meet, elect officers, hold discussions, and issue publications to forge unity behind their legislative proposals.

Caucus rooms

TWO GRANDLY ornate rooms in the Cannon House Office Building and Russell Senate Office Building are designated as caucus rooms. The title suggests that they were originally reserved for political party meetings, but the rooms gained more notoriety as the setting for major congressional investigations. In 1912 the Senate caucus room was the site of an investigation into the sinking of the *Titanic*. It was followed by the Teapot Dome investigation, the Wall Street investigation, the Truman Committee investigation of the national defense program, the Army-McCarthy hearings, the Watergate investigation, and the Iran-

Contra scandal investigation. Beginning with Estes Kefauver's organized crime investigation in 1950, television covered the bigger Senate investigations, making the room and its unusual furnishings familiar to millions of viewers.

The House, similarly, used its caucus room for major investigations, such as the House Un-American Activities Committee's Hiss-Chambers hearings in 1948, when Whittaker Chambers testified that former State Department official Alger Hiss had secretly been a member of the Communist party and had engaged in espionage. But Speaker Sam Rayburn refused to allow television to cover House hearings. Not until 1970 did the House permit radio and television coverage of its committee hearings. In addition to committee hearings, members of Congress have used the caucus rooms to announce their Presidential candidacies, to host foreign visitors, and to sponsor assorted exhibits and receptions.

President Woodrow Wilson picks the first draft number of World War I in the Senate Caucus Room.

Censure

BY CENSURING someone, Congress formally rebukes that member for wrongdoing. However, members who are censured do not lose their seat, their committee assignments, or their seniority. A simple majority vote can censure,

SENATORS WHO WERE CENSURED

Timothy Pickering (Federalist–Massachusetts), 1811, for reading confidential documents in a public session of the Senate

Benjamin Tappan (Democrat–Ohio), 1844, for releasing to the press a still-secret treaty

Benjamin Tillman and **John McLaurin** (Democrats–South Carolina), 1902, for fighting in the Senate chamber

Hiram Bingham (Republican–Connecticut), 1929, for bringing a lobbyist to a closed hearing

Joseph R. McCarthy (Republican–Wisconsin), 1954, for abuse of Senate committees and practices

Thomas J. Dodd (Democrat–Connecticut), 1967, for personal use of campaign funds

Herman Talmadge (Democrat–Georgia), 1979, for improper financial conduct

David Durenberger (Republican–Minnesota), 1990, for improper financial conduct

Senator Benjamin Tillman was censured for fistfighting in the Senate chamber.

REPRESENTATIVES WHO WERE CENSURED

William Stansbery (Democrat–Ohio), 1832, for insulting the Speaker

Joshua Giddings (Whig–Ohio), 1842, for defending the slave mutineers on the *Creole*

Laurence Keitt (Democrat–South Carolina), 1856, for complicity in Representative Preston Brooks's assault on Senator Charles Sumner

Benjamin Harris (Democrat–Maryland), 1864, for treasonable remarks

Alexander Long (Democrat–Ohio), 1864, for treasonable remarks

John W. Chanler (Democrat–New York), 1866, for an insult to the House

Lovell Rousseau (Republican–Kentucky), 1866, for an assault on Representative Josiah Grinnell in the Capitol

John Hunter (Independent–New York), 1867, for offensive remarks

Edward Holbrook (Democrat–Idaho), 1868, for offensive remarks

Fernando Wood (Democrat–New York), 1868, for offensive remarks

Roderick Butler (Republican–Tennessee), 1870, for corruption

John Deweese (Democrat–North Carolina), 1870, for corruption

Benjamin Whittemore (Republican–South Carolina), 1870, for corruption

Oakes Ames (Republican–Massachusetts), 1873, for corruption

James Brooks (Democrat–New York), 1873, for corruption

John Brown (Democrat–Kentucky), 1875, for offensive remarks

William Bynum (Democrat–Indiana), 1890, for offensive remarks

Thomas Blanton (Democrat–Texas), 1921, for publishing offensive material in the *Congressional Record*

Charles Diggs (Democrat–Michigan), 1979, for misuse of official funds

Charles Wilson (Democrat–California), 1980, for financial misconduct

Daniel Crane (Republican–Illinois), 1983, for sexual misconduct

Gerry Studds (Democrat–Massachusetts), 1983, for sexual misconduct

In 1842, the House nearly censured Representative John Quincy Adams (Whig–Massachusetts) for presenting an antislavery petition in violation of House rules. But Adams successfully fought back and the House took no vote. Other representatives suffered censure for insulting the Speaker, making treasonable utterances, assaulting fellow members of Congress, and corruption.

In 1811, the Senate censured Timothy Pickering (Federalist–Massachusetts) for reading a still-secret document in a public session. In 1902 two senators from South Carolina were censured for having a fistfight in the Senate chamber. Senators have also been censured for the misuse of campaign funds and other financial irregularities.

The most infamous censure case involved Joseph R. McCarthy (Republican–Wisconsin). McCarthy's reckless charges and bullying tactics had long troubled senators, but they hesitated to act because of the popularity of his anticommunist crusade. When McCarthy launched an irresponsible attack on the U.S. Army in 1954, public opinion turned against him. Following the Army-McCarthy hearings, the Senate by a vote of 67 to 22 found McCarthy guilty of conduct unbecoming a senator and of bringing the Senate into disrepute.

Since the resolution used the word *condemn*, McCarthy's supporters argued that he had not been censured. Other senators pointed out that the two words had identical meanings. In later cases involving financial misconduct, the Senate "denounced" offenders. Both the Senate and House have also "reprimanded" members for lesser offenses.

On only one occasion has Congress censured a President. In 1834 the Whig-dominated Senate censured President Andrew Jackson for not opening certain cabinet records for Senate inspection. Three years later, after Democratic senators had regained the majority, they voted to expunge (remove) the censure from the Senate journal.

SEE ALSO
Discipline; Expulsion; McCarthy, Joseph R.

FURTHER READING
Griffith, Robert. *The Politics of Fear: Joseph R. McCarthy and the Senate.* Lexington: University Press of Kentucky, 1970.

Chairs of committees

THROUGH SENIORITY, or length of service, members of the majority party advance to become committee chairs. Since most legislative work is done in committee, chairmen are extremely influential on Capitol Hill. The chair controls a committee's operating funds, appoints much of its staff, refers legislation to subcommittees, and sets the schedule for committee business. It is difficult for legislation to leave a committee without the chair's approval. In the past, committee chairs acted like autocratic barons of legislative fiefdoms, but modern reforms have whittled down their power and made committee operations more democratic. Junior members now chair subcommittees, and all members have staff on the committees on which they serve. Committee chairs must work harder to accommodate other members—particularly the ranking minority member—to establish as much unity and agreement as possible within their committee before reporting bills to the floor. Senator Bob Dole (Republican–Kansas), who chaired the powerful Finance Committee from 1981 to 1984, noted that "a chairman leads by consensus, not command."

A committee chairmanship has been described as "a blank check" to be filled out by the personality and skill of each individual who holds the job. As a result of their seniority, chairs are extremely familiar with the subject areas over which their committee has jurisdiction. Other members frequently defer to their judgment on the issues, and the heads of executive agencies consult with committee chairs in matters of common interest as well as to request increases in appropriations for their agencies. Some committee chairs gain respect and even inspire fear through their force of personality and parliamentary skill. All of these factors determine a chair's success in managing bills through to passage.

SEE ALSO
Ranking members; Seniority

FURTHER READING
Smith, Stephen S., and Christopher J. Deering. *Committees in Congress.* Washington, D.C.: Congressional Quarterly, 1984.

Chambers, House and Senate

THE SENATE and House of Representatives occupy impressive chambers on the north and south ends of the Capitol building, respectively. The galleries of these chambers are open to visitors, and the proceedings that take place there are televised, making them increasingly familiar to the public.

The Senate moved into the smaller of the two chambers in 1859. Today, it has 100 desks arranged in semicircular rows, with the parties divided by the central aisle. At the front of the chamber, the presiding officer sits at a raised desk. The various clerks and parliamentarians sit at a lower desk. Senators speak from their desks and vote by voice.

Since 1857, the House has occupied the larger chamber and therefore hosts all joint sessions, such as State of the Union addresses. House members sat at desks until 1911, when the membership reached 435 and the chamber became too crowded. The desks were replaced by semicircles of padded benches, with the parties divided by the center aisle. Representatives address the house from podiums in the "well" in front of the Speaker's rostrum or from two tables on either side of the aisle. They vote electronically, using voting cards, and the tallies are illuminated on the wall above the Speaker. The Speaker sits at an elevated rostrum above two rows of desks for the various clerks and a podium for the President and other heads of state who occasionally address the Congress.

Over the years, both chambers have undergone extensive remodeling. Electric lighting made the original glass ceilings unnecessary, and recessed panels were removed to improve acoustics. But the chambers also retain many symbols of their past. Long after senators ceased to use snuff, the Senate has kept two small snuffboxes filled with ground tobacco. Ringing the Senate chamber are marble busts of the first 20 Vice Presidents, who served as the Senate's presiding officers.

The House chamber features 23 marble medallions of the great lawgivers of history, ranging from the Babylonian king Hammurabi to Thomas Jefferson, author of the Declaration of Independence. On either side of the Speaker's podium are full-length portraits of George Washington, the first U.S. President, and the Marquis de Lafayette, the first foreign dignitary to address the House.

SEE ALSO
Capitol building

The House of Representatives chamber, showing the electronic scoreboard that records members' votes.

The Senate used this ornate chamber from 1810 until 1859.

Chaplain

CHAPLAINS, THE official clergymen of Congress, open the daily sessions of the House and Senate with prayer. Begun by the Continental Congress in 1774, this practice was continued by the 1st Congress. On April 25, 1789, the Senate elected Samuel Provoost, an Episcopalian bishop, as its first chaplain. On May 1, the Reverend William Lynn was elected chaplain of the House.

When Congress first moved to Washington, there were few churches in the new city, so the House and Senate chaplains alternated conducting Sunday services in the House chamber. Chaplains have also performed marriages and funerals for members of Congress. Although all chaplains have been Christians, Congress has invited religious leaders from many other faiths to deliver opening prayers. In 1860, Rabbi Morris Jacob Raphall became the first Jewish clergyman to pray at the opening of a House session. In 1971, a Native American holy man brought his peace pipe to open a Senate session. And in 1992, the imam Wallace D. Mohammed became the first Muslim to offer an invocation.

Occasional lawsuits have charged that the congressional chaplains violate the separation of church and state. However, the courts have ruled that the Constitution grants each house of Congress the power to elect its own officers and manage its own internal affairs as the majority sees fit.

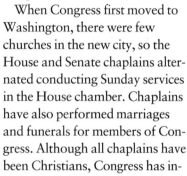

Episcopal bishop Samuel Provoost was the first chaplain of the Senate.

FURTHER READING

Byrd, Robert C. "Senate Chaplain." In *The Senate, 1789–1989: Addresses on the History of the United States Senate.* Vol. 2. Washington, D.C.: Government Printing Office, 1991.

Checks and balances

"AMBITION MUST be made to counteract ambition," explained James Madison when defining how the framers intended the U.S. Constitution to work. According to that reasoning, the Constitution divided the powers and responsibilities of the federal government among the legislative, executive, and judicial branches and also between the two houses of Congress. Each part of the government provides a check and balance on the ambition of the others, preventing any one part from becoming too powerful or autocratic.

For example, the President serves as commander in chief of the armed forces, but Congress appropriates the funds for the military and votes to declare war, and the Senate must ratify any peace treaties. The President nominates federal officials, but the Senate must confirm those nominations. The President may veto legislation, but Congress can override that veto by a two-thirds vote. The Supreme Court may declare executive actions or acts of Congress unconstitutional, but new legislation can reverse Court decisions.

Both houses of Congress must pass a bill in the same form for it to become law, and both must cast a two-thirds vote to override a Presidential veto. The House alone initiates revenue bills; the Senate alone confirms nominations and treaties. The House votes to impeach federal officials, and then the Senate sits as a court to convict or acquit them.

"If men were angels"

The system of checks and balances requires Congress and the President to work together if they wish to accomplish anything. The system also creates friction

President John Adams nominated his son, John Quincy Adams, as U.S. minister to Prussia (Germany).

among the branches, and it has sometimes appeared dangerously inefficient in times of national crisis. Yet the system has worked through war and peace, depression and prosperity, for more than two centuries. Checks and balances remain a reflection of the political realism of the framers of the Constitution.

"If men were angels, no government would be necessary," Madison wrote in the *Federalist Papers*. "If angels were to govern men, neither external nor internal controls on government would be necessary. In framing a government which is to be administered by men over men, the great difficulty is this: You must first enable the government to control the governed; and in the next place, oblige it to control itself."

SEE ALSO
Bicameral; Constitution; Separation of powers

FURTHER READING
Ritchie, Donald A. *The U.S. Constitution.* New York: Chelsea House, 1989.

Chisholm, Shirley

☆ *Born: Nov. 30, 1924, New York, N.Y.*
☆ *Political party: Democrat*
☆ *Representative from New York: 1969–83*

THE FIRST African-American woman elected to the House of Representatives, Shirley Chisholm represented a poor, inner-city district in Brooklyn, New York. So she was shocked when her party assigned her to the House Agriculture Committee. Because that committee had little to do with the desperate needs of her constituents, she refused to serve on it. Party leaders reassigned her to the Veterans' Affairs Committee and eventually to her first choice, the Education and Labor Committee.

Unafraid of a good fight, Chisholm went to Congress determined to right the wrongs that she had personally witnessed and experienced. In the House she championed equal rights for women and minorities, an Equal Rights Amendment to the Constitution, extension of the minimum wage to domestic workers, and federal day-care facilities.

SEE ALSO
African Americans in Congress

FURTHER READING
Chisholm, Shirley. *The Good Fight.* New York: Harper & Row, 1973.
Chisholm, Shirley. *Unbought and Unbossed.* Boston: Houghton Mifflin, 1970.

"Christmas tree" bills

SEE Pork barrel politics

Civil rights legislation

FOR A CENTURY after the Civil War, Congress debated, filibustered against, and finally enacted significant civil rights legislation to guarantee the equal rights of African Americans and other minorities. In 1866, Congress passed the first Civil Rights Act over President Andrew Johnson's veto. This act granted African Americans full citizenship, thereby reversing the Supreme Court's *Dred Scott* decision of 1857, which had stated that blacks, whether slave or free, were not citizens.

When Southern states passed laws requiring segregation by race, Senator Charles Sumner (Republican–Massachusetts) sponsored the Civil Rights Act of 1875, which provided for equal accommodations in hotels, restaurants, trains, and other public facilities. In 1896, the Supreme Court, ruling in *Plessy v. Ferguson*, declared this act unconstitutional and upheld racial segregation. The Court ruled that "laws permitting, and even requiring their separation in places where they are liable to be brought into contact do not necessarily imply the inferiority of either race to the other." Although segregationists never had the votes in Congress to write segregation into national law, they were able to protect it by filibustering—or blocking by extended debate and other legislative tactics—against all civil rights legislation in the Senate.

In 1957, Senate majority leader Lyndon B. Johnson (Democrat–Texas) took credit for passing the first civil rights bill since Reconstruction, but Southern opponents had severely weakened this measure by adding an amendment that required jury trials for offenders. Since Southern juries were still likely to be all white, few convictions could be expected. As President in 1964, Johnson led the effort to achieve cloture and stop the filibuster against a much stronger civil rights bill that outlawed discrimination in any form of interstate commerce. The next year Johnson proposed, and Congress enacted, the Voting Rights Act to provide federal protection for African Americans' right to vote. The Civil Rights Act of 1964 and Voting Rights Act of 1965 had a profound impact on American politics, especially in the South, where Southern Democratic officeholders became more attuned to minority constituents, where African Americans were elected to Congress, and where the Republican party once again became a real challenge to the once solid Democratic South.

SEE ALSO

Cloture; Filibuster; Johnson, Lyndon B.; "Solid South"; Sumner, Charles

FURTHER READING

Whalen, Charles, and Barbara Whalen. *The Longest Debate: A Legislative History of the 1964 Civil Rights Act.* Washington, D.C.: Seven Locks Press, 1985.

President Lyndon B. Johnson gives the Reverend Martin Luther King, Jr., the pen he used to sign the Voting Rights Act of 1965.

Clark, James Beauchamp ("Champ")

☆ *Born: Mar. 7, 1850, Lawrenceburg, Ky.*
☆ *Political party: Democrat*
☆ *Representative from Missouri: 1893–95, 1897–1921*
☆ *Speaker of the House: 1913–19*
☆ *House minority leader: 1909–13, 1919–21*
☆ *Died: Mar. 2, 1921, Washington, D.C.*

BY LEADING the fight to limit Speaker Joseph G. Cannon's power over the House in 1909, Democratic minority leader Champ Clark limited himself as well. "Although I am going to be Speaker next time," said Clark, "I am going to sacrifice the Speaker's power to change the rules." Clark forged an alliance with progressive Republicans to win a majority of votes for his resolution to enlarge the House Rules Committee and prohibit the Speaker from serving on that powerful committee. The next year, when Democrats won the majority in the House, Clark replaced Cannon as Speaker. Clark served chiefly as the House's presiding officer and left it to Majority Leader Oscar W. Underwood (Democrat–Alabama) to lead his party's floor fights. Clark accepted a further reduction in power when the Democratic Caucus took away the Speaker's power to make committee appointments. Although Champ Clark reduced the powers of his own office, he made sure that the House would not return to "one-man rule."

SEE ALSO
Cannon, Joseph G.

FURTHER READING
Clark, Champ. *My Quarter Century of American Politics.* 2 vols. New York: Harper, 1920.

Clay, Henry

☆ *Born: Apr. 12, 1777, Hanover County, Va.*
☆ *Political party: Democratic-Republican, Whig*
☆ *Senator from Kentucky: 1810–11, 1831–42, 1849–52*
☆ *Representative from Kentucky: 1811–14, 1815–21, 1823–25*
☆ *Speaker of the House: 1811–14, 1815–20, 1823–25*
☆ *Died: June 29, 1852, Washington, D.C.*

KNOWN AS the "Great Compromiser," Henry Clay dominated the House and Senate for more than four decades yet lost the election every time he ran for President. After a brief term in the Senate, he went to the House, where he was elected Speaker on his first day. Clay put forward an ambitious program of federally funded roads, canals, and other internal improvements, a national bank, and a protective tariff. His American System program took him into battle with President Andrew Jackson and the Democrats and led to the formation of the Whig party.

Clay also worked for years in Congress to achieve compromises between the North and South to reduce sectional tensions over slavery. From the Missouri Compromise to the Compromise of 1850, Clay played a major role. Although a pragmatic politician, he could also show passion and let his temper get the best of him. Members of Congress either adored or hated him. "I don't like Clay," said John C. Calhoun. "He is a bad man, an imposter, a creature of wicked schemes. I won't speak to him, but, by God, I love him!" Voters showed similarly mixed feelings.

SEE ALSO
Compromise; Compromise of 1850; Missouri Compromise (1821)

FURTHER READING
Remini, Robert. *Henry Clay: Statesman for the Union.* New York: Norton, 1991.

A bronze statue of Henry Clay in the Capitol's Statuary Hall

Clerk of the House

SINCE 1789, the clerk of the House has served as administrative officer of the House of Representatives. Elected by the members, although not a representative himself, the clerk purchases stationery and office supplies, disburses salaries, and supervises the staff necessary for the functioning of House sessions. (In the Senate, similar functions are performed by the secretary of the Senate.)

House rules stated that whenever it passed a bill, "it shall be certified by the clerk, noting the day of its passing" at the bottom of the page. The clerk was also assigned to read to the members any bills referred to the House as a committee of the whole. The clerk was put in charge of all the records of the House, especially the keeping and printing of the House journals. Two centuries after John Beckley was elected the first clerk of the House, his successors continue to be responsible for these duties and many more, including purchasing electrical and mechanical equipment, compiling the activity reports that all congressional lobbyists must file each year according to federal law, and issuing other reports that the House requires.

In 1992, following scandals involving the House bank and post office, the House of Representatives created the new post of director of non-legislative services. The director was assigned to handle all payrolls, office supplies, inside mail, restaurants, barber and beauty shops, and other administrative business that had once been supervised by the clerk of the House and sergeant at arms.

SEE ALSO
Committee of the whole; Director of non-legislative services; Journals; Officers of the House and Senate; Secretary of the Senate; Sergeant at arms

Cloakrooms

L-SHAPED ROOMS at the rear of the House and Senate chambers, on either side of the central door, provide cloakrooms for Democratic and Republican members. Once rooms where senators and representatives could hang their hats and cloaks before they entered the chambers, the cloakrooms have become informal meeting rooms. Members meet there to work out legislative compromises, use the phones, or simply rest on the leather couches behind the swinging doors to the chambers. The cloakrooms have become synonymous with backstage political dealing, away from public view. As majority leader, Lyndon B. Johnson (Democrat–Texas) shifted much of the Senate's real deliberations from the floor to the cloakrooms. Johnson once advised Senator Hubert Humphrey (Democrat–Minnesota):

> Now you don't just come right out on the floor and lay important bills right out in front of God and all those voters. That's not the way it's done, and you could lose before you get started, which doesn't look good to the folks back home. You have to take it slow and easy, working your colleagues over like gentlemen—not on the floor but in the cloakrooms—explaining and trading, but always letting them see what's in it for them. Then when you're sure—Ivory soap sure, and you know you have the votes buttoned up in your back pocket—you come out statesmanlike on the Senate floor and, in the spirit of democracy, have a little debate for the people.

Closed rule

WHEN A BILL comes before the House, the Rules Committee may set a "closed rule" for its debate and final vote. Under a closed rule, no additional amendments or substitutes to the bill may be offered from the floor.

Closed sessions

S E E Executive sessions

Cloture

IN THE Senate, when opponents of a bill try to delay and defeat its passage, supporters of the bill will seek to vote cloture, to cut off debate and bring the bill to a vote. The House of Representatives, because of its larger number of members, made majority rule easier to achieve. In 1842, the House adopted a standing rule that no member could speak for more than one hour on any issue under debate. Subsequent five-minute rules and one-minute rules reduced even further the time that members could speak on amendments. The House Rules Committee controls how long the House will debate a bill, prohibits non-germane (irrelevant) amendments, and sets the time for a vote.

The Senate has remained more tolerant of the right to unlimited debate. Until 1917, the Senate had no effective way of shutting off a filibuster, or delaying tactics. During the closing days of the session that year, a group of isolationist senators, who were opposed to the United States entering World War I, filibustered against a bill to arm U.S. merchant ships. President Woodrow Wilson denounced them as a "little group of willful men" and called on the Senate to change its rules. The Senate responded by adopting Rule 22, which provided that a two-thirds vote of all senators could cut off debate.

Cloture difficult to achieve even with Rule 22

The Senate tried eleven times between 1917 and 1964 to invoke (or achieve) cloture but failed each time. Southern senators especially relied on the filibuster to block civil rights legislation. They gained allies in senators from smaller states who refused to vote for cloture because they themselves might need to filibuster to protect their states' interests. In 1957, Senate majority leader Lyndon B. Johnson (Democrat–Texas) won passage of the first civil rights legislation since Reconstruction but at the price of a severely watered-down bill. As President in 1964, Johnson called for stronger civil rights legislation. With the support of Republican minority leader Everett Dirksen, Northern Democrats and Republicans at last were able to invoke cloture and break the Southern filibuster.

In 1975, the Senate reduced the number of votes necessary for cloture from two-thirds (67) to three-fifths (60) of the 100-member Senate. Some senators wanted to change the rule to require

This 1960s cartoon depicted "unlimited debate" as the Senate's best weapon against "majority rule."

only a simple majority (51), but Majority Leader Mike Mansfield (Democrat–Montana) objected. Mansfield believed it was important to retain some way for the minority to check the majority. By then, even moderate and liberal senators had resorted to filibusters to block legislation they found offensive.

Post-cloture tactics

Invoking cloture does not automatically stop all delaying tactics. In the 1970s, after rule changes made cloture easier to achieve, Senator James Allen (Democrat–Alabama) invented the post-cloture filibuster. Opponents load a bill up with amendments before cloture because under the terms of cloture they will have 100 hours to debate any amendment. But in 1977 Senate majority leader Robert C. Byrd (Democrat–West Virginia) arranged for the Vice President, as presiding officer, to declare a long list of such amendments out of order. However, a minority of senators can still find enough loopholes in the Senate's cloture rule to stall a bill long enough to amend or kill it.

S E E A L S O
Filibuster

F U R T H E R R E A D I N G
Oleszek, Walter J. *Congressional Procedures and the Policy Process.* Washington, D.C.: Congressional Quarterly, 1989.

Comity

S E E Decorum

Commemoratives

CONGRESS HAS designated practically every week of the year to commemorate something. A large number of bills enacted each session name a day, a week, or a month in honor of some worthy cause. Congress has declared commemoratives for country music, diseases, ethnic groups, flowers, sports, trees, and war veterans. Although commemoratives often appear to pander to special interests, members of Congress consider these resolutions a popular and inexpensive way to recognize groups that have done good work or issues that deserve national attention.

Commerce power

S E E Regulation of commerce

Committee assignments

APPOINTMENT TO a particular committee determines the areas of legislation over which a senator or representative will have the greatest say. Members try hard to persuade their party's steering committees to put them on committees that match their own interests and their constituents' needs. Until the 1950s, freshmen members routinely were assigned to such minor committees as the District of Columbia Committee and had to wait their turn for assignment to such major committees as Armed Services or Appropriations. Today, each new member joins at least one major committee. All members are limited to the number of major committees on which they can serve. Since individuals move up in seniority within a committee toward the chairmanship, they tend to retain the same committee assignments from year to year. But if their interests change, they might give up one committee for another. On the average, a senator serves on three committees, one select

Carol Moseley-Braun received assignments on the Banking, Housing, and Urban Affairs; Judiciary; and Small Business Committees as a new senator in 1993.

or special committee, and seven subcommittees. A representative usually has two standing committee assignments, one special or select committee, and four subcommittees. Since House members serve on fewer committees, they tend to become specialists in those areas, whereas senators, who serve on more committees, are more likely to be generalists.

S E E   A L S O
Committees

Committee of the whole

TO SUSPEND its rules and move ahead speedily on major bills, to which a committee may have added many amendments, the House of Representatives frequently becomes a committee of the whole (the official title is the Committee of the Whole House on the State of the Union). All House members serve on the committee of the whole, and it meets in the House chamber. A member of the majority other than the Speaker presides over the committee of the whole, and the House mace is moved to a lower pedestal than usual to indicate that the House is no longer in regular session. Although in a regular session 218 members are needed to provide a quorum—the number of members required to be present to conduct business—only 100 members are needed for a quorum in the committee of the whole. Debate is limited to five minutes on each side for each amendment. The committee of the whole may vote on these amendments but not on the final version of the bill. At the end of the debate, the bill's floor manager makes a motion to report the legislation. The House then returns to regular session and votes on the bill. The Senate does not

conduct business as a committee of the whole.

Committees

WHEN A BILL is introduced, the House or Senate parliamentarian determines its jurisdiction and refers it to the appropriate committee. Within the committee, the bill is usually considered by a subcommittee, which may hold hearings to collect testimony and other evidence. The subcommittee then reports the bill to the full committee for further debate and amendment. If the committee approves, it will report the bill to the House or Senate. The committee chairman or another designated floor manager from the committee will attempt to defend the bill against crippling amendments and win its passage. Once a bill becomes law, the same committee exercises oversight over the executive department agency that carries out the law.

Legislation is shaped more in committee than on the floor of the House and Senate. Bills tend to pass in a form so close to that in which they are reported (voted on and sent to the floor) by committees that the committees have been called "little legislatures." Members therefore have the most influence over bills considered in their own committees.

Select committees

The first House and Senate were small bodies that often debated legislative proposals as a committee of the whole and then appointed a select (temporary) committee to perfect the bill's language. Select committees went out of existence as soon as they reported their specific legislation. The first standing (permanent) committees dealt with such housekeeping items as enrolled bills (en-

A meeting of the Senate Finance Committee in the 1920s.

rolled bills are the final versions of enacted bills that have been checked for typographical errors and inconsistencies) and contested congressional elections. During the early Congresses, the House and Senate created hundreds of select committees. Committee members were elected by the entire chamber, and whoever received the most votes chaired the committee. Under this system, some members served on many committees, while others served on few or none.

Standing committees

In 1792, the House created the Ways and Means Committee to consider and enact Treasury Secretary Alexander Hamilton's proposals for an ambitious national financial program. A Committee on Public Lands was established following the Louisiana Purchase of 1803. After the disastrous War of 1812, for which both the executive and legislative branches seemed unprepared, both houses of Congress saw the need for more legislative expertise and for conducting their business more efficiently. In December 1816, the Senate created a dozen standing committees, including Foreign Relations, Judiciary, and Fi-

nance, which continue to operate today. By 1816, the House had created 16 standing committees. Over time, the number of committees increased steadily, and then various legislative reorganizations reduced their number and settled their jurisdiction—which bills would be referred to them.

By the late 19th century, congressional committees had become powerful instruments of government. Committees conducted most of their work in secret, and committee rooms became the domain of chairmen so autocratic that they were sometimes described as barons. The most influential committees were the four "money" committees—Finance and Appropriations in the Senate—Ways and Means and Appropriations in the House—which determined how all federal money would be raised and spent. Other committees held authority over such areas as the military, foreign policy, the federal judiciary, commerce, and the interior. A few committees existed only to give their chairmen a room and a clerk and never received any legislation to consider. For example, the Senate established a Committee on Woman Suffrage decades before the all-male Sen-

CONGRESSIONAL COMMITTEES
103RD CONGRESS, 1993–95

Standing Committees of the Senate

Agriculture, Nutrition, and Forestry

Appropriations

Armed Services

Banking, Housing, and Urban Affairs

Budget

Commerce, Science, and Transportation

Energy and Natural Resources

Environment and Public Works

Finance

Foreign Relations

Governmental Affairs

Judiciary

Labor and Human Resources

Rules and Administration

Small Business

Select and Special Committees of the Senate

Select Committee on Ethics

Select Committee on Indian Affairs

Select Committee on Intelligence

Special Committee on Aging

Joint Committees

Joint Committee on the Library

Joint Committee on Taxation

Joint Economic Committee

Standing Committees of the House

Agriculture

Appropriations

Armed Services

Banking, Finance, and Urban Affairs

Budget

District of Columbia

Education and Labor

Energy and Commerce

Foreign Affairs

Government Operations

House Administration

Interior and Insular Affairs

Judiciary

Merchant Marine and Fisheries

Post Office and Civil Service

Public Works and Transportation

Rules

Science, Space, and Technology

Small Business

Standards of Official Conduct

Ways and Means

Select and Special Committees of the House

Permanent Select Committee on Intelligence

Select Committee on Aging*

Select Committee on Children, Youth, and Families*

Select Committee on Hunger*

Select Committee on Narcotics Abuse and Control*

*Early in the 103rd Congress, the House abolished these select committees.

ate took that issue seriously and maintained a Committee on Revolutionary Claims into the early 20th century, long after any revolutionary war veterans and widows were still living to file claims for pensions. Party caucuses selected committee members, who then advanced by seniority.

Committee reforms

Reforms in the 20th century reduced the power of committee chairmen, provided for discharge of bills from committees that failed to report them, assigned staff to all committee members, and threatened uncooperative chairmen with removal by a majority vote of the majority caucus. "Sunshine" rules required all committee hearings, including markup sessions, to be open to the public.

SEE ALSO

Chairs of committees; Committee assignments; Conference committees; Investigations; Joint committees; Oversight; Ranking members; Referrals to committee; Seniority; Subcommittees

FURTHER READING

Byrd, Robert C. "The Committee System." In *The Senate, 1789–1989: Addresses on the History of the United States Senate.* Vol. 2. Washington, D.C.: Government Printing Office, 1991.
Smith, Stephen S., and Christopher J. Deering. *Committees in Congress.* Washington, D.C.: Congressional Quarterly, 1984

Compromise

"COMPROMISE IS the name of the game in the legislative process," argued Representative Richard Bolling (Democrat–Missouri). Henry Clay (Whig–Kentucky) gained fame as the "Great Compromiser," but "Battling Bob" La Follette (Republican–Wisconsin) pre-

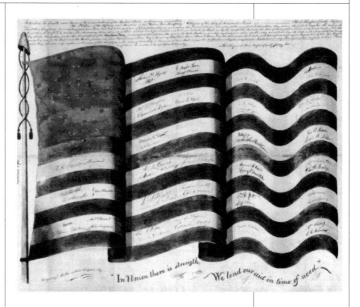

In 1861, Congress received this petition in support of the Crittenden Compromise, which sought to avoid a civil war.

ferred to lose rather than to compromise. Most members of Congress want to win without sacrificing their principles, but they recognize that because Congress represents such a diverse nation, conflicts over legislation are inevitable. To accomplish anything, they have to accommodate many conflicting positions and forge a consensus. Senate majority leader Alben Barkley (Democrat–Kentucky) insisted that "all legislation is a matter of compromise" and that no member should expect a bill to be enacted exactly as he introduced it. Other senators and representatives, in committee or on the floor, would see things differently and offer amendments to correct whatever problems or deficiencies they found. Very few bills become law with more than 50 to 75 percent of what their authors originally proposed. However, a bill's sponsors must decide when too much compromise might defeat their purposes and make their bill ineffective.

FURTHER READING

Bolling, Richard. *Power in the House: A History of the Leadership of the House of Representatives.* New York: Dutton, 1968.

Compromise of 1850

AFTER THE United States won vast southwestern territories from Mexico in 1848, Congress was faced with the question of whether to permit slavery in this region. Antislavery Northerners endorsed the Wilmot Proviso, an amendment to ban the spread of slavery, while Southerners insisted that any restriction on slavery would split the Union. The House of Representatives was so divided that it could not even elect a new Speaker, so solving the territorial problem fell to the Senate. Henry Clay (Whig–Kentucky) returned from retirement to craft one more compromise to save the Union. Clay put together an omnibus bill that would admit California to the Union as a free state, allow New Mexicans to decide whether they wanted slavery, preserve slavery in the District of Columbia, and enact a tough fugitive slave law to allow slave owners to hunt down runaway slaves in the North. Daniel Webster (Whig–Massachusetts) delivered an eloquent appeal for the compromise, warning Southerners who threatened to secede from the Union that there could be "no such thing as peaceable secession." By contrast, John C. Calhoun (Democrat–South Carolina) spent the last days of his life fighting against the compromise. Clay's strategy was to have the Senate vote upon his compromise as a whole, so that senators would have to accept even the portions of the package they disliked. When this tactic failed, an exhausted Clay left Washington to rest. In his absence, the young Stephen A. Douglas (Democrat–Illinois) took apart the omnibus bill, put together different majorities for each of its parts, and won their passage separately. Although not popular in any sec-

tion of the country, the Compromise of 1850 delayed civil war in the United States for another decade.

SEE ALSO

Benton, Thomas Hart; Calhoun, John C.; Clay, Henry; Webster, Daniel; Wilmot Proviso

FURTHER READING

Hamilton, Holman. *Prologue to Conflict: The Crisis and the Compromise of 1850.* New York: Norton, 1964.

Concurrent resolution

A CONCURRENT resolution is a formal statement passed by both houses of the Congress, stating the opinion of Congress or permitting some action that does not require the President's approval. A concurrent resolution must pass both the House and Senate in the same language, but because it does not have the President's signature, it does not have the force of law. Instead, Congress uses concurrent resolutions (designated as H. Con. Res. or S. Con. Res.) for such housekeeping functions as creating joint committees, authorizing the printing of congressional documents, and setting the date for Congress to adjourn. Concurrent resolutions also express the sense, or opinion, of Congress on many matters of foreign and domestic policy.

SEE ALSO

Bills; Joint resolutions; Resolutions

Conference committees

FOR A BILL to become law, both houses of Congress must pass it in exactly the same form, word for word. But the Senate and House usually pass different versions of the same bill. One house may authorize more money to be spent or make the bill tougher or add some entirely new provision. After each house has voted on its version of a bill, the party leaders appoint a conference committee of House and Senate members to reconcile the differences. Members of the conference committee are usually members of the committees that first handled the legislation. Once the conference agrees on a single bill, it issues a conference report, which the Senate and House then vote to adopt—or to reject.

If the chief disagreement is about how much money to spend, conference committees tend to split the difference. Issues are more subject to bargaining, and the conference may simply drop the most controversial portions of the bill. Sometimes the bill's floor managers have accepted controversial amendments simply as "trading material," knowing that the conference committee will eventually reject them.

Success in conference

House members often succeed in conference because they serve on just one major committee and have specialized in the issue at hand. "Before the conference committee, the House members usually meet to plan their strategies, their tactics," observed Howard Shuman, a veteran Senate staff member. "They stay together. They're tough in conference." But senators can also present a united front because the Senate usually works to achieve a bipartisan consensus on legislation rather than voting by party line. Conference reports tend to resemble the last version of the bill enacted, whether by the House or the Senate. Lobbyists from both inside and outside the government will concentrate on the later bill to correct whatever problems they find with the earlier one.

SEE ALSO
Bicameral; Lobbying

FURTHER READING
Baker, Ross K. *House and Senate.* New York: Norton, 1989.

Conferences

SEE Caucuses

Congress

CONGRESS IS the collective identity of the Senate and House of Representatives. The word is derived from the Latin for "coming together." Just as representatives of the American colonies came together in the 1st Continental Congress, the elected representatives of the American people continue to meet together in the U.S. Congress. Sometimes *Congress* is applied incorrectly to the House of Representatives alone because representatives use the alternate title of congressman and congresswoman (whereas senators are always addressed as senators).

The term *Congress* also refers to the two sessions between each congressional election. For instance, the 1st Congress met from 1789 to 1791, and the 101st Congress met from 1989 to 1991. Although the House and Senate do most of their work independently of each other, they must eventually come together to pass all legislation. Bills that were debated as S. Res. 45 or H. Res. 230 become an act of Congress when passed.

The fact that Congress represents the nation coming together can be heard in the many regional accents spoken in its chambers. Every state sends two senators and at least one representative. These legislators bring local concerns to

Representative Alphonso Bell (Republican–California) meets with constituents at a picnic.

national debates, and they work to make sure that the particular needs and concerns of their constituents are addressed in national legislation. These varying needs sometimes pit different sections of the country against each other, whether industrial versus agricultural, energy-producing versus energy-consuming, or the Sun Belt of the Southeast and Southwest versus the Rust Belt of the Northeast and Midwest. Congress provides the forum where the people's elected representatives can debate these conflicting positions and forge some legislative solutions.

Popularity of Congress

As a collective entity, Congress has never been popular. Many members of Congress even run for reelection by running *against* Congress—by emphasizing their differences with the congressional majorities. This accounts for the contradiction that Congress as a whole rates low in public opinion polls while the individual members of Congress are reelected at a high rate. People like their own senators and representatives, who reflect their views and fight for their interests. They have less admiration for senators and representatives who represent other constituencies and promote other interests.

In 1925 House Speaker Nicholas Longworth (Republican–Ohio) noted that he had been a member of Congress for 20 years:

> During the whole of that time we have been attacked, denounced, despised, hunted, harried, blamed, looked down upon, excoriated, and flayed. I refuse to take it personally. I have looked into history. . . . We were unpopular when Lincoln was a Congressman. We were unpopu-

lar when John Quincy Adams was a Congressman. We were unpopular even when Henry Clay was a Congressman. We have always been unpopular. From the beginning of the Republic, it has been the duty of every free-born voter to look down upon us, and the duty of every free-born humorist to make jokes at us.

SEE ALSO

Articles of Confederation; Bicameral; Continental Congress; House of Representatives; Senate

FURTHER READING

Josephy, Alvin M., Jr. *On the Hill: A History of the American Congress.* New York: Simon & Schuster, 1979.

Congressional Budget Office

CONGRESS'S GROWING distrust of the executive branch during the administration of Richard Nixon led to the creation of the Congressional Budget Office (CBO) in 1974. Economist Alice Rivlin served as the CBO's first director. She and her successors were chosen by the leadership of both houses of Congress. Rather than rely on the President's economic assessments, Congress now had its own independent, nonpartisan budget office. Members of the CBO staff spend much of their time preparing cost estimates of all bills reported out of committee—that is, they calculate how much the bill would cost over time. The CBO works closely with the House and Senate Budget Committees, as well as with other committees, and prepares many special reports on the costs of issues that the committees are studying. Congress also looks to the CBO to scrutinize the President's annual budget and other requests for funds from executive branch agencies. Although often critical of the administration's figures and statistics, the CBO tries diligently not to take sides with either political party.

SEE ALSO

Budget and Impoundment Control Act, Congressional (1974); Legislative agencies

FURTHER READING

Penner, Rudolph G., ed. *The Congressional Budget Office after Five Years.* Washington, D.C.: American Enterprise Institute, 1981.

Congressional Cemetery

ALTHOUGH THE Capitol Hill cemetery belongs to an Episcopalian church, Congress gave it the name Congressional—inscribed across its arched iron gate—in honor of the many early members of Congress who are buried there. Fourteen senators and 42 representatives are interred in Congressional Cemetery, together with Vice President Elbridge Gerry; the designer of the Capitol, William Thornton; and various congressional staff members, diplomats, journalists, and American Indian chiefs who died while in Washington. From 1820 to 1870, Congress erected stubby-looking sandstone cenotaphs (empty tombs) in Congressional Cemetery in memory of deceased members who were not buried there. The practice ended after Senator George F. Hoar (Republican–Massachusetts) complained that the cenotaphs were so ugly that they added a new terror to death. Establishment of Arlington National Cemetery during the Civil War made Congressional Cemetery less fashionable, and over time it became one of the least known and least visited historical sites in Washington. Congressional

Cemetery is located at Potomac Avenue and E Street in Southeast Washington.

Congressional Directory

THE INDISPENSABLE guide to each session of Congress is the *Congressional Directory,* which contains biographical sketches of members of Congress, their committee assignments, seniority rankings, and seating charts in the chambers, as well as statistical data and other information about sessions, committees, staff, the Capitol, the press galleries, the diplomatic corps, and the executive and judicial branches of the federal government.

Begun as a private publication in the 1820s, the first directories listed the Washington residences of senators and representatives at a time when members lived in hotels or rented rooms in boardinghouses. Since the boarders ate their meals together, as at a military mess hall, these residences were known as "messes." The directories listed members' addresses as the Washington Mess at Mrs. Wilson's boardinghouse or Dowson's Crowd at Mrs. Dowson's of Capitol Hill.

In 1860, journalist Benjamin Perley Poore published an expanded *Congressional Directory* that established many of the volume's current features. Poore later became clerk of the Senate Committee on Printing, which in 1865 made the *Congressional Directory* a government publication. The Joint Committee on Printing continues to edit the annual *Congressional Directory,* which the Government Printing Office publishes and sells.

FURTHER READING

Young, James Sterling. *The Washington Community, 1800–1828.* New York: Columbia University Press, 1966.

Congressional Medal of Honor

IN THE name of Congress, the President of the United States awards medals of honor to members of the armed services who have distinguished themselves through bravery in combat, risking their lives above and beyond the call of duty.

President Calvin Coolidge presented the Congressional Medal of Honor in 1928 to a sailor who rescued crewmates after an explosion on their ship.

Congress created the medals by legislation during the Civil War, and the first medals were awarded in March 1863. Each branch of the armed services nominates those soldiers, sailors, marines, and aviators most deserving of the honor. Veterans who have received the medal are also entitled to a special pension.

FURTHER READING
The Congressional Medal of Honor: The Names, the Deeds. Forest Ranch, Calif.: Sharp & Dunnigan, 1984.

Congressional Quarterly Inc.

SINCE 1945, Congressional Quarterly, a private editorial research service, has studied Congress from an objective, nonpartisan perspective and published a variety of journals and books—everything except a quarterly. CQ issues a *Weekly Report* that profiles members, legislation, media coverage, and institutional issues relating to Congress. This weekly information is combined into an annual *Congressional Quarterly Almanac,* a handy compilation of data on legislation, including voting statistics, for each session of Congress. Information from the almanacs is further synthesized into a multivolume series called *Congress and the Nation,* which traces the development of legislation over time. CQ's *Guide to Congress* is a one-volume reference book on the history, powers, and procedures of Congress.

Congressional Record

REPORTERS OF debate record everything said and done in the House and Senate chambers and publish an edited version of the proceedings the next day in the *Congressional Record.* Members may edit and revise their remarks and may include full texts in place of the condensed speeches they delivered on the floor. The *Record* reflects Congress's attitudes and legislative intent, making it the first place to begin any research on Congress and the legislative process.

The Constitution does not require the House and Senate to keep a verbatim, or word-for-word, record, only that

The cover of a daily edition of the Congressional Record

SENATOR TILLMAN'S ALLEGORICAL COW.

Senator Tillman's cow, the only cartoon ever printed in the Congressional Record, *appeared on October 3, 1913.*

they publish journals from time to time. These legislative and executive journals are short minutes of the proceedings. So the *Congressional Record* is not a legal requirement but something that evolved from the notes that journalists made of the speeches and published in their newspapers. Joseph Gales and William Seaton recorded the debates for their Washington newspaper, the *National Intelligencer*. In 1824, Gales and Seaton began publishing these as the *Register of Debates*. They also compiled the speeches of the earliest Congresses in a series called the *Annals of Congress*. In 1833, Francis Blair and John C. Rives launched a rival publication, the *Congressional Globe*. Because Gales and Seaton were Whigs and Blair and Rives were Democrats, members of Congress sometimes viewed reporters from their publications as partisans who deliberately distorted congressional speeches. But it was not partisanship so much as primitive stenography and poor acoustics that hobbled the reporters.

Beginning in 1848, Congress put the reporters of debate on its payroll to en-

sure impartiality. That same year, the new Pitman system of stenography greatly improved the reporters' accuracy. The *Congressional Globe* remained a private publication until 1873, when the Government Printing Office took over the project and began publishing the *Congressional Record* as a government document.

Over time the *Congressional Record* has undergone many stylistic changes. In addition to their speeches, members are permitted to reprint newspaper and magazine articles and other items that they want their colleagues to read. It is against the rules, however, to reprint editorial cartoons. That rule was made in 1913 after Senator Benjamin Tillman (Democrat–South Carolina) put in the *Record* a cartoon of a cow being fed by western farmers and milked by eastern financiers.

Remarks that representatives do not actually read on the floor are printed in the "Extensions of Remarks" section at the back of the *Record*. Senators rarely use this section and instead ask for unanimous consent that their remarks be included in the *Record* as if they had been delivered on the floor. Such provisions speed up proceedings on the floor while still allowing members to compile a comprehensive record on the issues.

Since 1947, a Daily Digest has appeared at the back of the *Congressional Record* as a summary and index of floor proceedings and committee business of the day. Once a Congress has ended, the Government Printing Office combines the daily *Congressional Record*s into a fully indexed, permanent edition.

SEE ALSO
Daily Digest; Reporters of debate

FURTHER READING
Ritchie, Donald A. *Press Gallery: Congress and the Washington Correspondents.* Cambridge: Harvard University Press, 1991.

Congressional Research Service

WITH CONGRESS ever hungry for information, the Congressional Research Service (CRS) provides a ready source of nonpartisan, thorough, and reliable data. During the Progressive Era, reformers advocated that state and national governments hire experts to assist in the drafting of legislation. In 1914, the Legislative Reference Service was established as part of the Library of Congress. The service remained relatively small until the Legislative Reorganization Act of 1946 doubled its appropriation and provided for the appointment of senior specialists for each of the fields covered by the standing committees. Renamed the Congressional Research Service in 1970, the agency grew to include several hundred experts in government, law, agriculture, energy, economics, environment, housing, defense, foreign policy, and taxation.

CRS staff members prepare "issue briefs" stating the pros and cons of major issues before Congress and giving legislative histories of bills under consideration. They also compile specific information for individual members of Congress who plan to introduce legislation. Senior specialists regularly brief members and congressional staff on current issues, and the CRS occasionally loans members of its staff to congressional committees to assist with hearings and other legislative matters.

SEE ALSO
Library of Congress

FURTHER READING
Simpson, Andrew L. *The Library of Congress.* New York: Chelsea House, 1989.

Conkling, Roscoe

☆ *Born: Oct. 30, 1829, Albany, N.Y.*
☆ *Political party: Republican*
☆ *Representative from New York: 1859–63, 1865–67*
☆ *Senator from New York: 1867–81*
☆ *Died: Apr. 18, 1888, New York, N.Y.*

HANDSOME, INTELLIGENT, and eloquent but also vain, pompous, and overbearing, Senator Roscoe Conkling built one of the most powerful political machines (a tightly run political organization based on patronage) of the Gilded Age. Representative James Garfield (Republican–Ohio) once observed that Conkling was "inspired more by his hates than his loves." When Garfield won the Presidency, he took on the New York senator. Conkling's machine depended upon patronage—awarding government jobs in return for political support—and the richest source of patronage was the collector of the port of New York, the person who collected tariff revenues at the nation's busiest port.

An editorial cartoon depicting the vainglorious Senator Roscoe Conkling.

Conkling wanted his own man in the post, but Garfield instead nominated Conkling's rival, Judge William Robertson. When a Senate clerk read out Robertson's nomination, Conkling "raged and roared like a bull," according to a fellow Republican senator. Estimating that Garfield had the votes to confirm the nomination, Conkling and fellow New York Republican Senator Thomas C. Platt resigned from the Senate. They expected the New York legislature to reelect them as a show of support. But in a tragic twist of fate, an assassin sympathetic to Conkling shot and fatally wounded President Garfield. The New York legislature declined to reelect either Conkling or Platt, and Conkling's machine collapsed, ending his political career. Garfield's death spurred Congress to enact the first civil service laws aimed at ending the abuses of federal patronage.

SEE ALSO
Patronage

FURTHER READING
Jordan, David M. *Roscoe Conkling of New York: Voice in the Senate.* Ithaca, N.Y.: Cornell University Press, 1971.

Constituent services

FIRST AND foremost, members of Congress represent their constituents, the residents of their district or state who vote them into office. Senators and representatives assist constituents who have problems with Social Security payments, Medicare, veterans' pensions, or with other federal programs and agencies. Constituent needs vary widely, depending on whether a member represents a farming district or a densely populated city and depending on the social, cultural, and political leanings of the people in that district or state. Members cast their votes on national issues with an eye to how the legislation will affect their own constituents.

Constituent services offer members much visibility in their district or state. "I sent all graduating high-school seniors in the Sixth District a certificate to mark their commencement," Bob Dole (Republican–Kansas) recalled of his service in the House. "No bride walked down the aisle without a copy of *The Congressional Cookbook.* I once mistakenly extended congratulations on the birth of a baby to a couple observing their golden wedding anniversary."

Members of Congress now maintain offices in their home state as well as in Washington. Recesses of Congress are called "district work periods." Members return home as often as possible to gauge their constituents' opinions on national issues and to determine their needs. They employ caseworkers to handle mail and telephone requests from constituents. "Some members devote nearly all of their personal energies to such matters and little or none of their time to legislation beyond answering roll calls," Representative Richard Bolling (Democrat–

Missouri) observed. But members of Congress can also use their staff to attend to their constituents, freeing them to devote more of their time to legislation.

FURTHER READING

Bolling, Richard. *Power in the House: A History of the Leadership of the House of Representatives.* New York: Dutton, 1968.

Fenno, Richard F. *Home Style: House Members in Their Districts.* Boston: Little, Brown, 1978.

Constitution

THE CONSTITUTION created and defined Congress, listing its responsibilities, outlining its powers and its limitations, and setting the qualifications for its members. Under the Articles of Confederation, adopted in 1781, the federal government consisted entirely of a single-body legislature. Under the Constitution, ratified in 1788, Congress was divided into two houses and power was distributed among the legislative, executive, and judicial branches of the federal government and the states.

The two compromises critical to the success of the Constitutional Convention of 1787 both involved Congress. In the Great Compromise, the states were assured equal representation in the Senate and proportional representation (representation in proportion to their population) in the House of Representatives. The Three-fifths Compromise, which allowed a slave to be counted as three-fifths of a person, satisfied the Southern states because it meant their slaves (called "other persons")

Counting money in a Treasury Department vault in 1907. The Constitution grants Congress the power to coin money.

would be counted for purposes of taxation and representation in Congress.

Defining congressional power

Article 1, the longest part of the Constitution, deals exclusively with Congress. It grants the House and Senate together the power to collect taxes, borrow and coin money, raise and support an army and navy, declare war, set up a federal court system, establish rules for the naturalization of foreigners seeking citizenship, fix standard weights and measurements, establish post offices and post roads, make copyright and patent laws to protect authors and inventors, and pass legislation to govern the District of Columbia. The Constitution also authorizes Congress "to make all laws which shall be necessary and proper for carrying into execution the foregoing powers." Because this provision is so broad and sweeping, it is known as the "elastic clause."

The Constitution placed some restrictions on congressional power. Congress could not stop the slave trade until 1808 nor could it restrict habeas corpus (the right of a person accused of a crime to know the charges against him), pass ex post facto laws (make something a crime after the fact), give preference to any port of commerce, or grant or allow any federal officeholder to accept a title of nobility. Nor could members of Congress serve simultaneously in any other civil office. The first 10 amendments to the Constitution, known as the Bill of Rights, further specify areas that Congress can make no laws to limit.

The Constitution's instructions were not detailed, and the first members of Congress had to grope for their way. Over the years, practice and precedent shaped government, and the courts have further interpreted the proper role of Congress. Various amendments to the Constitution changed the means of electing senators from a vote of state legislatures to a direct vote of the people and shifted the date that Congress convenes from December, at the end of the year, to January, at the beginning of that year.

SEE ALSO
Amendments, constitutional; Bill of Rights

FURTHER READING
Bowen, Catherine Drinker. *Miracle at Philadelphia: The Story of the Constitutional Convention, May to September 1787.* Boston: Little, Brown, 1966.
Ritchie, Donald A. *The U.S. Constitution.* New York: Chelsea House, 1989.

Contempt of Congress

CONTEMPT OF Congress is any improper attempt to obstruct the legislative process, usually by a refusal to provide information that Congress has requested. The contempt power is critical to Congress's ability to investigate the activities of the executive branch or any issue about which it is considering enacting legislation. Congress can use contempt citations against witnesses who refuse to testify or to produce required evidence. Those found guilty of contempt of Congress may go to prison.

There are three methods of prosecuting for contempt of Congress. First, Congress can try contempt cases itself. In 1848 and 1871 the Senate did just that, imprisoning newspaper reporters in the Capitol for not revealing the source of the Senate secrets they had published. Congress can also turn contempt cases over to the Department of Justice for criminal prosecution. However, juries have often acquitted individuals charged with contempt, especially if it appears that the congressional committee abused its power. For example, between 1950 and 1966 the House Un-American Activities Committee issued 133 contempt citations, but only nine people were convicted. Finally, the Senate or House can also file civil charges of contempt. Using this procedure, a federal judge determines whether a question asked by Congress was legitimate. If the judge orders a witness to answer and the witness refuses, then the witness would be in contempt of court and could be fined or imprisoned. For example, during the Watergate investigation the House cited G. Gordon Liddy for contempt for refusing to testify before a House committee. A federal judge gave Liddy a suspended six-month sentence.

The Supreme Court has upheld Congress's power to punish for contempt but has specified some limitations against its unreasonable use. In the case of *McGrain v. Daugherty* in 1927, the Court ruled that "a legislative body cannot legislate wisely or effectively in the absence of information. . . . Experience has taught that mere requests for such information often are unavailing, and also that information which is volunteered is not always accurate or complete; so some means of compulsion are essential to obtain that which is needed."

Although Congress has issued hundreds of contempt citations against witnesses, it has found only one executive agency head in contempt. In 1982, the House voted Environmental Protection Agency administrator Anne Gorsuch Burford in contempt for refusing to provide documents that the House Committee on Public Works and Transportation had requested. She later agreed to give the documents to the committee. Other actions against cabinet members and high-ranking officials have been resolved before either the House or Senate voted.

SEE ALSO
Investigations

FURTHER READING
Hamilton, James. *The Power to Probe: A Study of Congressional Investigations.* New York: Vintage, 1976.

Continental Congress

THE FIRST national American government was the Continental Congress. Colonial leaders came together in this Congress to oppose British policies that restricted their rights and taxed them without representation in Parliament. Called by the Virginia House of Burgesses, delegates from all of the thirteen colonies except Georgia gathered in Philadelphia in September 1774.

The 1st Continental Congress urged Americans not to import British goods and to form armed militia. But rather than advocate revolution, Congress called for "peace, liberty and security" within the British empire. The British Parliament saw the Congress as treasonous and ordered colonial governors to prevent another election. Yet the 2nd Continental Congress met in May 1775.

The 2nd Congress established the Continental army and chose George Washington as the army's commander in chief. A committee that included Thomas Jefferson, John Adams, and Benjamin Franklin drafted the Declaration of Independence.

The Congress negotiated with foreign nations, established a postal system, borrowed money to support the army, and printed currency known as "continentals." However, the government's poor finances led to the expression "not worth a continental." Since the Continental Congress lacked any formal constitution, in 1777 a committee drafted a charter for a more permanent form of government. The Articles of Confederation were ratified in 1781, at which time the Continental Congress became "The United States in Congress Assembled."

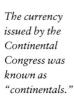

The currency issued by the Continental Congress was known as "continentals."

SEE ALSO

Articles of Confederation

FURTHER READING

Morgan, Edmund S. *The Birth of the Republic, 1763–89.* Chicago: University of Chicago Press, 1977.

Continuing body

IT IS SAID that "the Senate never dies." Senators are separated into three classes with staggered terms so that at any congressional election only one-third of the seats are up for election. Meanwhile, two-thirds of the senators remain in office. For this reason, the Senate is considered to be a "continuing body." The Senate's rules remain in place and are not readopted at the beginning of a new Congress.

By contrast, all House members stand for reelection every two years, House rules are reconsidered at the beginning of each term, and all House officers, including the Speaker, must be elected or reelected when the new Congress convenes. By carrying over a majority of senators through every election, the Constitution insulated the Senate from sudden shifts in public opinion. Because the Senate is a continuing body, Senate committees can also continue to hold hearings—with the Senate's authorization—even after Congress has adjourned at the end of a session.

SEE ALSO

Adjournment; Senate

Court-packing plan (1937)

PRESIDENT FRANKLIN D. Roosevelt's landslide reelection in 1936 gave the Democrats overwhelming majorities in the Senate and House, which Roosevelt sought to use to reorganize the Supreme Court. He wanted to reduce the power of conservative justices who had ruled that major New Deal programs for social and economic reform were unconstitutional. Roosevelt asked Congress for authority to make a new appointment for every justice over the age of 70, to help shoulder the work load for the "nine old men." These appointments might have increased the Court to as many as 15 members. Opponents angrily accused Roosevelt of trying to "pack" the Court with liberal justices.

The Senate considered the bill first, and the tiny Republican minority wisely chose to remain silent. "Let them [the Democrats] do the talking," advised Republican leader Charles McNary, "and we'll do the voting." The Democratic party split, with conservatives fearing that Roosevelt's plan would make the President "absolute boss" over Congress and the Court. Majority Leader Joseph Robinson used all his legislative skills to hold his party together, but in July 1937 Robinson died and the Court plan collapsed. The Senate sent the bill back to the Judiciary Committee, which killed it. Although the retirement of several justices soon enabled Roosevelt to appoint a majority of the Court, defeat of his plan had shattered his congressional majority and halted the New Deal's legislative program. The coalition of conservative Democrats and Republicans forged during the Court plan fight remained the effective majority in Congress for the next two decades.

SEE ALSO

Judicial review; McNary, Charles L.; Robinson, Joseph T.

FURTHER READING

Baker, Leonard. *Back to Back: The Duel between FDR and the Supreme Court.* New York: Macmillan, 1967.

A cartoon version of the "Nine Old Men" of the Supreme Court in 1937.

Coxey's army

THE FIRST amendment to the Constitution states that Congress shall not abridge the "right of the people peaceably to assemble, and to petition the Government for a redress of grievances." Whenever demonstrators have protested at the Capitol, Congress has had to balance the right of peaceful assembly against the need to maintain public safety. During the severe depression of 1893–94, Ohio businessman Jacob Coxey proposed that Congress enact a "good roads bill" to put people back to work building roads and other public works. When Congress failed to act, Coxey organized an "army" of unemployed men to march on Washington. "We'll send a petition to Washington with boots on," he declared. Coxey's army attracted much newspaper publicity, and eventually some 500 marchers reached Washington. Doubting the peaceable nature of the approaching mob, a fearful Congress called out the police and federal troops to stop the marchers before they reached the Capitol building. Jacob Coxey slipped through police lines and raced toward the Capitol steps, where he tried to speak. He was arrested, fined, and imprisoned for walking on the grass. Although unsuccessful, Coxey's army revealed the depth of unrest among the unemployed and their frustration with an unresponsive government.

SEE ALSO

Protest

FURTHER READING

Schwantes, Carlos. *Coxey's Army: An American Odyssey.* Lincoln: University of Nebraska Press, 1985.

Credit Mobilier scandal (1872–73)

IN THE BOOM years after the Civil War, Congress made large land grants and appropriated funds to help the privately owned Union Pacific Railroad build a transcontinental railroad line. Union Pacific organized a construction company called Credit Mobilier to lay the track. Union Pacific's chief Washington agent, Representative Oakes Ames (Republican–Massachusetts), distributed stock in Credit Mobilier to key members of Congress, where, as he explained, "it will do the most good for us." The company expected that those members who got the stock would look favorably on the project and support the company's future needs. The story did not break in the newspapers until the Presidential election of 1872. "How the Credit Mobilier Bought Its Way Through Congress," read one headline in the *New York Sun.* The press revealed that stocks had gone to the Vice President, the Speaker of the House, and leading members of the House and Senate. House and Senate investigations led to the censure of Representatives Ames and James Brooks (Democrat–New York). The Credit Mobilier scandal damaged or destroyed many other political reputations and left a stigma of corruption on the Congress of the Gilded Age.

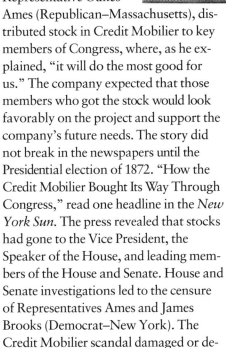

Key members of Congress received stock in the Credit Mobilier company.

SEE ALSO

Scandals, congressional

FURTHER READING

Wilbur, W. Allan. "The Credit Mobilier Scandal, 1873." In *Congress Investigates: A Documented History, 1792–1974,* edited by Arthur M. Schlesinger, Jr., and Roger Bruns. New York: Bowker, 1975.

Crockett, David

☆ *Born: Aug. 17, 1786, Greene County, Tenn.*
☆ *Political party: Whig*
☆ *Representative from Tennessee: 1827–31, 1833–35*
☆ *Died: Mar. 6, 1836, San Antonio, Tex.*

PERHAPS THE most colorful personality ever elected to Congress was the legendary bear hunter Davy Crockett, who represented Tennessee in the House of Representatives for three terms. Although he had commanded a battalion of riflemen under General Andrew Jackson in campaigns against the Creek Indians in 1813 and 1814, Crockett ran for office against Jackson's financial policies and became an outspoken Whig. The frontiersman Crockett often felt impatient with Congress's slow pace of business. "We generally lounge and squabble the greater part of the session, and crowd into a few days of the last term three or four times the business done during as many preceding months," he complained. When his constituents failed to reelect him, Crockett told them: "I am going to Texas and you can go to hell." He joined the Texans' struggle for independence from Mexico and died fighting at the Alamo.

Davy Crockett, bear hunter and Congressman

FURTHER READING

Crockett, David. *A Narrative of the Life of David Crockett of the State of Tennessee.* Knoxville: University of Tennessee Press, 1973.
Shackford, James Atkins. *David Crockett: The Man and the Legend.* Chapel Hill: University of North Carolina Press, 1956.

C-SPAN

YOU CAN watch House and Senate debates on television over C-SPAN, the Cable Satellite Public Affairs Network. Beginning in 1979, the House of Representatives allowed television to cover its floor proceedings. The Senate opened its chamber to television in 1986. Since then, C-SPAN has broadcast the daily proceedings of the House and Senate "gavel to gavel"—that is, from the moment the presiding officer gavels the chamber into session to the moment it adjourns. C-SPAN was created and continues to be funded solely by the cable television industry. C-SPAN expanded the congressional galleries into millions of homes, allowing citizens to follow the floor debates as well as the more important committee hearings. Videotapes of the proceedings are deposited at the National Archives for future research use.

FURTHER READING

Lamb, Brian. *C-SPAN: America's Town Hall.* Washington, D.C.: Acropolis Books, 1988.

C-SPAN broadcasts the House and Senate debates.

Daily Digest

AT THE BACK of each daily issue of the *Congressional Record* is the Daily Digest. Since 1947 the Digest has served as a handy index to the *Record,* listing the bills and resolutions introduced and what measures were passed or rejected in each chamber and giving the page numbers where the reports can be found. The Daily Digest also lists all nominations received, confirmed, or rejected, together with page references to messages from the President, amendments, co-

The Daily Digest provides a summary of the day's events in Congress.

---

sponsors, and related information. In addition to floor activities, the Daily Digest catalogs the previous day's committee meetings, including a brief description of topics of hearings, witnesses, and votes. The Digest concludes with announcements of the hearings that will be held the next day, listing the subject, time, and location of these meetings.

SEE ALSO
Congressional Record

Davis, Jefferson

☆ *Born: June 3, 1808, Fairview, Ky.*
☆ *Political party: Democrat*
☆ *Representative from Mississippi: 1845–46*
☆ *Senator from Mississippi: 1847–51, 1857–61*
☆ *President of the Confederate States of America: 1861–65*
☆ *Died: Dec. 6, 1889, New Orleans, La.*

Jefferson Davis's statue in the U.S. Capitol

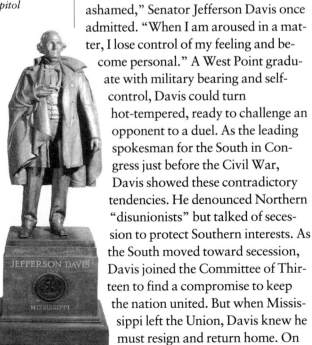

"I HAVE an infirmity of which I am ashamed," Senator Jefferson Davis once admitted. "When I am aroused in a matter, I lose control of my feeling and become personal." A West Point graduate with military bearing and self-control, Davis could turn hot-tempered, ready to challenge an opponent to a duel. As the leading spokesman for the South in Congress just before the Civil War, Davis showed these contradictory tendencies. He denounced Northern "disunionists" but talked of secession to protect Southern interests. As the South moved toward secession, Davis joined the Committee of Thirteen to find a compromise to keep the nation united. But when Mississippi left the Union, Davis knew he must resign and return home. On January 21, 1861, he spoke in the

Senate for the last time, forgiving his opponents for their offenses toward him and offering his apologies for any offenses he had given them. Applauded from both sides of the aisle, Davis left the Senate chamber looking "inexpressively sad." A month later he became President of the Confederacy.

FURTHER READING
Davis, William C. *Jefferson Davis: The Man and His Hour.* New York: HarperCollins, 1991.

"Dear Colleague" letters

TO ALERT fellow members to a particular issue or event, or encourage them to cosponsor legislation, senators and representatives send out "Dear Colleague" letters. These form letters are circulated through internal mail (rather than through the postal system) to all members' offices. "Dear Colleague" letters identify the sender with a certain issue and form an important unofficial link in the information chain around Capitol Hill.

SEE ALSO
Sponsoring and cosponsoring legislation

Debate

DEBATES IN Congress are aimed at winning votes from other members, swaying public opinion, forcing the opposition into politically embarrassing positions, and establishing a record of legislative intentions. Under the "speech and debate" clause of the Constitution (Article 1, Section 6), any member can speak on any issue in Congress without fear of being prosecuted for libel or slander (that is, defaming someone else's character).

Beginning in the 1840s, the growing size of the House caused representatives to adopt rules that limited debate. Under House rules, no member can hold the floor for more than an hour. During some debates members are allowed only five minutes to speak. Often the House considers a bill under a "suspension of the rules," which limits the entire debate on a bill, by both sides, to 40 minutes. By contrast, the Senate, which is smaller, has retained unlimited debate, allowing members to speak as long as they feel necessary on any issue. However, when senators filibuster, or speak excessively in order to block passage of a bill, a vote of three-fifths of the Senate can enact cloture, which cuts off debate and forces a vote.

Many observers have questioned whether speeches really change any votes. In 1806, Senator William Plumer (Federalist–New Hampshire) commented, "I have for sometime been convinced that speeches in the Senate in most cases have very little influence upon the vote." And in 1820, former President Thomas Jefferson complained, "If the present Congress err in too much talking, how can it be otherwise, in a body to which the people send 150 lawyers, whose trade is to question everything, yield nothing, and talk by the hour?"

SEE ALSO

Decorum; Filibuster; Oratory

Decorum

CONGRESS USES extremely polite, old-fashioned language and decorum (or etiquette) during its debates. Officially, members do not even address each other

but speak always to the presiding officer: "Mr. President" in the Senate or "Mr. Speaker" in the House. They call other members by title rather than by name. References to "my esteemed colleague," "the very able senior senator from . . . ," and "the distinguished representative from . . ." litter the *Congressional Record.* House and Senate rules prohibit any speaker from questioning another member's motives or referring offensively to other states. If a senator breaks these rules, the presiding officer can require that senator to sit down and not speak again without the permission of the Senate. The Speaker may similarly call the name of any House member causing commotion and order that person to sit down.

When the French writer Alexis de Tocqueville visited Congress in 1831, he described the Senate as a body "of eloquent advocates . . . whose language would at times do honor to the most remarkable parliamentary debates in Europe," but he was dismayed by the "vulgar demeanor" of the House. Although often more boisterous in debate, the House, just as much as the Senate, expects its members to maintain proper decorum. Members of Congress call this comity (courtesy). In 1989, Representative Mickey Edwards (Republican–Oklahoma) described the rules of comity as "this kind of nineteenth-century Victorian etiquette which is very important to keep us working together and helps bridge some of the partisan and deeply felt divisions between us."

SEE ALSO

Debate

FURTHER READING

Baker, Ross K. *House and Senate.* New York: Norton, 1989.
Mathews, Donald R. *U.S. Senators & Their World.* New York: Vintage, 1960.

Delegates

EACH U.S. TERRITORY can elect a delegate to the House of Representatives. In the 3rd Congress, from 1794 to 1795, the first nonvoting delegate, James White, represented the "territory south of the River Ohio," which later became Tennessee. During the 103rd Congress, from 1993 to 1995, five delegates represented American Samoa, the Commonwealth of Puerto Rico, the District of Columbia, Guam, and the Virgin Islands. Delegates receive office space and staff, serve on committees, and have traditionally worked to promote statehood for their territory. They can vote in committee, and in the 103rd Congress, rules were changed so that delegates can also vote when the House meets as a committee of the whole, to debate and vote on amendments. Delegates can participate in all legislative business except the final vote on bills.

In the Senate, only states can be represented. Some territories and the District of Columbia have elected "shadow senators" to lobby for statehood, but they are not officially part of the Senate. They neither serve on committees nor participate in other proceedings.

SEE ALSO

Committee of the whole; Shadow senators

Desks

BOTH SENATORS and representatives were originally assigned desks in their chambers. But after the 1910 census, when House membership grew to 435, the House no longer had room for a desk for every member. House desks were re-placed by rows of leather-upholstered seats, where representatives sit at random (Republicans to the left of the center aisle, Democrats to the right of the aisle).

In the Senate, each of the 100 members has a desk in the chamber. Some of these mahogany desks date back to 1819, and the rest were built as new states joined the Union. Some senators carve their name inside the desk drawers to show the desk's lineage. Several desks are notable. Daniel Webster's desk is the only one with no writing table fixed to its top. Writing tables with hinged tops that open to provide additional storage space were added in the 1840s, but Webster refused to have his desk altered, and none of his successors has chosen to change it. By resolution, the Webster desk always goes to the senior senator from New Hampshire (Webster's original home state). Jefferson Davis's desk bears a small scar from the bayonet of a Union soldier who in 1861 took out his anger on the desk where the Confederate president once sat. A small block of mahogany has been inlaid in the desk to fill the scar. Since 1965, Republican senators have maintained a "candy desk" in the back row near the entrance to the chamber. Each senator assigned to that desk has dutifully kept its drawer filled with assorted candies for the benefit of other legislators.

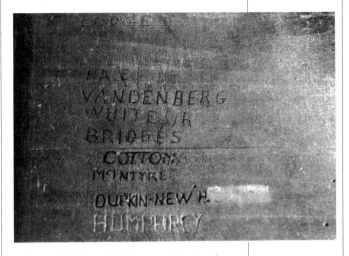

Senators carve their names in their Senate chamber desks. This one was once used by Daniel Webster.

Direct election

SEE Elections; Senate

Director of non-legislative services

ROCKED BY a series of scandals involving management of the House of Representatives bank and post office, House members voted to create the new post of director of non-legislative services. In 1992, with bipartisan support, retired army general Leonard P. Wishart III was appointed as the first director. His office was assigned a variety of functions once performed by the clerk of the House, the sergeant at arms, and the House postmaster. These responsibilities include handling the House payroll, all internal mail, office supplies, restaurants and cafeterias, and the barber and beauty shops that operate out of the House office buildings to serve the members and staff.

SEE ALSO
Clerk of the House; Sergeant at arms

Dirksen, Everett McKinley

☆ *Born: Jan. 4, 1896, Pekin, Ill.*
☆ *Political party: Republican*
☆ *Representative from Illinois: 1933–49*
☆ *Senator from Illinois: 1951–69*
☆ *Senate minority leader: 1959–69*
☆ *Died: Sept. 7, 1969, Washington, D.C.*

CALLED THE "Wizard of Ooze," Everett Dirksen used his deep baritone to great effect as Senate Republican minority leader. "He was a natural-born orator—eloquent, persuasive, and forceful," said Senator Norris Cotton (Republican–New Hampshire), who cited Dirksen's careful use of words, enormous vocabulary, and seemingly endless supply of stories and anecdotes. More than just talk, Dirksen possessed skills at legislative maneuvering. He fostered mutual ties between Republicans and conservative Southern Democrats and maintained a close friendship with Democratic majority leader and later President Lyndon B. Johnson. Both sides bargained for his support, which gave Dirksen influence far beyond his minority party status. Dirksen made his influence most keenly felt in 1964, when Southerners filibustered to block Johnson's Civil Rights Bill. Declaring the end of segregation "an idea whose time has come," Dirksen dramatically chose to support cloture to cut off the filibuster. Enough Republicans joined Dirksen and the liberal Democrats to cut off debate and pass the bill. For such reasons, other senators called Minority Leader Dirksen "the most powerful member of the Senate."

SEE ALSO

Civil rights legislation; Cloture; Filibuster; Johnson, Lyndon B.; Leadership

FURTHER READING

Loomis, Burdett. "Everett M. Dirksen: The Consummate Minority Leader." In *First among Equals: Outstanding Senate Leaders of the Twentieth Century*, edited by Richard A. Baker and Roger A. Davidson. Washington, D.C.: Congressional Quarterly, 1991.
MacNeil, Neil. *Portrait of a Public Man.* New York: World, 1970.

Because Senator Everett Dirksen promoted the marigold as the national flower, a variety of the flower was named in his honor.

Discharging a bill

WHEN LEGISLATORS try to get a bill out of a committee that refuses to report it, or refer it to the full House or Senate, the procedure is called discharging the bill. Legislators generally prefer to let the committees do the bulk of the work on a bill, but sometimes a committee will not report out a bill that the majority of the full house favors but the majority of the committee does not. When this happens, members attempt to discharge bills, but only rarely do such attempts succeed. However, sometimes just the threat of a discharge petition persuades the committee to act.

As part of the progressive revolt against Speaker Joseph G. Cannon's dictatorial leadership in 1910, the House of Representatives adopted the discharge petition. Once a majority of the House has signed the petition, it goes on the Discharge Calendar. After seven days, any member who signed the petition can make a motion to discharge the bill from committee. If a majority votes for the motion, the bill becomes the immediate business of the House and can be debated, amended, and voted upon.

The Senate uses a different procedure, in which members can make discharge motions during morning business, at the beginning of a day's session. The motion must remain at the clerk's desk for one day before it can be debated and adopted by a majority vote. However, other members may filibuster or use other delaying tactics to block a vote on the discharge motion.

SEE ALSO
Cannon, Joseph G.; Committees; Morning business

FURTHER READING
Oleszek, Walter. *Congressional Procedures and the Policy Process.* Washington, D.C.: Congressional Quarterly, 1989.

Discipline

CONGRESS FINDS it painful to discipline its own members. Seeking to maintain alliances on so many different issues and to remain on good terms with each other, legislators prefer not to question their colleagues' ethics. They prefer to leave such judgments to the voters in the next election. But pressure from the press and public outrage over alleged misconduct often force the House or the Senate to act.

The Constitution permits each house to punish its own members for disorderly behavior. The most serious offenses can result in expulsion: a member can be expelled by a two-thirds vote. Alternatively, the Senate or House can censure (rebuke) a member by a majority vote. For lesser offenses, members may simply be reprimanded. The House has a Committee of Standards of Official Conduct, and the Senate a Select Committee on Ethics, which monitor the activities of members and staff and advise them on compliance with the rules and laws affecting behavior, ethics, and finances.

SEE ALSO
Censure; Ethics; Expulsion; Impeachment; Scandals, congressional

District of Columbia

THE CONSTITUTION (Article 1, Section 8) gives Congress authority to make laws for the District of Columbia, the seat of the federal government. This power has its origins in events that took place in 1783, when soldiers angry about not being paid surrounded the Congress under the Articles of Confederation in Philadelphia, where local officials offered no protection. To ensure that the new federal government would never be as helpless, the framers of the Constitution called for a district, not exceeding 10 square miles, to serve as the seat of government.

As a result of a deal in which Southern members of Congress agreed to support the repayment of American revolutionary war debts, Northerners agreed to locate the new capital in the South. Congress approved a location for the district on the Potomac River, on a 10-square-mile site that included the existing cities of Georgetown, Maryland, and Alexandria, Virginia. Commissioners in charge of the project named the district in honor of Christopher Columbus, and the new capital city within the district in honor of President George Washington, whose home, Mount Vernon, lay just 20 miles south of the new district. In 1800, the federal government moved to the district.

In 1846, the citizens of the Virginia side of the district voted to return their area to Virginia, so that the current District of Columbia occupies only the land that Maryland ceded. Congress has established several different kinds of government in the district, both with elected mayors and appointed commissioners. For many years, House and Senate committees really ran the district. Dominated by Southerners, the committees did not address the needs of the city's African-American majority.

In 1968, following the assassination of the civil rights leader Dr. Martin Luther King, Jr., riots broke out in Washington. There was extensive looting and destruction of property. These events hastened plans to establish an elected city government with a mayor and city council. However, Congress retained a veto on all of the city finances. The House has a standing committee on the District of Columbia, and the Senate assigns these functions to a subcommittee of the Governmental Affairs Committee.

Although the 23rd Amendment to the Constitution, ratified in 1961, allowed district residents to vote for President, they still cannot elect senators or representatives. The District of Columbia sends only a delegate to the House of Representatives. In 1990, the district also elected two shadow senators, including the nationally prominent African-American leader Jesse Jackson, to work for its statehood.

SEE ALSO
Delegates; Shadow senators

FURTHER READING
Bowling, Kenneth R. *The Creation of Washington, D.C.: The Idea and Location of the American Capital.* Fairfax, Va.: George Mason University Press, 1991.
Lewis, David L. *The District of Columbia: A Bicentennial History.* New York: Norton, 1976.

Divided government

DIVIDED GOVERNMENT occurs when different parties control the House and Senate or when the majority in Congress is not from the President's party. These divisions differentiate the Ameri-

Republican President Ronald Reagan (left) confers with the Democratic Senate majority leader, Robert C. Byrd, during a period of "divided government."

can government from parliamentary systems such as Great Britain's, where the prime minister always heads the majority party. There, if the prime minister's party loses its majority, or loses a "vote of confidence," the country must hold new elections. Under the U.S. Constitution, the President remains in office for a set term, even if his party loses control of Congress.

During the 19th century, voters faithfully cast straight-party ballots, electing Presidents and congressional majorities from the same party. However, the President's party frequently lost seats in the midterm congressional election two years later. In the 20th century, party loyalty and the custom of voting for straight-party tickets declined, and it became more common for the President and congressional majority to represent different parties. Divided government existed for 26 out of the 40 years between 1952 and 1992. Since 1955, Democrats have held the longest continuous majority in the House of Representatives of any party in American history, and they lost the Senate for only six years, from 1981 to 1987. Yet during these same years, Republicans more often won the White House.

Why do voters choose divided government? They often select Presidential candidates based on national issues and congressional candidates based on what a candidate can do for their state or district. The high cost of running for Congress and the advantages that incumbents enjoy have also tended to insulate Congress from the frequent switches of party majority that occurred in the past.

During long periods of divided government, Congress grew more suspicious of the executive branch, expanded its own staff, and developed its own independent sources of data and analysis. Divided government deprived Congress of Presidential leadership and pitted the ex-

ecutive and legislative branches against each other. Presidents could veto legislation they opposed but had great difficulty enacting their own legislative initiatives. As a result, while not efficient or entirely effective, divided government has further strengthened the U.S. system of checks and balances.

SEE ALSO
Checks and balances; Separation of powers

Dole, Robert J.

☆ Born: July 22, 1923, Russell, Kans.
☆ Political party: Republican
☆ Representative from Kansas: 1961–69
☆ Senator from Kansas: 1969–
☆ Senate majority leader: 1985–87
☆ Senate minority leader: 1987–

THERE IS nothing wrong with partisanship, Bob Dole believes, as long as it remains constructive and focused on issues rather than personalities. Dole never shies away from partisan politics. He entered the Senate with the Republican party in the minority in both houses of Congress, but with the Republican Richard Nixon in the White House. Having little influence in his committees as a freshman, Dole spent much time on the Senate floor defending the President's programs. Barry Goldwater (Republican–Arizona) called Dole "the first fellow we've had around here in a long time who can grab 'em by the hair and haul 'em down the aisle." Dole's outspoken partisanship, tough debating style, and sense of humor all gained him recognition. In 1971 President Nixon endorsed him for chairman of the Republican National Committee. Gerald Ford chose him to be the Vice Presidential running mate in 1976, and Senate Republicans elected Dole as their leader in 1985.

Although he lost the Republican Presidential nomination to George Bush in 1988, Dole led Senate Republicans in support of the Bush administration's programs. He rallied the Republican party's forces to prevent Bush's vetoes of Democratic-sponsored legislation from being overridden.

SEE ALSO

Leadership

FURTHER READING

Dole, Bob, and Elizabeth Dole, with Richard Norton Smith. *The Doles: Unlimited Partners.* New York: Simon & Schuster, 1988.

Doorkeepers

VISITORS WAITING for seats in the House and Senate galleries are supervised by doorkeepers. These doorkeepers enforce the rules of the chamber, maintain decorum, and regulate the flow of traffic. They also make sure that only those with floor privileges enter the floor of the chamber, and they bar all visitors during closed executive sessions. The doorkeepers operate under the supervision of the Senate sergeant at arms and the House doorkeeper. During the President's State of the Union message, it is the House doorkeeper who announces loudly, "Mr. Speaker, the President of the United States."

SEE ALSO

Dress; Executive sessions; Floor privileges; Galleries

FURTHER READING

Miller, William "Fishbait." *Fishbait: The Memoirs of a Congressional Doorkeeper.* New York: Warner, 1977.

Douglas, Stephen A.

☆ *Born: Apr. 23, 1813, Brandon, Vt.*
☆ *Political party: Democrat*
☆ *Senator from Illinois: 1847–61*
☆ *Died: June 3, 1861, Chicago, Ill.*

THE FRAGILE compromises that glued the Union together began to dissolve in January 1854, when Senator Stephen A. Douglas introduced the Kansas-Nebraska Bill. His bill aimed to organize the territorial governments of Kansas and Nebraska for eventual statehood. The Kansas-Nebraska territory lay north of the Missouri Compromise line, where slavery was prohibited. Douglas promoted the bill because it would allow construction of a transcontinental railroad out of Chicago, in his state of Illinois. To win Southern support, his bill canceled the Missouri Compromise and allowed the residents of the territories to decide for themselves whether to permit or prohibit slavery—a plan he called "popular sovereignty" (rule by the people). Douglas expected these territories to remain free, assuming that slavery could never be economical there. A skillful politician, known popularly as the "Little Giant," Douglas knew that his bill would raise a storm of protest, but even he was surprised by the ferocity of Northern opposition. The Kansas-Nebraska Bill led to the formation of a Republican party dedicated to opposing the spread of slavery into the territories. Rather than uniting the nation, as he had hoped, Douglas's plan divided it even further.

In 1858, Douglas was challenged for reelection to the Senate by Republican Abraham Lincoln. The Lincoln-Douglas debates, held throughout Illinois and focusing largely on the slavery issue, drew national attention. Although Douglas defeated Lincoln in that Senate race, two

Senator Stephen A. Douglas was called the "Little Giant."

years later in 1860 he lost to Lincoln in the campaign for President. Douglas fell political victim to the forces he had unleashed by repealing the Kansas-Nebraska Act.

SEE ALSO
Missouri Compromise (1821)

FURTHER READING
Johannsen, Robert W. *Stephen A. Douglas.* New York: Oxford, 1973.

Dress

HOUSE SPEAKER Thomas P. ("Tip") O'Neill, Jr. (Democrat–Massachusetts) once advised a representative wearing a yellow suit to go home and change, which he did. Tradition, more than rules, determines appropriate dress for members of Congress. At first, members of the House wore their hats in the chamber, carrying on a tradition of the British House of Commons to show its independence from the king. But in 1837, the House adopted a rule prohibiting wearing a hat in the chamber, and that rule remains in effect for both men and women members.

By the late 19th century, members of Congress—then all men—wore formal attire: striped pants, vests, and cutaway coats. Today, formal wear is seen only at Presidential inaugurations. The last senator to dress daily in this manner was Clyde Hoey (Democrat–North Carolina), who died in office in 1954. Long after, however, editorial cartoonists continued to depict congressional characters dressed in formal attire.

Earmarking

SEE Pork barrel politics

Elections

IN CONGRESS an election is never more than two years away. Representative government requires that the citizens elect the people who will represent them. The Constitution specified that the House of Representatives be directly elected by the people. The entire House stands for election every two years. Senators are elected for six-year terms. The Senate is divided into three groups, so that one-third of the Senate stands for election every two years. Initially, senators were chosen by state legislatures, but in several instances state legislators were unable to agree on a candidate and Senate seats went vacant for an entire Congress. Other problems involving the election process led progressives to advocate direct election of senators. As a result, the 17th Amendment to the Constitution was ratified in 1913, and senators stood for popular election for the first time in 1914.

Before the direct election of senators, the House was more likely than the Senate to respond to shifts of public opinion. During the late 19th century, as many as 200 House seats might change

Barbara Boxer (Democrat– California) campaigning for a seat in the U.S. Senate.

party in a single election. The Senate was more insulated from popular passions and frenzy. But a century later, House incumbents enjoyed a high rate of reelection, and shifts in party became more pronounced in the Senate. House members sought to spend their careers in Congress, aided in their reelections by their visibility in the media, their franking (free mail) privileges, and their ability to raise more campaign contributions than their challengers could.

SEE ALSO

Campaign committees; Campaign financing; Incumbents

Electoral college

THE ELECTORAL college is the formal body, created by the Constitution (Article 2, Section 1), that elects the President of the United States. Each state has as many electors in the electoral college as it has senators and representatives in Congress. When citizens participate in a Presidential election, they are actually voting for electors pledged to vote for their candidate. Political parties choose a slate of electors made up of party loyalists who are most likely to vote for their party's candidate. However, no law binds these electors, who may cast their ballot for another candidate. Those who stray from their party—a very infrequent occurrence—are known as "faithless electors."

After the popular election the electors vote, and their ballots are sent to Congress. The Senate then marches in procession to a joint session in the House chamber, where the Vice President or president pro tempore counts the electoral ballots. If no candidate receives a majority in the electoral college, the House chooses the President. When this happens, each state has one vote, and a majority vote is necessary for election.

The Senate and House meet in joint session to count the electoral ballots in 1969.

The Senate chooses the Vice President.

In 1800, the Democratic-Republican candidates Thomas Jefferson, running for President, and Aaron Burr, running for Vice President, received a tie vote in the electoral college. The election then went to the House of Representatives, where Federalists held the majority. Some Federalists voted for Burr for President, and House members cast 36 ballots before they finally elected Jefferson. As a result, the 12th Amendment was added to the Constitution in 1804, requiring that each elector cast a single ballot for a combined slate of President and Vice President.

In 1824, when no candidate received a majority of electors, the House chose John Quincy Adams for President, even though Andrew Jackson had received a higher popular vote. In 1836, Virginia electors refused to vote for Richard M. Johnson for Vice President, denying any candidate a majority. The Senate then voted to make Johnson Vice President. In 1876, when Southern Democrats were contending with radical Republicans for control of their state governments, three Southern states submitted contradictory sets of electoral ballots, one set for the Republican candidate, Rutherford B. Hayes, and another for the Democratic candidate, Samuel J. Tilden. Republicans held the majority in the Senate and wanted the president of the Senate to count the ballots. Democrats, who held the majority in the House, objected that the Senate president pro tempore (who was presiding because the Vice President had died) would count only the Republican ballots. To break this stalemate, a joint committee recommended creating a special electoral commission to judge which ballots were valid. The commission, composed of five senators, five representatives, and five Supreme Court justices, voted 8 to 7 in favor of Hayes, who became President.

FURTHER READING
Schlesinger, Arthur M., Jr., and Fred L. Israel, eds. *Running for President*. New York: Simon & Schuster, 1993.

Enacting clause

EACH BILL before Congress begins with the phrase "Be it enacted by the Senate and House of Representatives," which is the enacting clause. If a majority votes to strike, or remove, the enacting clause, then the entire bill is automatically killed, without requiring a vote on the bill as a whole.

Ervin, Samuel J., Jr.

☆ *Born: Sept. 27, 1896, Morganton, N.C.*
☆ *Political party: Democrat*
☆ *Representative from North Carolina: 1946–47*
☆ *Senator from North Carolina: 1954–74*
☆ *Died: Apr. 23, 1985, Winston-Salem, N.C.*

WHEN IT became clear that the Watergate break-in had been more than just a "third-rate burglary" and that Congress needed to investigate the Nixon administration's tactics during the 1972 Presidential election, Senate majority leader Mike Mansfield (Democrat–Montana) wisely chose North Carolina senator Sam Ervin to chair the special investigating committee. The 76-year-old Ervin called himself "just a country lawyer." But despite his grandfatherly appearance, Ervin was a shrewd politician, constitutional scholar, and relentless investigator.

As a conservative Southern Democrat, Ervin had opposed civil rights legislation, but as the chairman of the Senate Subcommittee on Constitutional Rights, he had labored long in defense of civil liberties. From his reading of the Bill of Rights, Ervin opposed excessive government secrecy and defended individual privacy and freedom of the press. When he became chairman of the Select Committee on Presidential Campaign Activities, formed to investigate Watergate, Ervin captivated national attention with his folksy sayings and Southern drawl. At the same time, his probing of witnesses from the Nixon administration exposed the "dirty tricks" they had employed during the election. Ervin's persistence led to the indictment and conviction of many government officials and eventually to the resignation of President Richard M. Nixon.

SEE ALSO

Bill of Rights; Investigations; Watergate investigation (1973)

FURTHER READING

Dabney, Dick. *A Good Man: The Life of Sam J. Ervin.* Boston: Houghton Mifflin, 1976.
Ervin, Sam. *Preserving the Constitution: An Autobiography of Senator Sam Ervin.* Charlottesville, Va.: Mitchie, 1984.

Ethics

THE PUBLIC expects its elected officials to have high ethical standards. But standards of ethical behavior have changed over time. When Daniel Webster served as a senator in the 1830s and 1840s, he carried on a private legal practice and argued cases before the Supreme Court. Since Congress met for only half the year, it was commonplace for members to continue their other business activities during the months of adjournment. Questions arose about members' conflict of interest, and Congress began to meet year-round. The Senate and House revised their rules to prohibit members

Ralph Nader testified in favor of improving congressional ethics.

Failed banker Charles Keating's large campaign contributions raised questions about Senate ethics.

from representing legal clients and engaging in other outside activities. The old practice of a member putting his wife and children on the congressional payroll was banned. Ethics laws also prohibited the use of campaign funds for personal expenses. No set of ethics laws will ever be final, however, because political and financial practices, and public opinion, are constantly changing.

Some private groups, including Common Cause and Ralph Nader's Citizens' Watch on Congress Project, keep close watch on congressional behavior and publicize ethics lapses and abuses of position. The press also scrutinizes congressional ethics. The Senate Select Committee on Ethics and the House Standards of Official Conduct Committee advise members and staff and investigate charges of impropriety.

From time to time, scandals have stirred public opinion and caused Congress to reexamine its rules of behavior. In the 19th century, such lobbying scandals as the one involving Credit Mobilier in 1872—when high-ranking members of both houses accepted stock from a railroad company receiving subsidies from the federal government—began the movement to restrict members' outside business and financial activities. Similarly, the 1970s investigation of Abscam (in which an FBI agent posed as an Arab sheikh and offered bribes to members of Congress) and the savings and loan scandals of the 1990s—which caught some members offering their influence in return for campaign contributions—further tightened congressional rules of ethics. The public has also seen excessive perks of Congress, including travel junkets and check bouncing at the House bank, as indications of the need for continued reform.

SEE ALSO

Campaign financing; Credit Mobilier scandal (1872–73); Discipline; House bank scandal (1992); Junkets; Perks

FURTHER READING

Jennings, Bruce, and Daniel Callahan, eds. *Representation and Responsibility: Exploring Legislative Ethics.* New York: Plenum, 1985.

Executive privilege

PRESIDENTS CITE executive privilege—their right as head of a separate branch of government to withhold information—when they decline to turn over executive branch documents that Congress has requested. Although executive privilege is not specified in the Constitution, Presidents have argued that the concept of separation of powers among government branches protects their correspondence with their staff and other internal documents from congressional scrutiny.

George Washington established the precedent in 1796, when he denied a request from the House for correspondence dealing with the controversial Jay Treaty. In 1834, Andrew Jackson refused a Senate request for certain cabinet records dealing with his feud with the Bank of the United States. In a message to the Senate, Jackson stated, "The Executive is a co-ordinate and independent branch of the Government equally with the Senate; and I have yet to learn under what constitutional authority that branch of the Legislature has to require of me an account of any communication, either verbally or in writing, made to the heads of department acting as a cabinet council."

In the 1934 case *United States v. Curtiss-Wright Corporation,* the Supreme Court upheld the concept of executive privilege, ruling that Congress could not demand executive branch information whose "premature disclosure" might cause "harmful results" to the nation's foreign policy. During Senator Joseph McCarthy's anticommunist crusade against alleged spies in the executive branch, President Dwight Eisenhower expanded executive privilege even further when he decreed that to protect executive branch employees' candid dealings with each other, "it is not in the public interest that *any* of their conversations or communications, or *any* documents . . . concerning such advice be disclosed."

President Richard M. Nixon repeatedly invoked executive privilege. For instance, the President bypassed the Department of State and conducted foreign

President Richard Nixon tried to use executive privilege to keep Congress from learning the contents of his secret tape recordings.

policy through his national security adviser, Henry Kissinger, but would not permit congressional committees to call Kissinger to testify. Nixon also used executive privilege to deny the Senate Watergate committee access to secret tape recordings of his conversations. "No president could function if the private papers of his office, prepared by his personal staff, were open to public scrutiny," Nixon protested. In the 1974 case *United States v. Nixon,* the Supreme Court ruled unanimously that while executive privilege was a fundamental aspect of separation of powers, it was not an absolute power. The Court said that a President could withhold information to protect military, diplomatic, or national security secrets but not from a criminal investigation. The Supreme Court ordered Nixon to turn over the tapes, whose revelations led to his resignation as President.

SEE ALSO

Jay Treaty (1795); Separation of powers; Watergate investigation (1973)

FURTHER READING

Hamilton, James. *The Power to Probe: A Study of Congressional Investigations.* New York: Vintage, 1976.
Schlesinger, Arthur M., Jr. *The Imperial Presidency.* Boston: Houghton Mifflin, 1973.

Executive sessions

AN EXECUTIVE session of a committee or of the full House or Senate once meant a closed session, from which the public and the press were excluded. In committee, these closed sessions often dealt with the final marking up of bills, in which the substance and language of a bill were prepared to be reported to the floor. Committees also held closed sessions to hear information of a sensitive nature, notably reports containing classified information relating to national security. The term *executive* also refers to executive business, such as treaties and nominations, which the Senate handles exclusively. Until 1929, the Senate debated and voted on executive business in closed session. Since then, the Senate has conducted these executive sessions in public, closing the doors only on rare occasions when dealing with highly classified, or confidential, information.

Expulsion

THE MOST severe form of punishment for a member of Congress is expulsion, which requires a two-thirds vote of the Senate or House. In 1797 the Senate expelled William Blount of Tennessee for treason, and during the Civil War it expelled another 14 senators for supporting the Confederacy. The House similarly expelled three of its members during the Civil War. In 1980 the House expelled Michael ("Ozzie") Myers (Democrat–Pennsylvania) for corruption. However, most members of Congress convicted in court of a crime have resigned rather than face expulsion.

Senator Jesse D. Bright (standing, right) defended himself against efforts to expel him from the Senate in 1862.

SEE ALSO

Censure; Discipline

SENATORS WHO WERE EXPELLED

William Blount (Independent–Tennessee), 1797, for treason

Thomas Bragg (Democrat–North Carolina), 1861, for support of the rebellion

John Breckinridge (Democrat–Kentucky), 1861, for support of the rebellion

James Chestnut (States Rights–South Carolina), 1861, for support of the rebellion

Thomas Clingman (Democrat–North Carolina), 1861, for support of the rebellion

John Hemphill (States Rights–Texas), 1861, for support of the rebellion

Robert Hunter (Democrat–Virginia), 1861, for support of the rebellion

James Mason (Democrat–Virginia), 1861, for support of the rebellion

Charles Mitchel (Democrat–Arkansas), 1861, for support of the rebellion

Alfred Nicholson (Democrat–Tennessee), 1861, for support of the rebellion

William Sebastian (Democrat–Arkansas), 1861, for support of the rebellion

Louis Wigfall (Democrat–Texas), 1861, for support of the rebellion

Jesse D. Bright (Democrat–Indiana), 1862, for support of the rebellion

Waldo Johnson (Democrat–Missouri), 1862, for support of the rebellion

Trusten Polk (Democrat–Missouri), 1862, for support of the rebellion

REPRESENTATIVES WHO WERE EXPELLED

Henry Burnett (Democrat–Kentucky), 1861, for support of the rebellion

James Clark (Democrat–Missouri), 1861, for support of the rebellion

John Reid (Democrat–Missouri), 1861, for support of the rebellion

Michael ("Ozzie") Myers (Democrat–Pennsylvania), 1980, for corruption

Extraordinary sessions

SEE Special sessions

Families in Congress

THE POLITICAL impulse often passes from one generation to the next within the same family, so that many senators and representatives can claim family members who served in Congress before them. Younger family members win election in part because of their name recognition, voters' emotional ties to their family, and their strong identification with a particular state or region.

The Breckinridge family of Kentucky, for instance, began its congressional tenure when John Breckinridge served as a senator from 1801 to 1805. A grandson, John C. Breckinridge, was a senator from 1851 to 1855 and again in 1861; another grandson, William C. Breckinridge, served in the House from 1885 to 1895. A great-great-grandson, John B. Breckinridge, was a House member from 1973 to 1979.

The Bayard family of Delaware, similarly, had four generations in the

Brothers Robert, Edward, and John Kennedy all served in the U.S. Senate.

House and Senate. Henry Dodge (Democrat–Wisconsin) and Augustus Caesar Dodge (Democrat–Iowa) have been the only father and son to serve in the Senate at the same time. Frances Bolton and her son Oliver (Republicans–Ohio) served simultaneously in the House of Representatives—Frances's late husband, Chester Bolton, had also served in the House. When Senator Huey P. Long (Democrat–Louisiana) was assassinated in 1935, his widow, Rose Long, was appointed to fill the vacancy. Their son, Russell Long, was elected in 1948, making them the only father, mother, and son to sit in the Senate.

Carrying on the tradition

Sometimes family members come to Congress to carry on the tradition of a famous predecessor, as did "Young Bob" La Follette (Republican/Progressive–Wisconsin), who followed his crusading father, "Battling Bob" La Follette, in the Senate. Or they may deliberately chart a different course. Henry Cabot Lodge, Jr. (Republican–Massachusetts) won fame as an internationalist, although his grandfather, Henry Cabot Lodge, Sr., had led the fight against the Treaty of Versailles and fostered isolationism.

Among the most notable congressional families was the dynasty founded by John Fitzgerald (Democrat–Massachusetts), who served in the House from 1895 to 1901. His grandson John Fitzgerald Kennedy (Democrat–Massachusetts) served in the House from 1947 to 1953 and in the Senate from 1953 to 1960 before being elected President. John Kennedy's brothers Robert Kennedy (Democrat–New York) and Edward Kennedy (Democrat–Massachusetts) were also elected senators, and his nephew Joseph Kennedy (Democrat–Massachusetts) has continued the family tradition as a member of the House.

SEE ALSO

Kennedy, Edward M.; Lodge, Henry Cabot, Sr.; Long, Huey P.

FURTHER READING

Goodwin, Doris Kearns. *The Fitzgeralds and the Kennedys.* New York: Simon & Schuster, 1987.

Klotter, James C. *The Breckinridges of Kentucky: Two Centuries of Leadership.* Lexington: University Press of Kentucky, 1986.

Felton, Rebecca Latimer

☆ Born: June 10, 1835, Decatur, Ga.
☆ Political party: Democrat
☆ Senator from Georgia: 1922
☆ Died: Jan. 24, 1930, Atlanta, Ga.

THE FIRST woman senator, 87-year-old Rebecca Felton was also the oldest person to become a senator, and her single-day term set the record as the shortest. Two years after the 19th Amendment granted women the right to vote in 1920, the governor of Georgia appointed her to fill out the remaining days of a deceased senator's term. The appointment was a symbolic gesture because the Senate was not expected to be in session before her successor would be chosen in a special election. But when the Senate met in special session, Rebecca Felton persuaded her elected successor, Walter George (Democrat), to withhold his credentials and allow her to serve just briefly. The Senate debated for a day whether to accept her credentials. At last she took the oath of office and delivered a short speech in which she promised senators that "when the women of the country come in and sit with you, though there may be but very few in the next few years, I pledge you that you will get ability, you will get integrity of purpose, you will get exalted patriotism, and you will get unstinted usefulness." The

Rebecca Latimer Felton was the first woman senator.

next day, her elected successor replaced her, and Rebecca Felton returned to Georgia.

SEE ALSO
Women in Congress

FURTHER READING
Talmadge, John E. *Rebecca Latimer Felton: Nine Stormy Decades.* Athens: University of Georgia Press, 1960.

Filibuster

THE USE of delaying tactics to block legislation is called a filibuster. The expression, from a Dutch word meaning "pirate," became popular in the 1850s when American adventurers went filibustering around the Caribbean, trying to overthrow governments and seize power for themselves. The word was soon applied to Congress, where it was used to describe roguish efforts to seize the floor and prevent the majority from acting.

Even in the 1st Congress, minority members delivered long speeches and used the rules to obstruct legislation they opposed. At first, representatives as well as senators could filibuster, but as the House grew larger, it tightened its rules on how long individuals could speak. The Senate, which had fewer members, retained the right of unlimited debate. Senators felt it important that every member have the ability to speak for as long as necessary on any issue.

One of the Senate's first organized filibusters took place in 1841, when the Democratic minority sought to prevent action on a bank bill promoted by Henry Clay (Whig–Kentucky). After many days of speeches and delaying maneuvers, Clay threatened to change the Senate's rules to permit the majority to act. But Thomas Hart Benton (Democrat–Missouri) angrily accused Clay of trying to "stifle debate," and John C. Calhoun (Democrat–South Carolina) denounced any attempt

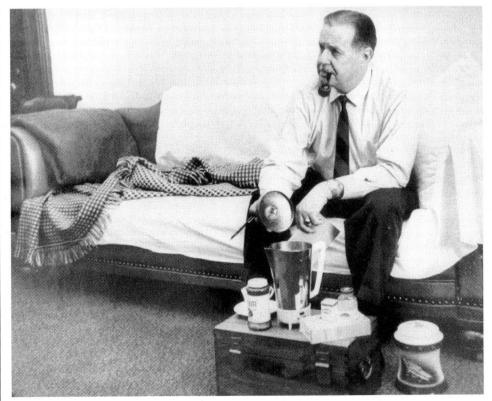

Senator Hugh Scott (Republican–Pennsylvania) resting in his office during a filibuster.

"to infringe the right of speech." Clay retreated and conceded defeat.

Cloture

Until 1917 the Senate had no way to cut off debate. At the urging of President Woodrow Wilson, the Senate adopted a rule that permitted a two-thirds vote of the Senate to end debate. In 1919 the Senate invoked cloture for the first time to shut off a filibuster against the Treaty of Versailles. But cloture proved difficult to achieve and filibusters flourished, especially during lame-duck sessions, which take place between the November election and the beginning of the next Congress. During these sessions, many members would be leaving Congress shortly and were therefore easily influenced by special interests. With only days left in the session, any member could disrupt business by filibustering or even threatening to filibuster. For this reason, Senator George Norris (Republican–Nebraska) sponsored the 20th Amendment to the Constitution, ratified in 1933, which effectively ended lame-duck filibustering by moving the opening of Congress from December of the following year back to January of that year so that lame ducks would have much less time to serve after they had been replaced by election. Since then, Congress has rarely met during the months between a November election and the convening of a new Congress on January 3.

Famous filibusters

During the 1930s, Senator Huey P. Long (Democrat–Louisiana) frequently filibustered against bills that he thought gave away too much to the wealthy. Long frustrated the Senate and entertained the nation by reciting Shakespeare, the Bible, and recipes for "potlikker" (a Southern dish of boiled roots or greens whose liquid is used for dipping cornbread in) for hours on the Senate floor. He once held the floor for 15 hours. The longest individual speech was delivered by J. Strom Thurmond (Democrat/Republican–South Carolina), when he filibustered for 24 hours and 18 minutes against the Civil Rights Act of 1957.

More commonly, groups of senators conduct filibusters by working in teams to hold the floor for days and weeks. They will object to unanimous consent agreements, force the previous day's journal entry to be read aloud, suggest the absence of a quorum (the minimum attendance to conduct business), and otherwise insist that all the rules be observed as a means of slowing down business and wearing out the majority. For many years, Southern senators were especially skillful in filibustering against civil rights legislation. Not until 1964 was the Senate able to invoke cloture against an anti–civil rights filibuster. In 1975, the Senate reduced the number of senators needed to invoke cloture from two-thirds to three-fifths.

Absences and arrests

Along with making long-winded speeches, another favorite device of filibustering senators is simply to absent themselves from the chamber. If the minority party does not answer quorum calls, then the majority has to stay near the chamber at all times, day or night, to establish a quorum and keep business moving. At such times, the Senate majority leader will order that the sergeant at arms arrest absent senators. Deputy sergeants at arms go to the absent senators' offices and homes to accompany them to the chamber, and on occasion they have even physically carried senators in the door.

The Senate tolerates filibusters as a necessary evil. The ability to filibuster makes every senator, even the most junior member of the minority party, an important force in Senate proceedings. Even more important, contrary to the general belief that in a democracy the majority should rule, the filibuster offers a defense of the minority's rights and opinions.

SEE ALSO
Cloture; Debate; Lame-duck sessions

FURTHER READING
Byrd, Robert C. "The Cloture Rule," "Extended Debate," and "Filibusters." In *The Senate, 1789–1989: Addresses on the History of the United States Senate.* Vol. 2. Washington, D.C.: Government Printing Office, 1991.

First branch of government

AS THE subject of the first and longest article of the Constitution, Congress has been called the "first branch of government." This phrase also reflects the Jeffersonian concept that the legislative branch is superior to the executive and judiciary because it more accurately reflects the needs and opinions of the people.

First hundred days of the New Deal

AT THE depth of the Great Depression, Franklin D. Roosevelt took office as President on March 4, 1933, and called Congress into special session. Lasting from March 9 to June 15, 1933, this session became known as the "first hundred days" of the New Deal. Responding to the economic crisis, Congress passed an extraordinary amount of major legislation in a remarkably short period. Sometimes, members did not even have a chance to read the legislation before they voted for it. During the hundred days, Congress enacted emergency banking

President Franklin D. Roosevelt (seated) with Representative Jennings Randolph during the "first hundred days."

legislation to restore stable banking, emergency relief legislation, a public works bill, a Civilian Conservation Corps bill to provide relief and create jobs, the National Industrial Recovery Administration to establish federal economic planning, the Federal Securities Act to regulate the sale of stocks, the Agricultural Adjustment Act and Farm Credit Act to help farmers, and the Tennessee Valley Authority to provide electrical power and jobs. These laws were designed to bring recovery, relief, and reform.

Although some of these programs had originated in Congress, the first hundred days in general represented congressional yielding to strong Presidential leadership. In later years other Presidents' legislative successes have been measured against—but few have come close to matching—Roosevelt's first hundred days. Acutely conscious of this pressure, John F. Kennedy said in his inaugural address, "It won't be done in the first hundred days...." By comparison, Ronald Reagan consciously sought to establish his policies during the important first hundred days of his administration.

FURTHER READING
Israel, Fred L. *Franklin Delano Roosevelt.* New York: Chelsea House, 1985.

Floor managers

AFTER A COMMITTEE reports out legislation, floor managers guide the bill to a final vote of the House and Senate. Usually, the committee or subcommittee chairman serves as floor manager, while the ranking minority member leads the opposition. Floor managers make the opening statements and schedule other members who want to debate the bill. They try to prevent any crippling amendments but will negotiate to reach whatever compromises are necessary to get a majority vote.

In the House, floor managers sit at the large tables on either side of the center aisle and may address the chamber from that location. In the Senate, floor managers move forward to occupy the leaders' front-row desks. The floor managers normally serve on the conference committee that determines the bill's final form, and they are traditionally photographed standing behind the president as their work is signed into law. Some sponsors and floor managers become so identified with legislation that it takes their names, such as the Taft-Hartley or Humphrey-Hawkins bills.

Floor privileges

HOUSE AND Senate rules limit who can go onto the floor of the chambers when Congress is in session. Those regularly admitted include members and their staff, committee staff, the staff who work at the front desks, and the pages. Floor privileges are also extended to the President and Vice President, members of the cabinet, governors, Supreme Court justices, senior military officers, the Architect of the Capitol, and the mayor of the District of Columbia. House and Senate doorkeepers direct all other visitors to the galleries. Former members of Congress also have floor privileges, which for a while gave them considerable advantage as lobbyists. But since 1945 the House has followed the Rayburn Rule, named after former Speaker Sam Rayburn, which bars former members from the floor during any debate or vote in which they have any personal or business interest. The Senate, similarly, discourages former members from using their floor privileges to lobby.

SEE ALSO
Doorkeepers; Lobbying; Rayburn, Sam

Foley, Thomas S.

☆ *Born: Mar. 6, 1929, Spokane, Wash.*
☆ *Political party: Democrat*
☆ *Representative from Washington: 1965–*
☆ *House majority leader: 1987–89*
☆ *Speaker of the House: 1989–*

THE RESIGNATION under fire of Jim Wright in 1989 (due to alleged financial misconduct) elevated Majority Leader Tom Foley to Speaker of the House. Foley assumed the Speaker's chair at a difficult time of divided government (a Republican President but Democratic majorities in both the House and Senate), which led to legislative stalemate and frustration. In contrast to Wright's tendency to act aggressively and independently, Foley had built a reputation for achieving consensus through negotiation and conciliation.

Speaker Foley had begun his career as a member of the congressional staff.

From 1961 to 1963 he served as assistant chief clerk and special counsel to the Senate Committee on Interior and Insular Affairs, chaired by Henry Jackson (Democrat–Washington). Foley left the staff to run for Congress himself in 1964. He rose through the leadership as a result of his even-tempered approach to legislative problems and his skills in bringing people together.

Gerald R. Ford during his service in the House of Representatives.

Ford, Gerald R.

☆ *Born: July 14, 1913, Omaha, Nebr.*
☆ *Political party: Republican*
☆ *Representative from Michigan: 1949–73*
☆ *House minority leader: 1965–73*
☆ *Vice President: 1973–74*
☆ *President: 1974–77*

GERALD FORD'S party called on him in time of trouble. In 1965, after the Republican party suffered a major defeat in the Presidential and congressional elections, House Republicans ousted Charles Halleck and elected the younger and more aggressive Gerald Ford as minority leader. Ford proved an aggressive and successful leader who helped his party regain much of its lost stature.

In 1973, Vice President Spiro Agnew was convicted of accepting bribes and resigned from office. President Richard Nixon then appointed Ford as Vice President, both to rebuild the Nixon administration's crumbling relations with Congress and because the Senate would be likely to confirm him. This was the first time that the 25th Amendment was used to fill a Vice Presidential vacancy. When Nixon resigned in 1974 because of the Watergate scandal, Ford became President. President Ford was often at odds with the Democratic Congress. He vetoed many bills and had many of his vetoes overridden. Yet members of

Congress respected Ford as one of their own, which helped calm the nation and restore the government to working order after the shock of Watergate.

FURTHER READING

Ford, Gerald R. *A Time to Heal: The Autobiography of Gerald R. Ford.* New York: Harper & Row, 1979.
Witcover, Jules. *Crapshoot: Rolling the Dice on the Vice Presidency.* New York: Crown, 1992.

Franked mail

MEMBERS OF Congress can send official correspondence by frank—or free of postage (from the Latin word *francus,* meaning "for free"). A member's printed signature on an envelope takes the place of stamps. This privilege dates back to both the British House of Commons and the American Continental Congress. In 1789, members of the 1st Congress granted the frank to themselves, the President, and members of the cabinet. Originally, members simply signed their name on envelopes; today their signatures are printed on all franked envelopes.

During the 19th century there were numerous charges that members of Con-

This 1860 cartoon suggests that members of Congress used the frank to mail their laundry home for cleaning.

gress were abusing the frank. Some mailed their laundry home, and others sent household goods. One senator supposedly signed his name to his horse's saddle and had the post office deliver the animal to his home. Incumbents were accused of bombarding their constituents with transcripts of speeches, government documents, packages of seeds (from the Department of Agriculture), and other items designed to win their reelection. So many objections were raised that in 1873 Congress suspended the use of the frank. However, others defended the frank as essential for "free and unrestrained communications between the people and their representatives." Acting in stages, Congress restored the frank by 1891. Since then, various revisions of the ethics code have limited the amount of franked mail that members can send each year and set restrictions on the newsletters and other types of mail that can be legitimately sent via the frank.

Freedmen's Bureau Acts (1865 and 1866)

AS THE Civil War ended in 1865, Congress created the Bureau of Refugees, Freedmen, and Abandoned Land, popularly known as the Freedmen's Bureau, to help former slaves make the transition to freedom. Throughout the South, the Freedmen's Bureau established schools and hospitals, helped negotiate labor contracts, leased or sold confiscated lands to the freedmen, and generally tried to protect them from their former masters.

The unpopularity of the Freedmen's Bureau among white Southerners caused President Andrew Johnson to veto an 1866 bill to extend the life of the bureau.

The veto outraged both moderate and radical Republicans in Congress and united them against the President. Congress passed the second Freedmen's Bureau Act over the President's veto and started down the collision course that would result in Johnson's impeachment in 1868.

SEE ALSO
Impeachment of Andrew Johnson (1868); Reconstruction, congressional

FURTHER READING
Benedict, Michael Les. *A Compromise of Principle: Congressional Republicans and Reconstruction, 1863–1868.* New York: Norton, 1974.

Fulbright, J. William

☆ *Born: Apr. 9, 1905, Sumner, Mo.*
☆ *Political party: Democrat*
☆ *Representative from Arkansas: 1943–45*
☆ *Senator from Arkansas: 1945–74*

IN 1964, as chairman of the Senate Foreign Relations Committee, J. William Fulbright led the effort to pass the Gulf of Tonkin Resolution. The resolution gave congressional support to President Lyndon B. Johnson to retaliate against any hostile military acts by North Vietnam. Fulbright assured other senators that the resolution was not an act of war and that President Johnson would consult with Congress before escalating the conflict. The next year, however, when

Senator J. William Fulbright (left) of Arkansas succeeded Senator Theodore Francis Green (right) of Rhode Island as chair of the Foreign Relations Committee.

President Johnson sent U.S. Marines to intervene in a rebellion within the Dominican Republic, Senator Fulbright became concerned that the President was not telling Congress and the public the full truth. If Johnson had exaggerated the situation in the Dominican Republic in order to justify sending troops, Fulbright wondered, might he be doing the same in Vietnam? In 1966, the Foreign Relations Committee launched a series of "educational" hearings on the Vietnam War, inviting both defenders and critics of the war to testify. The hearings began a national debate on the war and made Senator Fulbright one of the leading dissenters against American foreign policy.

SEE ALSO

Gulf of Tonkin Resolution (1964); Johnson, Lyndon B.

FURTHER READING

Berman, William C. *William Fulbright and the Vietnam War: The Dissent of a Political Realist.* Kent, Ohio: Kent State University Press, 1988.

"Gag rule"

IN 1836 the House of Representatives established a "gag rule" to try to stop citizens from submitting antislavery petitions. Previously, the House and Senate had simply referred such petitions to committee without ever acting on them. But when petitioners called for Congress to abolish slavery in the District of Columbia, which Congress supervised, Southern representatives sought to put an end to this "agitation." Together with sympathetic Northerners, they voted 117 to 68 to adopt a "gag rule" that required the House to lay antislavery petitions on the table (meaning to put them aside) immediately, without printing them, referring them to committee, or in any way

debating them. Representative John Quincy Adams (Whig–Massachusetts) led the opposition to what he called an unconstitutional attempt to suppress the freedom to petition. Adams lost repeated battles and came close to being censured. By 1844, enough Northerners had changed their position, and the House voted 105 to 80 to repeal the "gag rule."

SEE ALSO

Adams, John Quincy; Petition, citizens' right to

FURTHER READING

Richards, Leonard L. *The Life and Times of Congressman John Quincy Adams.* New York: Oxford, 1986.

Galleries

VISITORS WATCH the proceedings of the House and Senate from galleries, or balconies, surrounding the chambers. The House, elected directly by the people, opened a public gallery when it first met in 1789, but the Senate, whose members were elected by state legislatures, saw no need for a gallery at first. The Senate's debates were closed until 1794, when a gallery at last was constructed. Today the galleries of both the House and Senate are open whenever that chamber is in session, at any hour of the day or night.

Congress appoints doorkeepers to supervise the galleries. Rules prohibit visitors to the galleries from taking notes or photographs. Visitors may not lean over the railing, a prohibition dating back to 1916, when President Woodrow Wilson addressed a joint session of Congress and activists draped a large banner down from the gallery that read, "Mr. President, What Will You Do For

Tickets to the Senate galleries were issued during the impeachment trial of President Andrew Johnson in 1868.

Woman Suffrage?" The rules of the Senate and House also forbid members from addressing the galleries or from calling attention to special visitors.

Before entering the galleries, visitors must obtain tickets from their senators or representatives. The first tickets were issued in 1868 to control the crowds seeking to witness the impeachment trial of President Andrew Johnson. Today, television cameras mounted in the galleries broadcast the proceedings live via C-SPAN. Television has become a nationwide extension of the House and Senate galleries.

In addition to the public galleries, the House and Senate also make gallery space available to their staff, to the members' families, to the foreign diplomatic corps, and to the press. To encourage the widest media coverage of its proceedings, Congress provides separate press galleries for newspaper correspondents, radio and television reporters, magazine writers, and press photographers.

SEE ALSO
C-SPAN; Doorkeepers; Media coverage of Congress

Garner, John Nance

☆ *Born: Nov. 22, 1868, Detroit, Tex.*
☆ *Political party: Democrat*
☆ *Representative from Texas: 1903–33*
☆ *Speaker of the House: 1931–33*
☆ *Vice President: 1933–41*
☆ *Died: Nov. 7, 1967, Uvalde, Tex.*

THE ELECTION of 1930 made "Cactus Jack" Garner the first Democratic Speaker in a dozen years. With the nation sliding into a terrible economic depression, Garner seemed uncertain about what course to follow. At first he encouraged Democratic support for Republican President Herbert Hoover's programs,

but when these seemed too limited and unsatisfactory, Garner looked for Democratic alternatives. In 1932, Garner proposed that the federal government spend billions of dollars on public works programs to put the unemployed back to work. Hoover vetoed this plan, but the following year it became a major initiative of the new Democratic President, Franklin D. Roosevelt. By then, Speaker Garner had become Vice President Garner. Presiding over the Senate was a far less powerful post than that of House Speaker, but Garner continued to play an active role in promoting Roosevelt's New Deal in the Senate.

SEE ALSO
First hundred days of the New Deal

FURTHER READING
Bolling, Richard. *Power in the House: A History of the Leadership of the House of Representatives.* New York: Dutton, 1969.

General Accounting Office (GAO)

SINCE 1921 the General Accounting Office has been Congress's financial watchdog. Congress exercises its "power of the purse" by raising and appropriating all the money that the government spends. But Congress is also concerned about how well the numerous departments and agencies of the government handle those funds. Headed by the comptroller general, GAO accountants audit the books of government agencies in search of problems and wrongdoing. Congressional committees may request the GAO to evaluate particular government programs to determine how efficiently they are administered and to recommend reforms. GAO staff members work closely with the House and Senate

Appropriations and Budget Committees and often assist congressional investigating committees.

SEE ALSO
Legislative agencies

FURTHER READING
Trask, Roger R. *GAO History, 1921–1991.* Washington, D.C.: Government Printing Office, 1991.

Germaneness

TO BE germane, or relevant, an amendment must have something to do with the rest of the bill it seeks to amend. House rules require that all amendments be germane. The rules of the Senate are different, and senators can attach favored amendments onto completely unrelated bills. These are sometimes called "riders" because they ride along on the larger bill. The Senate requires germaneness only for amendments to general appropriations bills and after cloture, the end of debate, has been voted on a bill. The Senate might also require germaneness as part of a unanimous consent agreement that sets the conditions under which a bill can be debated and voted upon.

SEE ALSO
Riders

Gerrymandering

WHEN ELBRIDGE Gerry was governor of Massachusetts in 1812, his party redrew the state's congressional districts deliberately to favor its own candidates. One district had such an odd shape that it resembled a salamander, a lizardlike

This 1812 cartoon of "The Gerry-Mander" showed voting districts in Massachusetts.

creature. Combining *Gerry* and *salamander* created *Gerrymander,* which came to mean any unfair and extremely partisan form of reapportionment of election districts.

SEE ALSO
Reapportionment

Goldwater, Barry M.

☆ *Born: Jan. 1, 1909, Phoenix, Ariz.*
☆ *Political party: Republican*
☆ *Senator from Arizona: 1953–65, 1969–87*

AS A SENATOR during the 1950s, Barry Goldwater objected to what he called "me too" Republicanism. He meant that under President Dwight D. Eisenhower, Republicans had embraced many of the social and economic programs of Democratic Presidents Franklin D. Roosevelt and Harry S. Truman. Goldwater rejected the idea of big government, social welfare programs, and regulation of business. "My aim is not to pass laws, but to repeal them," he insisted. "It is not to inaugurate new programs, but to cancel old ones that do violence to the Constitution."

Goldwater used the Senate as a pul-

This Barry Goldwater doll was made for his 1964 Presidential campaign.

pit to preach his conservative creed and became the nation's leading conservative spokesman. In 1964 he won the Republican nomination for President, but his views seemed extreme and he lost to Lyndon B. Johnson in a landslide. Goldwater's followers retained control of the Republican party and steered it in the direction that led eventually to the election of Ronald Reagan on a platform of cutting back social programs and deregulating business. Goldwater himself returned to the Senate in 1969, where he continued to speak his mind, bluntly and provocatively.

FURTHER READING

Goldwater, Barry M. *The Conscience of a Conservative.* Washington: Regnery Gateway, 1990.
Goldwater, Barry M. *With No Apologies.* New York: Morrow, 1979.

Great Compromise (1787)

THE BASIC structure of the Senate and House of Representatives resulted from the Great Compromise of 1787. A dangerous stalemate had developed at the Constitutional Convention between delegates from the larger states, who wanted representation in both houses of Congress according to the size of a state's population, and delegates from the smaller states, who demanded equal representation for each state.

When the convention recessed to celebrate the Fourth of July, a special committee met to break the deadlock. The committee proposed a compromise, strongly advocated by the delegates from Connecticut, under which the House membership would be apportioned by population and the Senate would have

an equal number of representatives from each state. William Samuel Johnson of Connecticut explained that the two houses of Congress would be "halves of a unique whole." The Great Compromise (sometimes called the Connecticut Compromise) saved the Constitution. Equality was so essential for the smaller states that they added a clause to the Constitution to make sure they would never lose it. Article 5 states that "no state without its consent, shall be deprived of its equal suffrage in the Senate." Today, as a result of the Great Compromise, California's 30 million people send 52 representatives to the House, and Wyoming's one-half million people send only one. Yet both states elect two senators apiece.

FURTHER READING

Ritchie, Donald A. *The U.S. Constitution.* New York: Chelsea House, 1989.

Gulf of Tonkin Resolution (1964)

EVEN THOUGH Congress never officially declared war against North Vietnam during the 1960s, President Lyndon B. Johnson cited the Gulf of Tonkin Resolution as congressional authorization for American military intervention in Vietnam. On August 4, 1964, U.S. naval vessels were reportedly attacked by torpedo boats in the Gulf of Tonkin, off the coast of North Vietnam. President Johnson asked Congress for a resolution allowing him to take "all necessary measures" to repel any further armed attacks. Congress had previously passed similar resolutions to show support for Presidents in confronting such trouble spots as Formosa (now Taiwan), the Middle East, Berlin, and Cuba. Although

Using charts and maps, Defense Secretary Robert S. McNamara explained the Gulf of Tonkin incident to the press.

some senators worried that these resolutions were "blank checks" and "predated declarations of war," no President had actually put one of these resolutions to use. The Gulf of Tonkin Resolution was rushed through Congress with little debate. The House voted unanimously in its support. Only two senators, Wayne Morse (Democrat–Oregon) and Ernest Gruening (Democrat–Alaska), voted against it. J. William Fulbright (Democrat–Arkansas), chairman of the Senate Foreign Relations Committee, assured senators that the resolution was not a declaration of war and that the President would consult with Congress before expanding U.S. military efforts in Vietnam.

In 1965, President Johnson escalated the war, using the Gulf of Tonkin Resolution as proof that Congress endorsed his actions. Later congressional investigations revealed that Johnson's staff had drafted the resolution well before the Gulf of Tonkin incident. These investigations also raised questions about whether an attack had even taken place. Evidence strongly suggested that the American naval vessels had reacted to radar signals caused by weather conditions rather than by the North Vietnamese. In 1970, Congress repealed the resolution, but by then Johnson's successor, President Richard M. Nixon, argued that the Gulf of Tonkin Resolution was not necessary to continue the war. Displeasure with the Gulf of Tonkin Resolution led Congress to enact the War Powers Act of 1973, over President Nixon's veto. The War Powers Act requires Presidents to withdraw troops from combat after 60 days unless Congress has approved the military action.

SEE ALSO
Fulbright, J. William; War powers

FURTHER READING
Herring, George C. *America's Longest War: The United States and Vietnam, 1950–1975.* New York: Knopf, 1986.

Hart, Philip A.

☆ *Born: Dec. 10, 1912, Bryn Mawr, Pa.*
☆ *Political party: Democrat*
☆ *Senator from Michigan: 1959–76*
☆ *Died: Dec. 26, 1976, Washington, D.C.*

KNOWN AS the "conscience of the Senate," Philip Hart was a quiet man who never ducked a fight. As chairman of the antitrust subcommittee, Hart took on big business and the trend toward corporate mergers that he believed would stifle competition. He fought his own state's largest industry, the automobile manufacturers. Hart promoted handgun control laws, although his state had many hunters opposed to any form of gun control. He fought for truth-in-packaging and other consumer rights. He urged the Senate to liberalize its own rules, to make it easier to achieve cloture and shut off filibusters—especially against civil rights bills. Hart's children helped change his opinion about the Vietnam War, and he became sympathetic toward student antiwar protests. As a sign of his support for antiestablishment protest, Hart grew the only beard in the Senate during his era. When he was dying of cancer in 1976, his Senate colleagues recognized his valiant career by naming the newest Senate office building after him.

Head counting

CONGRESSIONAL LEADERS rarely expect a straight party-line vote—one in which all Democrats vote on one side and all Republicans on the other side of a bill. Modern senators and representatives feel free to vote their conscience or to vote for the good of their constituents, regardless of their party's position on an issue. So "head counters" regularly poll the members of their party (and even members of the opposition) to find out how many are in favor, how many opposed, and how many might be leaning either way before a roll call vote. The party whips and party secretaries do most of the head counting, and some gain a special reputation for their accurate predictions.

Head counters expect many members to cast predictable votes because of their ideology, district, or other political reasons. But they also know that personal considerations may sway a member's vote. "You can't just say because Barry Goldwater is a conservative therefore he will vote for a conservative position," one Republican head counter explained. "There may be a personality problem. There may be something somebody did for him and he's going to pay back a favor." The information gathered from head counting enables the party leadership to decide when best to schedule a vote and when to try to delay a vote to avoid defeat.

Hearings

COMMITTEES AND their subcommittees hold hearings to collect testimony and evidence in favor of or against proposed legislation, nominations, and treaties. Committees generally schedule hearings in the mornings, when the House and Senate are not in session. Since many hearings take place at the same time, they therefore compete with each other for attention from the press and even from their own members. Senators and representatives serve on a number of committees and subcommittees whose scheduling conflicts force them to decide which hearings to attend and which to skip.

Committee staffs prepare for hearings by inviting witnesses from the executive branch and various experts who favor or oppose the issue at hand. Citizens' groups and private individuals may also request time to give testimony. Committees often invite movie stars, former high-ranking officials, and other celebrities to testify to draw public attention—and to generate public support for a bill.

The committee chair calls the hearing to order, introduces and sometimes swears in the witnesses, and begins the questioning. Other members of the committee are allotted time, usually according to their seniority, to question the witness. Reporters take down whatever is said, which the committee will publish as a transcript of the hearings. The committee will also prepare a report on the information gathered in the hearings to issue to the full Senate or House.

For many years committees held many hearings and markup sessions—to prepare the final version of a bill—in executive, or closed, session. Since the adoption of "sunshine" rules in the 1970s, which required open committee meetings, the public can attend most congressional hearings and markup sessions. Washington, D.C., newspapers publish lists of those committees holding hearings each day, and visitors may attend without tickets. The more important hearings, however, draw large crowds of newspaper and broadcast reporters, lobbyists, and others, creating long lines of people waiting for available seating. C-SPAN televises many congressional hearings, and the major networks also record segments of the testimony for broadcast on news programs.

SEE ALSO

Committees; Executive sessions; Markup sessions; "Sunshine" rules

Hideaway offices

SENIOR MEMBERS of Congress, particularly senators, occupy "hideaway" offices in the Capitol building. Regardless of their seniority, all members have offices in the office buildings. There, they and their staffs conduct legislative business and greet visitors. But when space becomes available, senior members receive an extra room closer to the House or Senate floor. No names are posted on the doors, and the locations of these hideaways are not announced. Some members rarely use their hideaway, or they assign them to overflow staff. Others retreat to their hideaway to get a few moments of peace and quiet, while remaining near the chambers. Hideaway offices range from windowless rooms in the Capitol's basement to spacious suites with panoramic views of the Mall.

SEE ALSO

Capitol building

Hispanic Americans in Congress

Hispanic Americans are a small but steadily increasing group in Congress, although their proportion there is less than it is in the general population. In 1877 Governor Romualdo Pacheco (Republican–California) became the first Hispanic American to serve in Congress when he was elected to the House of Representatives. He served two terms and chaired the Committee on Private Land Claims. The first Hispanic-American senator was Octaviano Larrazolo (Republican–New Mexico), who was elected to fill the remaining three months of a vacant Senate seat. In 1935 Representative Dennis Chavez (Democrat–New Mexico) was appointed to fill another Senate vacancy. Chavez was reelected four times and became chairman of the Committee on Public Works. After Chavez's death the state of New Mexico sent a statue of him to stand in the Capitol. Herman Badillo (Democrat–New York) became the first Puerto Rican-born representative, and Ilena Ros-Lehtinen (Republican–Florida) became the first Cuban-born representative.

In 1976 as the number of Hispanic members of Congress grew, they formed the Congressional Hispanic Caucus. Drawing its members largely from California, Florida, Texas, and New Mexico, the Hispanic Caucus has also included the nonvoting delegates from Samoa, Puerto Rico, Guam, and the Virgin Islands.

After the 1990 census Congress enacted legislation requiring states to give racial and ethnic minorities greater voting strength in the newly drawn congressional districts. A number of largely Hispanic districts was created, and in 1992 seven new Hispanic candidates won election to the House.

Dennis Chavez of New Mexico

FURTHER READING

Conmy, Peter Thomas. *Romualdo Pacheco: Distinguished Californian of the Mexican and American Periods.* San Francisco: Native Sons of the Golden West, 1957.

Hold

ANY SENATOR who objects to a particular bill can have the party leader place a "hold" on that bill. A hold suspends action and may freeze a bill for weeks or months. At the end of a session, when time is running out, such holds can kill a bill. Managers of the bill will try to negotiate with senators who have placed holds to make whatever changes they can agree upon. If they reach a compromise, the senator will notify the party leadership to lift the hold. Because the hold is an informal arrangement, the leadership can decide at any time to ignore the hold and bring the legislation to the floor. However, the bill's managers know that the senator who placed the hold might object to any unanimous consent agreements and might even launch a filibuster or other delaying tactics. Senators sometimes place reciprocal holds on each other's bills so they can offer to lift one hold in return for lifting the other.

SEE ALSO
Filibuster; Unanimous consent agreements

House bank scandal (1992)

IN 1992, angry about stalemated government, soaring deficits, and economic recession, the public focused its attention on check bouncing in the House bank as a symbol of government perks, or special privileges. For 150 years the House sergeant at arms had operated a bank in the Capitol, where members could write checks based on their deposited salaries. A General Accounting Office (GAO) investigation revealed that many representatives had written checks with insufficient funds in their accounts to cover those checks, but the bank had taken no action to suspend or penalize those who bounced checks. Extensive media coverage caused the House to abolish the bank and reveal the names of more than 300 members who had bounced checks. An unusually large number of representatives chose not to run for reelection, and several other check bouncers were defeated. The bank scandal spurred the House to establish the position of director of non-legislative services, who would serve as a general manager of financial and other administrative activities.

SEE ALSO
Director of non-legislative services; General Accounting Office (GAO); Perks; Scandals, congressional

House of Representatives

THE HOUSE of Representatives has been called the "people's body." No one ever became a member of the House by appointment or any means other than standing for election by the people. Because of the House's close connection to the voters, the Constitution gave the House authority to originate all bills to levy taxes and spend government money.

Representatives serve two-year terms. Each state has at least one representative. States with larger populations are divided into districts, whose lines are redrawn every ten years according to the latest federal census. The House has sole authority to determine any disputed elections and to expel members by a two-thirds vote.

Sheer numbers have shaped the House. The original House consisted of 65 members, one for every 30,000 citizens. After the first census the number rose to 105, and it grew steadily as the population increased and new states were added. In 1910 Congress fixed the membership at 435, and districts are reapportioned every ten years following a new census.

As its membership grew, the House changed its rules to limit time for debate and to strengthen majority rule. When Asher Hinds compiled the first volumes of House precedents in 1907, he observed that "the pages of these volumes show a constant subordination of the individual to the necessities of the whole House as the voice of the national will." Nearly a century later, in 1992, House majority leader Richard Gephardt (Democrat–Missouri) reconfirmed that "the Senate is a collection of individuals, while the House, by virtue of its size, forces you to function in a group."

Leadership in the House

The House sets its own rules and elects its own officers, headed by the Speaker. Depending upon the personality and philosophy of the various Speakers, they have acted as impartial presiding officers or as strong partisan leaders. Speakers of the stature of Henry Clay, James G. Blaine, Thomas B. Reed, Joseph G. Cannon, Nicholas Longworth, John Nance Garner, Sam Rayburn, and Thomas P. ("Tip") O'Neill, Jr., have shaped the development of the House. So, too, have strong committee chairs, notably of the powerful Rules Committee and of the "money" committees: Appropriations and Ways and Means. Traditionally, a small number of committee chairs, ranking minority members, and other senior representatives have dominated the House, and junior members have had little influence. Committee re-

forms in 1975 opened the chairmanships, particularly of subcommittees, to more members and gave members of the majority party the opportunity to vote to remove committee chairs who acted arbitrarily.

Constituent services

House members often receive less national press attention than do senators, and they tend to devote more time to constituent services. If effective, they assure that their district will have a voice in national—and international—affairs and that the federal government will be responsive to its needs, whether in road building, federal water projects, public housing, military bases, Social Security payments, or any number of other areas.

The atmosphere of the House chamber has traditionally differed from that of the more staid Senate. The larger body has often been the more boisterous one, with shouts of "Vote! Vote!" and other commotion on the floor, causing Woodrow Wilson to describe the House as a "mass of jarring elements." The Speaker, as presiding officer, holds the responsibility for keeping order. He is assisted by the sergeant at arms, who during particularly tumultuous moments has lifted the House mace, the symbol of

An 1841 debate in the House of Representatives over antislavery petitions.

the authority of the House, as a means of quieting the chamber.

After 200 years the House of Representatives remains the branch of government closest to the voters and the most conscious of operating with the "consent of the governed." Its members therefore constantly strive to make sure that their constituents' voices are heard and their interests are fairly considered within the federal system.

SEE ALSO
Committees; Congress; House-Senate relations; Mace of the House of Representatives; Speaker of the House

FURTHER READING
Currie, James T. *The United States House of Representatives*. Malabar, Fla.: Krieger, 1988.
Ragsdale, Bruce A. *The House of Representatives*. New York: Chelsea House, 1989.

House-Senate relations

ALTHOUGH THEY must work together to produce all legislation, the Senate and House of Representatives have very different rules, procedures, terms of election, and constituencies. These differences often cause tensions between the two bodies.

Some representatives, impatient with the many years that it will take them to achieve seniority and influence in the House, run for the Senate. In the 1940s and 1950s Speaker Sam Rayburn would try to persuade them to stay in the House, citing long lists of representatives who had gone to the Senate "and hadn't amounted to much." Those who choose to spend their entire legislative career in the House bristle at the notion that the Senate is an "upper body," or in any way superior. Donald Riegle (Republican/Democrat–Michigan), who served in both the House and Senate, observed that some of the older House members "detest the Senate and can always be counted upon to rise up indignantly any time someone suggests that the Senate is transgressing on House prerogatives, attempting to by-pass House rules or 'blackmailing' the House by attaching 'non-germane' [irrelevant] amendments to bills."

Checks and balances

House members often focus more closely on the needs and opinions of their home district, whereas senators, with statewide constituencies, develop a more national outlook on issues. House members also serve on fewer committees and tend to become specialists in a few areas,

House and Senate leaders during the 1950s. From left: Senate Republican leader William F. Knowland, House Republican leader Joseph W. Martin, Senate Democratic leader Lyndon B. Johnson, and House Speaker Sam Rayburn.

whereas senators, with many committee assignments, become generalists. House rules favor the majority; Senate rules give greater leeway to individual members, whether in the majority or the minority party. These disparities often come to a head in conference committees, when senators and representatives seek to merge the Senate and House versions of a bill into a single piece of legislation.

In the spirit of checks and balances, the two houses insist upon their equality. During the 1st Congress, the House rejected a Senate plan that would have paid senators a higher salary than representatives. Members of the 1st Congress also devised the elaborate procedures by which clerks still deliver bills and messages from one chamber to the next. The clerks appear in the center door of the chamber to be announced to the presiding officer. They bow as they enter the chamber, deliver the bill to the front desk, and bow again when they leave, demonstrating through this 18th-century ritual the respect of one house of Congress for the other.

SEE ALSO

Bicameral; Conference committees; Congress; House of Representatives; Senate

FURTHER READING

Baker, Ross K. *House and Senate*. New York: Norton, 1989.
Riegle, Donald. *O Congress*. New York: Popular Library, 1976.

Humor, congressional

HUMOR HAS always been a ready weapon for members of Congress but also one that has often been aimed against them. Debaters use humor to put down their opponents. "You speak for the present generation; I speak for posterity [future generations]," a long-winded representative asserted. "Yes," replied Henry Clay (Whig–Kentucky), "and you seem resolved to continue speaking until your audience arrives." When a Democratic member asked for unanimous consent to correct the printed version of a speech he had made attacking the Republicans, Speaker Thomas B. Reed (Republican–Maine) replied, "No correction needed. We didn't think it was so when you said it."

Senators and representatives have also used humor to grease the legislative process, to help defuse tensions, and to put their colleagues in a more cooperative mood. Members have been known to engage in pranks and horseplay to relieve the tension and sometimes the boredom. For instance, they initiate new pages, students who run errands and carry messages, by sending them in search of a mythical "bill stretcher."

Congress has also been the target of humorous abuse. "Suppose you were an idiot," said Mark Twain, "and suppose you were a member of Congress; but I repeat myself." Humorist Will Rogers claimed, "After I read that ancient Rome had a Senate, too, I knew then why it had declined." Editorial cartoons and comic strips have similarly poked fun at talkative senators, the enjoyment of perks or privileges of office, and other congressional foibles. House Speaker Carl Albert (Democrat–Oklahoma) speculated that Congress attracts such a large share of humorous abuse because it is less distant from the public than the other branches of government: "Congress is as near as the post office, as personal as an old neighbor. For that reason, it is Congress—not the courts, not the presidency—that usually bears the frustrations with government. And Americans are frustrated with government. They nearly always are."

A statue of humorist Will Rogers stands in the U.S. Capitol representing Oklahoma.

FURTHER READING

Boller, Paul F., Jr. *Congressional Anecdotes.* New York: Oxford, 1991.

Hogan, Bill, and Mike Hill. *Will the Gentleman Yield? The Congressional Record Humor Book.* Berkeley, Calif.: Ten Speed Press, 1987.

Pitch, Anthony. *Congressional Chronicles.* Potomac, Md.: Mino Publications, 1990.

Senator Hubert H. Humphrey speaking at a meeting of the Senate Budget Committee.

Humphrey, Hubert H.

☆ *Born: May 27, 1911, Wallace, S. Dak.*
☆ *Political party: Democrat*
☆ *Senator from Minnesota: 1949–65, 1971–78*
☆ *Senate majority whip: 1961–65*
☆ *Vice President: 1965–69*
☆ *Died: Jan. 13, 1978, Waverly, Minn.*

HUBERT HUMPHREY brought to the Senate a reputation as a liberal reformer. Because of his outspoken advocacy of civil rights legislation and other liberal concerns, conservative Southern senators at first would have nothing to do with Humphrey, and his legislative career seemed destined to be more talk than action. But Humphrey became an ally of Senator Lyndon B. Johnson, who advised him on the arts of legislative compromise and negotiation and helped him gain access to the Senate's "inner club." Johnson in turn relied on Humphrey as his liaison with the Senate's liberal wing.

Humphrey blossomed into an effective legislator and in 1961 became the Democratic whip. He served as floor manager of the Civil Rights Act of 1964 and other significant reforms. In 1964 President Lyndon B. Johnson selected Humphrey as his Vice Presidential running mate. Humphrey's loyalty to Johnson, however, proved his undoing. In 1968, Humphrey himself ran for President but lost the election, largely because of his support for Johnson's policies in Vietnam. He returned to the Senate, still

a "happy warrior" in politics and an indefatigable advocate of liberal causes.

SEE ALSO

"Inner club"; Johnson, Lyndon B.

FURTHER READING

Humphrey, Hubert H. *The Education of a Public Man.* Garden City, N.Y.: Doubleday, 1977.

Impeachment

IF A FEDERAL official commits a crime or otherwise acts improperly, Congress may impeach—formally charge—and remove that person from office. The House of Representatives votes to impeach, an action similar to an indictment in a court of law. Then the Senate sits as a court to determine guilt or innocence. It takes a two-thirds vote of the Senate to remove someone from office.

The Constitutional Convention decided that no one should be above the law and that even the President should be subject to impeachment. All civil (nonmilitary) officers of the government can be removed if impeached and convicted for "treason, bribery, or other high crimes and misdemeanors" (Article 3, Section 4). If a President is impeached, the Constitution specifies that the chief justice of the Supreme Court shall preside over the Senate trial.

The first impeachment case, in 1797, targeted a U.S. senator, William Blount of Tennessee, who was accused of conspiring with the British to prevent Spanish control of Florida and Louisiana. Although the House voted to impeach Blount, the Senate refused to try him because it had already expelled him from office under its internal rules. This case set the precedent that individuals cannot be impeached after they have left office. In 1974 the House Judiciary

Committee voted to recommend impeachment of President Richard M. Nixon for his role in the Watergate scandal, but Nixon's resignation stopped any further impeachment proceedings.

In 1804 Jeffersonian Republicans in Congress impeached an outspoken Federalist Supreme Court justice, Samuel Chase. But the lack of specific charges against Chase made their goals seem partisan and vindictive. Their failure to achieve a two-thirds vote in the Senate made the Jeffersonians abandon impeachment as a political tool. In 1868 the House impeached President Andrew Johnson for removing a cabinet officer in violation of the Tenure of Office Act—an act that Johnson considered unconstitutional. Johnson's impeachment reflected the bitter political disagreements between the President and congressional Republicans over Reconstruction policies rather than any criminal behavior. The Senate fell just one vote short of the two-thirds needed to remove Johnson from office.

To simplify matters, the Senate in recent years has delegated the responsibility of hearing evidence in impeachment cases to special committees, which then report their findings to the full Senate for a vote. A federal judge ruled in 1992 that the full Senate had not heard the full charges against Judge Walter Nixon and voided his impeachment. However, in 1993 the Supreme Court ruled in *Nixon v. United States* that the Senate had the sole power to decide how to try such cases and allowed Judge Nixon's impeachment to stand.

SEE ALSO

Impeachment of Andrew Johnson (1868); Watergate investigation (1973)

FURTHER READING

Byrd, Robert C. "Impeachment." In *The Senate, 1789–1989: Addresses on the History of the United States Senate.* Vol. 2. Washington, D.C.: Government Printing Office, 1991.

IMPEACHMENT CASES

1797: **William Blount**, U.S. senator, Tennessee. Expelled from Senate, charges dropped.

1803: **John Pickering**, federal judge. Guilty, removed from office.

1804: **Samuel Chase**, Supreme Court justice. Not guilty.

1830: **James H. Peck**, federal judge. Not guilty.

1862: **West H. Humphreys**, federal judge. Guilty, removed from office.

1868: **Andrew Johnson**, President. Not guilty.

1873: **Mark H. Delahay**, federal judge. Resigned, no action.

1876: **William Belknap**, secretary of war. Not guilty.

1904: **Charles Swayne**, federal judge. Not guilty.

1912: **Robert Archbald**, judge, U.S. Commerce Court. Guilty, removed from office.

1926: **George W. English**, federal judge. Resigned, charges dismissed.

1933: **Harold Louderback**, federal judge. Not guilty.

1936: **Halsted Ritter**, federal judge. Guilty, removed from office.

1986: **Harry Claiborne**, federal judge. Guilty, removed from office.

1988: **Alcee Hastings**, federal judge. Guilty, removed from office. (In 1992 Hastings was elected to the House as a Democrat from Florida.)

1989: **Walter Nixon**, federal judge. Guilty, removed from office.

Impeachment of Andrew Johnson (1868)

DURING CONGRESS'S long fight with President Andrew Johnson over the Reconstruction of the South, the House impeached Johnson and the Senate came

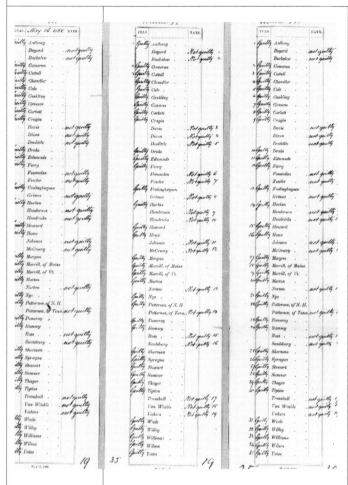

Senate vote tallies on the impeachment of President Andrew Johnson.

within one vote of removing him from office. Johnson favored a speedy return to the Union of the former Confederate states, while congressional Republicans wanted to make these states guarantee that they would protect the rights of the newly freed slaves. In 1867 Congress enacted the Tenure of Office Act, which required the Senate's consent whenever a president *removed* a federal official. Congress specifically wanted to protect Secretary of War Edwin Stanton, who supported a tough Reconstruction policy. But Johnson considered the law unconstitutional and fired Stanton anyway. The House then voted to impeach Johnson, and the Senate held a trial from March to May 1868. The Senate's vote of 35 to 19 was one vote short of the two-thirds margin needed to remove Johnson.

SEE ALSO

Impeachment; Reconstruction, congressional; Tenure of Office Act (1867)

FURTHER READING

Benedict, Michael Les. *The Impeachment and Trial of Andrew Johnson.* New York: Norton, 1973.

Impoundment of funds

SOME PRESIDENTS who objected to federal projects for which Congress had appropriated funds have impounded (withheld) those funds. President Richard M. Nixon accused Congress of being financially irresponsible and asserted that it was his right and duty not to spend money he considered wasteful. But Congress believed that it alone held the "power of the purse." In 1974, when Nixon was weakened by the Watergate scandal, Congress passed, over his veto, the Congressional Budget and Impoundment Control Act. It established the House and Senate Budget Committees and made it illegal for a President to impound appropriated funds.

Although it abolished impoundment, the Budget Act does allow a President to ask Congress to enact a recision (cutback) of appropriated funds if he believes that the money is no longer needed for a federal project. Congress has also considered giving the President an "enhanced recision," by which the President could withhold the appropriated money, subject to reversal by a majority vote of both the Senate and House.

SEE ALSO

Budget and Impoundment Control Act, Congressional (1974); Recision bills

FURTHER READING

Shuman, Howard E. *Politics and the Budget: The Struggle between the President and the Congress.* Englewood Cliffs, N.J.: Prentice-Hall, 1992.

Incumbents

MEMBERS CURRENTLY holding seats in Congress are the incumbents. Although *incumbent* is derived from the French word meaning "to lie down on," those who lie down on the job in Congress will not hold their job for long. Voters want to know, "What have you done for me lately?" Incumbents must demonstrate their ability to legislate effectively and to provide services for their constituents. But incumbents generally enjoy a high rate of reelection over their challengers because of their greater ability to raise campaign funds and their use of the frank (free mailing) and other privileges of office that make them better known to the voters.

Independents

Occasionally, senators and representatives who are independent of the major parties are elected to office. Independents, or third-party candidates, have become increasingly rare in modern times. In the 1950s, Oregon senator Wayne Morse quit the Republican party. Before he joined the Democrats, he demonstrated his independence by moving his chair into the aisle that divided the two parties. Generally, independent members choose to join one of the major party conferences, and they receive their committee assignments through that conference. For instance, James Buckley, elected to the Senate by the Conservative party in New York in 1970, joined the Republican conference. Bernard Saunders, elected as a Socialist in Vermont in 1990, joined the House Democratic Caucus. Independents have their greatest influence when the two major parties are closely balanced—then, third-party members can tip the scales one way or the other.

"Inner club"

DESCRIBED AS the most exclusive club in the world, the Senate for many years also contained an "inner club." Theoretically, all senators are equal, but members of the "inner club" were committee chairmen and other senior senators who held greater power and influence over legislation than the average senator did. Conservative Southern Democrats, because of their seniority, made up the largest share of this "inner club," which was also called the "Senate establishment." By contrast, Northern liberals were relegated to the "outer life of the Senate." By the 1970s committee reforms had given more senators subcommittee chairmanships and other access to power. Although some senators remained more powerful than others, the "inner club" faded away.

FURTHER READING

White, William S. *Citadel: The Story of the U.S. Senate.* New York: Harper, 1956.

Instruction of senators

BECAUSE STATE legislatures originally elected senators, they believed they held the power to instruct those senators how to vote. During the 1790s and 1800s several state legislatures sent formal instructions to their senators. Senators generally ignored these instructions, and a few denounced them as unconstitutional.

Senator Richard B. Russell was the undisputed leader of the Senate's "inner club."

FURTHER READING

Swanstom, Roy. *The United States Senate, 1789–1801: A Dissertation on the First Fourteen Years of the Upper House.* Washington, D.C.: Government Printing Office, 1989.

Insurgents

THOSE MEMBERS of Congress who revolt against their party leadership are known as insurgents—from the Latin word meaning "to rise up." Insurgents have often risen up against what they perceive as dictatorial behavior by the leadership or against the suppression of legislative reforms that they favor. Insurgents run the risk of being punished by the leadership for their defections.

The most famous insurgency took place in 1909, when progressive Republicans joined with Democrats to reduce the powers of Speaker Joseph G. Cannon. On an individual level, William Proxmire (Democrat–Wisconsin), a freshman senator in 1958, publicly denounced the powerful Senate majority leader, Lyndon B. Johnson, for his domineering behavior. Proxmire spoke on George Washington's birthday, a day when the Senate traditionally hears a reading of Washington's Farewell Address. Reporters joked that there were two farewell addresses that day: Washington's and Proxmire's. But Proxmire's insurgent spirit did not hurt him with the voters in his state, who regularly reelected him to the Senate.

SEE ALSO

Cannon, Joseph G.; Johnson, Lyndon B.

The insurgent Senator William Proxmire (Democrat–Wisconsin) challenged his own party's leadership.

Interns

DURING THE summer months, student interns swell the ranks of the congressional staff. These interns, working for pay or for college credit, gain experience in the legislative process. Most often, interns deliver messages, photocopy, and file. But some offices use interns to help with correspondence and to conduct preliminary legislative research. Most important, they observe the activities of Congress firsthand.

Though the majority of interns are undergraduates, others are graduate students and people at mid-career who receive fellowships from professional associations to spend a year working with Congress. Representative Steve Horn (Republican–California), for example, first came to Capitol Hill as a Congressional Fellow with the American Political Science Association. He then joined the Senate staff and eventually won a seat in Congress himself.

Interparliamentary relations

ALTHOUGH THE U.S. Congress is structured very differently from most legislatures around the world, it has sought to build goodwill and working ties with other legislative bodies. Members of Congress regularly attend sessions of the Inter-Parliamentary Union, which consists of delegates from many different national legislatures who meet to discuss common issues and problems. Congress also appoints delegations to the Canada–U.S. and Mexico–U.S. interparliamentary groups. Members of foreign parliaments regularly visit Congress to observe its proceedings and up-to-date technology. Since the end of the cold war, Congress has worked especially with the new legislative bodies in eastern Europe and the former Soviet republics to demonstrate how the U.S. system of separation of powers and checks and balances works.

Investigations

ASIDE FROM its legislative activities, Congress devotes much attention to investigations. Congressional investigations have uncovered wrongdoing within the executive branch, from obscure agencies up to the President's office. They have also focused on the military, private enterprise, and foreign agents. By uncovering this information and informing the public, investigations have often led to important reform legislation.

But critics have also dismissed congressional investigations as merely an opportunity for politicians to make headlines and appear on television. They accused some investigations of trampling on the rights of witnesses and interfering with court proceedings. Critics pointed out that many investigations produced no solid evidence and failed to lead to any legislation at all.

The first congressional investigation took place in 1792, when a special committee of the House looked into the disastrous expedition led by General Arthur St. Clair against the Shawnee and Miami Indians in Ohio, in which 657 American troops were killed. The House committee demanded that it see War Department records regarding this defeat. President George Washington complied with the committee's request, thereby acknowledging Congress's right to investigate.

In 1871 a Senate committee investigating the Ku Klux Klan heard from one of the Klan's victims.

Uncovering scandal

During the 19th century Congress investigated the military conduct of the Civil War, Ku Klux Klan violence against freedmen after the war, the circumstances surrounding the purchase of Alaska, and such railroad scandals as that involving Credit Mobilier, which involved the payment of bribes to key members of Congress. In the 20th century congressional investigating increased steadily. In 1923 the Senate's investigation of the Teapot Dome scandal discredited President Warren G. Harding's administration and sent his secretary of the interior, Albert B. Fall, to prison. During the 1930s the Senate banking committee drew many headlines with its investigation of the stock market crash of 1929 and the causes of the depression. Senator Harry S. Truman first rose to public notice by chairing an investigation of the national defense program during World War II.

During the cold war of the 1940s and 1950s, congressional investigations stirred up a "Red scare" by looking for communists in the government. The House Un-American Activities Committee (HUAC) made news when Whittaker

A joint committee of Congress investigated the Tennessee Valley Authority in 1938.

Chambers testified that former State Department official Alger Hiss had secretly been a communist and alleged that Hiss had engaged in espionage. Later, Senator Joseph R. McCarthy (Republican–Wisconsin) used his chairmanship of the Senate's Permanent Subcommittee on Investigations to pursue allegations that communists were operating in the military and other government agencies. Critics charged HUAC and Senator McCarthy with "witch hunting" and accused congressional investigators of bullying witnesses and ignoring their civil rights and liberties.

Court rulings on investigations

Periodically, the Supreme Court has helped to define the scope and limitations of Congress's power to investigate. In *McGrain v. Daugherty* (1927) the Court ruled that anyone, even private citizens, could be subpoenaed (compelled) to testify before a congressional committee. And in *Sinclair v. United States* (1929) the Court said that Congress had the power to investigate anything related to legislation or oversight, the monitoring of the activities of executive agencies. But in *Watkins v. United States* (1957)—which involved a witness who declined to give names of suspected communists to HUAC—the Court ruled that Congress's investigative powers are limited by the Bill of Rights and that witnesses do not lose those rights when they testify.

Public approval of congressional investigations was restored in 1973 by the Watergate investigation. Chaired by Sam Ervin (Democrat–North Carolina), the special Senate committee painstakingly interrogated witnesses to link the White House to the burglary of Democratic National Committee headquarters at the Watergate building in 1972. The investigation led to the resignations of many administration officials, including President Richard M. Nixon. The Watergate investigators established that in order for congressional investigations to be successful, investigators must treat witnesses seriously and with some degree of humanity; do their homework, no matter how much drudgery it entails; and persist until they have kept the issue in the media long enough to educate the public, expose wrongdoing, and suggest corrective action.

SEE ALSO

Ervin, Samuel J., Jr.; McCarthy, Joseph R.; Wall Street investigation (1932–34); Watergate investigation (1973)

FURTHER READING

Hamilton, James. *The Power to Probe: A Study of Congressional Investigation.* New York: Vintage, 1976.
Schlesinger, Arthur M., Jr., and Roger Bruns, eds. *Congress Investigates, 1792–1974: A Documented History.* 5 vols. New York: Bowker, 1975.

Iran-Contra investigation (1986)

Marine Lt. Col. Oliver North testified before the Iran-Contra committee.

IN 1986 a joint committee of Congress investigated charges that President Ronald Reagan's administration had sold weapons to Iran and diverted the money received to the Contra forces seeking to overthrow the government of Nicaragua. In 1982, Congress had enacted Representative Edward Boland's amendment to the defense appropriations bill, forbidding any U.S. aid to the Contras. But high-level officials of the Reagan administration, including Central Intelligence Agency director William Casey and National Security Council aide Lieutenant Colonel Oliver

North, bypassed the Boland Amendment by using money raised through secret arms sales to Iran. After the media and the joint committee revealed the details of the Iran-Contra scandal, a special prosecutor won indictments and convictions of North and other officials. However, the courts later overturned some of these convictions on the grounds that their televised testimony before the investigating committee, and grants of limited immunity to testify, had prejudiced their case.

FURTHER READING

Cohen, William S., and George J. Mitchell. *Men of Zeal: A Candid Inside Story of the Iran-Contra Hearings.* New York: Viking, 1988.

Jay Treaty (1795)

THE JAY Treaty with Great Britain ignited political fireworks in Congress. President George Washington sent Supreme Court chief justice John Jay to London to negotiate a treaty that would settle American disputes with Great Britain and avoid another war between the two nations. Britain opened some of its ports in the British West Indies to U.S. trade and agreed to remove British troops from the American Northwest Territory. But the treaty did nothing to stop British searches of American ships or to settle other American grievances. Jay's controversial treaty brought into the open the growing political rift between Federalists and Jeffersonian Democratic-Republicans in Congress.

After an angry debate, the Senate ratified the treaty by a vote of 20 to 10 on June 24, 1795. Because the treaty required the United States to pay some pre–revolutionary war debts, the House of Representatives would also have to vote for the needed appropriation of funds. Senators argued that because they had ratified the treaty, the House must fund it. Members of the House felt free to act as they saw fit but eventually appropriated the money. The House has never yet failed to fund a treaty approved by the Senate.

FURTHER READING

Josephy, Alvin M., Jr. *On the Hill: A History of the American Congress.* New York: Simon & Schuster, 1979.

Jefferson's manual

AS VICE PRESIDENT from 1797 to 1801, Thomas Jefferson occupied his time by compiling a handbook on parliamentary procedure. He finished the project shortly before becoming President, and his *Manual of Parliamentary Practice* was published in 1801. Jefferson combined his reading of British parliamentary practice with his personal observations of the debates in the Senate. He concluded that specific rules were less important than the fairness and consistency with which they were enforced. It was essential, he wrote, "that order, decency, and regularity be preserved in a dignified public body."

The Senate never officially made Jefferson's manual part of its rules but regularly printed it in the *Senate Rules Manual* until 1977. By contrast, the House of Representatives formally adopted Jefferson's manual in 1837 as a supplement to its own rules and continues to include it in the *House Rules Manual.*

FURTHER READING

Howell, Wilbur Samuel, ed. *Jefferson's Parliamentary Writings.* Princeton, N.J.: Princeton University Press, 1988.

Johnson, Lyndon B.

☆ *Born: Aug. 27, 1908, Stonewall, Tex.*
☆ *Political party: Democrat*
☆ *Representative from Texas: 1937–49*
☆ *Senator from Texas: 1949–61*
☆ *Senate majority whip: 1951–53*
☆ *Senate minority leader: 1953–55*
☆ *Senate majority leader: 1955–61*
☆ *Vice President: 1961–63*
☆ *President: 1963–69*
☆ *Died: Jan. 22, 1973, Johnson City, Tex.*

AS SENATE majority leader, Lyndon Johnson insisted that he had no power except the "power to persuade." But Johnson could be masterful in persuasion. A protégé of House Speaker Sam Rayburn, a fellow Texan, Johnson had moved from the House to the Senate in 1949, determined to rise to its leadership. By 1951 he was the Senate Democratic whip, and by 1953 the Democrats had made him their floor leader. With his aide Bobby Baker, Johnson made careful "head counts" to anticipate when he had a majority vote. He did frequent personal favors for senators and gave important committee assignments to those who voted with him. When Johnson sought to persuade another senator, wrote newspaper columnists Rowland Evans and Robert Novak, he would move in close, "his face a scant millimeter from his target, his eyes widening and narrowing, his eyebrows rising and falling. From his pockets poured clippings, memos, statistics." Mixing logic, humor, and bullying tactics, Johnson would leave his target "stunned and helpless."

As majority leader, Johnson established a remarkable record of legislation, including passage of the Civil Rights Act

Lyndon B. Johnson as a member of the House of Representatives.

of 1957, the first civil rights bill since Reconstruction. But when Johnson left to become Vice President, Senate Democrats were tired of "one-man rule" and turned to a very different type of leader, Mike Mansfield, who was willing to share power and allow more independence.

SEE ALSO

Leadership; Majority leader; Mansfield, Mike; Rayburn, Sam; Whip

FURTHER READING

Evans, Rowland, and Robert Novak. *Lyndon B. Johnson: The Exercise of Power*. New York: New American Library, 1966.
Shuman, Howard E. "Lyndon B. Johnson: The Senate's Powerful Persuader." In *First among Equals: Outstanding Senate Leaders of the Twentieth Century*, edited by Richard A. Baker and Roger Davidson. Washington, D.C.: Congressional Quarterly, 1991.

Joint committees

CONSISTING OF both senators and representatives, joint committees avoid the duplication of House and Senate committee hearings on the same subject. During the Civil War, Congress created a Joint Committee on the Conduct of the War. Later, it created a Joint Committee of Fifteen to oversee the reconstruction of the Southern states. The greatest effort to establish joint committees came from the Legislative Reorganization Act of 1946, which promoted joint committees as a means of streamlining and modernizing Congress. Several joint committees were established as a result of this act. At first, senators always chaired such joint committees, but the Joint Committee on Atomic Energy developed the practice of alternating the chairmanship and vice chairmanship of the committee between senators and representatives, a practice that other joint committees also adopted.

Members of the Joint Committee on Atomic Energy visit a nuclear site.

By the time of the Legislative Reorganization Act of 1970, however, members of both houses had found no indication that joint committees speeded up their work and recommended against continuing them. With the exception of the Joint Economic Committee and the Joint Committees on Taxation and on the Library, the use of joint committees was abandoned. During the Iran-Contra investigation of 1987 a joint committee was appointed, but its large membership made it unwieldy and reduced its effectiveness.

SEE ALSO

Committees; Legislative Reorganization Acts (1946 and 1970)

Joint meetings

SEE Joint sessions

Joint resolutions

CONGRESS USES joint resolutions to propose amendments to the Constitution and to address certain specific and limited issues. Joint resolutions are identified as H. J. Res. (House Joint Resolution) or S. J. Res. (Senate Joint Resolution) followed by their number. Like bills, joint resolutions require the President's signature, and they can be vetoed. However, joint resolutions proposing constitutional amendments require state ratification rather than a Presidential signature.

Congress has frequently used joint resolutions to express its sentiments on different policies and to encourage the administration to take a stand. For instance, Congress by joint resolution called on the United States to recognize Texas's independence from Mexico in 1836. Another significant joint resolution was the Gulf of Tonkin Resolution of 1964, by which the Congress authorized President Lyndon B. Johnson to take any military action necessary to prevent communist aggression in South Vietnam.

SEE ALSO
Bills; Gulf of Tonkin Resolution (1964); Legislation; Resolutions

in procession from their chamber through the Capitol to the House chamber, where seats at the front are reserved for them. Members of the cabinet and Supreme Court usually attend joint sessions. Since 1947, most joint sessions and joint meetings have been televised.

British prime minister Winston Churchill addressed a joint session of Congress during World War II.

Joint sessions

THE SENATE and House meet in joint session to hear the President's State of the Union message and to witness the counting of the electoral ballots for President and Vice President. The first joint session took place on April 6, 1789, for the counting of the electoral ballots that chose George Washington for President.

The Senate and House are in session during joint sessions. By contrast, the two bodies recess to attend joint meetings to hear distinguished speakers such as foreign heads of state and military heroes. Joint sessions and joint meetings take place in the House chamber, which is larger than the Senate. Senators march

Journals

THE CONSTITUTION (Article 1, Section 5) requires both houses of Congress to keep and publish journals of their legislative business. The Senate also keeps a journal of its executive business (treaties and nominations). Unlike the *Congressional Record,* with its lengthy speeches, the journals are short minutes that list such information as bills and resolutions introduced, committee referrals, amendments, and votes. The indexes to the journals provide a short history of all legislation, nominations, and treaties for easy reference. Journals are available for research in the government documents section of most large libraries throughout the country.

Each legislative day in the House

and Senate must begin with the reading of the journal, although this formality is usually suspended by unanimous consent. Journal clerks take notes on the proceedings and prepare the histories of bills and resolutions for publication in the annual journals.

Judicial review

ALTHOUGH THE Constitution says nothing about it, the Supreme Court has assumed the right to declare acts of Congress unconstitutional, a practice known as judicial review. In the case of *Marbury v. Madison* (1803), Chief Justice John Marshall declared one section of the Judiciary Act of 1789 to be unconstitutional and therefore null and void. Marshall argued that because the Constitution was the "supreme law of the land" (Article 6, Section 2) and because it was the duty of the courts to enforce the laws, the justices had the right to decide whether an act of Congress was consistent with or contrary to the Constitution. Since that time, the Supreme Court has reviewed the activities of both the executive and legislative branches to keep them from exceeding their constitutional powers.

Judicial review can also work in Congress's favor. In the case of *McCulloch v. Maryland* (1819), Marshall used judicial review to uphold an act of Congress as it applied to the states. The state of Maryland had sought to tax the federally chartered Bank of the United States. Since the tax would make it difficult for the bank to do business in Maryland, the Supreme Court ruled that the state had improperly interfered with a federal agency. This ruling promoted the supremacy of federal laws over state laws.

Checking and balancing

At times, the Supreme Court's use of judicial review has frustrated and angered both Presidents and Congress. Sometimes the federal judiciary lags behind public opinion—for instance, when conservative Supreme Court justices declared popular New Deal programs unconstitutional during the 1930s. Yet in 1937, when President Franklin D. Roosevelt proposed to "pack" the Court with extra justices to protect New Deal programs, Congress blocked the plan and defended the independence of the judiciary.

Sometimes the judiciary takes the lead in promoting new policies before the public—or their elected representatives in Congress—have accepted them. Many members of Congress were outraged over such decisions as *Brown v. Board of Education* (1954), which ended racially segregated schools, *Engle v. Vitale* (1962), which prohibited prayer in public schools, and *Roe v. Wade* (1971), which permitted abortion.

Congress can pass legislation to try to meet the Court's objections to a law it has overturned. Or two-thirds of Congress can propose a new amendment to the Constitution to overturn the Court's ruling. For instance, when the Supreme Court ruled a federal income tax unconstitutional, Congress responded with the 16th Amendment (ratified in 1913) to permit such a tax.

At other times, the Court changes by itself. Some have said that the Supreme Court "follows the election returns." This means that the Court has reversed some of its opinions because of shifts in national politics and public attitudes. For instance, even though Franklin Roosevelt failed to "pack" the Court, some of

Chief Justice John Marshall originated the practice of judicial review.

the conservative justices began to shift their votes in favor of the New Deal's liberal programs, which the public had endorsed by overwhelmingly reelecting Roosevelt and his supporters in Congress. New Presidents appoint new judges who often think differently about legal issues than the previous majority on the Court. Congress has the power to impeach federal judges, but it can do so only in cases of criminal misbehavior, rather than because of the way a judge thinks and votes. Instead, the Senate scrutinizes federal judges before they go on the bench and does not hesitate to reject a judge it considers too extreme or out of step with public opinion.

SEE ALSO

Court-packing plan (1937); Nominations, confirmation of

FURTHER READING

Friedman, Leon. *The Supreme Court.* New York: Chelsea House, 1987.
Keynes, Edward, with Randall K. Miller. *The Court vs. Congress: Prayer, Busing, and Abortion.* Durham, N.C.: Duke University Press, 1989.

Judiciary Act (1789)

THE CONSTITUTION (Article 3) outlined a judicial branch consisting of a Supreme Court and lower federal courts but left it to Congress to fill in the details. Setting up a federal court system became one of the 1st Congress's most significant accomplishments. The day after it established its first quorum on April 6, 1789, the Senate elected a special committee to draft the Judiciary Bill, numbered S. 1. This bill set up a Supreme Court, headed by a chief justice, with five associate justices. (In 1863 Congress increased the number to eight associate justices.) The bill also created 13 federal district courts and 3 traveling circuit courts. Greatly expanded and with the addition of appellate (appeals) courts, the basic structure of the federal judiciary remains today essentially the same as when S. 1 created it. The Senate passed S. 1 on July 17. The House passed the bill two months later, and President Washington signed the Judiciary Act into law on September 24, 1789.

Junkets

THE PRESS often criticizes members of Congress who travel abroad at government expense for taking "junkets." The term implies that the trip is as much or more for personal pleasure as for official business and is just another congressional perk, or privilege of office. Indeed, the origin of the word *junket* suggests a good time: it comes from an old English word, *jonket,* for the woven reed baskets used to carry foods for picnics and other outings. Some members travel more frequently than others, but most congressional travel is related to the members' committee assignments, including military policy, foreign relations, international commerce, and interparliamentary activities (that is, meetings with legislative branches in other countries).

To explain the purpose and findings of their trips to the public, members usually prepare a formal report for publication after their return. Advocates of congressional travel argue that regardless of the official reason, international travel is useful because it allows members to escape from parochialism (cultural and geographic narrowness) and broaden their perspectives on the world issues upon which they must vote.

SEE ALSO

Interparliamentary relations; Perks

Kansas-Nebraska Act

SEE Douglas, Stephen A.

Kennedy, Edward M.

☆ *Born: Feb. 22, 1932, Boston, Mass.*
☆ *Political party: Democrat*
☆ *Senator from Massachusetts: 1962–*
☆ *Senate majority whip: 1969–71*

EDWARD M. KENNEDY began his Senate career in the shadow of his famous brothers, John, who was President of the United States, and Robert, who was attorney general. All three Kennedy brothers served in the Senate, but in many ways Edward Kennedy became the most effective legislator among them. Despite personal tragedies that came close to derailing his political career, over time he surprised his critics by building one of the most effective staffs on Capitol Hill and taking strong leadership on a wide variety of legislation. When Kennedy speaks, whether against apartheid—the policy of racial segregation—

in South Africa or in favor of a jobs program or medical insurance, he attracts the media and focuses national attention on that issue. Nowhere did he demonstrate his ability to galvanize public opinion and frame the debate better than by his successful effort to block the Supreme Court nomination of Judge Robert Bork in 1986.

SEE ALSO
Families in Congress

FURTHER READING
Burns, James MacGregor. *Edward Kennedy and the Camelot Legacy.* New York: Norton, 1976.

Lame-duck sessions

IF THE outgoing Congress comes back into session between the November election and the beginning of the new Congress in January, it is called a lame-duck session. The British first used the term *lame duck* to refer to bankrupt businessmen, and eventually it was extended to defeated politicians. Members of Con-

Senator Edward M. Kennedy (center) at the Judiciary Committee's hearing on the nomination of Clarence Thomas to the Supreme Court.

LAME-DUCK SESSIONS SINCE RATIFICATION OF THE 20TH AMENDMENT (1933)

Dates	Reasons
Nov. 5, 1940– Jan. 3, 1941	Threat of war in Europe
Nov. 3, 1942– Dec. 16, 1942	World War II
Nov. 14, 1944– Dec. 19, 1944	World War II
Dec. 31, 1948	Formalities
Nov. 27, 1950– Jan. 2, 1951	Korean War
Nov. 8, 1954– Dec. 2, 1954	Censure of Joseph McCarthy
Nov. 16, 1970– Dec. 2, 1971	Domestic legislation and foreign aid
Nov. 18, 1974– Dec. 20, 1974	Legislation delayed by Watergate investigation
Nov. 12, 1980– Dec. 16, 1980	Budget and appropriations
Nov. 29, 1982– Dec. 23, 1982	Budget and appropriations

gress who lose or do not stand for reelection can still attend a postelection session and vote on legislation. But because they have been defeated or are about to retire, they are as hobbled as lame ducks in terms of influence.

Throughout the 19th century, Congress regularly held lame-duck sessions. But reformers believed that lame-duck legislators were less responsive to the public and more susceptible to influence by special interests. Led by Senator George Norris (Republican–Nebraska), reformers proposed the 20th Amendment to the Constitution, which in 1933 changed the opening of a new Congress

from the first Monday in December in odd-numbered years (13 months after the election) to January 3 (just two months after the election). Since then, Congress has held lame-duck sessions only on rare occasions, to address some important unfinished business.

SEE ALSO
Norris, George W.; Sessions

Laws

SEE Acts; Bills; Legislation

Leadership

THE TWO houses of Congress depend on many different types of leadership. The Constitution provides for presiding officers for both chambers: the Speaker of the House; the president of the Senate (who is the Vice President of the United States); and the president pro tempore of the Senate, who presides in the Vice President's absence.

Once political parties were established, their members in Congress formed party caucuses, each of which elected a chairman. In the Senate the caucus chairman often acted as a party floor leader. Over time the party leadership positions of majority and minority leader and majority and minority whip evolved as formal leadership posts. Leadership is also provided by the chairmen and ranking minority members of the House and Senate committees. Additionally, members of both Houses have formed blocs, or caucuses, united by region, race, or issues, whose leaders develop prominence and power within their chamber. Although leadership generally comes through seniority or election to a formal

Lyndon B. Johnson confers with Everett M. Dirksen.

party post, strong, assertive, and charismatic personalities have also exerted influence and leadership over their colleagues even without holding a formal position.

SEE ALSO

Majority leader; Minority leader; President pro tempore of the Senate; Speaker of the House; Vice President; Whip

---

Leaks

SEE Secrecy

Legislation

IN LATIN, *legis lator* means "a proposer of laws." Legislation is therefore proposed laws, in the form of bills and resolutions. Making legislation is Congress's chief function. Ideas for legislation originate with members of Congress, their staff, lobbyists, constituents, the media, and the executive branch. Once members have introduced legislation, it is referred to the appropriate committees, made the subject of hearings, voted upon, and re-

ported out to the full House or Senate. Both chambers must adopt the legislation in the same form for it to be sent to the President, who may sign or veto it. Once the President has signed the legislation, or Congress has overridden the veto, the legislation becomes law.

SEE ALSO

Acts; Bills; Resolutions

Legislative agencies

IN ADDITION to the staff of members and committees, several large agencies are part of the legislative branch of the federal government. The General Accounting Office (GAO) assists Congress by investigating how executive branch agencies handle federal funds. The Congressional Budget Office helps Congress assess the President's annual budget requests and estimates the cost of all bills reported out of committee. The Library of Congress provides a vast amount of reference and research materials for the Congress, both through its general collections and through the work of the

The book stacks
of the Library of
Congress.

lections and through the work of the Congressional Research Service. The Office of Technology Assessment analyzes scientific and technological policy issues for Congress. The Government Printing Office publishes the *Congressional Record,* hearing transcripts, and reports of Congress. It also publishes government documents for the executive and judicial branches. These agencies have nonpartisan, professional staffs who are all included in the legislative branch payroll.

SEE ALSO

Congressional Budget Office; Congressional Research Service; General Accounting Office (GAO); Library of Congress

Legislative assistants

EACH MEMBER of the House and Senate hires legislative assistants to work on different types of legislation in which that member is particularly interested. One legislative assistant might handle all agricultural and environmental issues, while another handles military and foreign policy issues. The larger a member's staff, the more a legislative assistant can specialize in certain types of legislation. Legislative assistants are responsible for following bills in their areas of specialization, briefing the senator or representative for whom they work, working with the staff of committees and with other members, and suggesting bills and amendments for their senator or representative to introduce. In general, legislative assistants make sure that their senator or representative is well informed when voting in committee or in the full chamber.

Legislative clerks

SITTING AT the front desk, below the presiding officer of the House or Senate, the legislative clerks serve as official readers of bills, resolutions, and amendments, as well as the journals. In the Senate, legislative clerks also call the roll for roll call votes and for quorum calls (to establish that enough members are present to conduct business), functions that have been automated in the larger House. Legislative clerks assign numbers to all bills and reports from the committees on those bills, and they publish the *Calendar of Business.* Because these clerks also maintain the official copies of all legislation under debate, they are responsible for preparing bills and resolutions for the *Congressional Record.*

SEE ALSO

Bills; Calendars; Journals; Resolutions; Voting

Legislative clerks sit below the Speaker's rostrum in the House of Representatives.

Legislative counsel

THE HOUSE and Senate each employ a nonpartisan legislative counsel to assist in drafting bills. These trained lawyers, appointed to the staff with the approval of the leadership of both parties, do not take sides on a bill but make sure that the legislation is correctly and coherently written and that its language achieves what its sponsors want to accomplish. Legislative counsels also work with conference committees on perfecting the final language of the bills.

Legislative day

CONGRESSIONAL DAYS sometimes last longer than 24 hours. In an average day the House and Senate convene in the morning and work through the late afternoon or early evening, when they adjourn. But sometimes, for tactical reasons, the House or Senate may recess rather than adjourn. When the members meet again on the next calendar day, the "legislative day" will not have changed. For instance, immediately following the date in the Senate section of the *Congressional Record* for Wednesday, July 2, 1980, was the notation "(Legislative day of Thursday, June 12, 1980)." That meant that while the calendar date for the rest of the world was July 2, the Senate was still operating on the legislative day of June 12. Especially in the Senate, this tactic of extending the legislative day reduces the amount of routine daily business, such as the reading of the journal, that opponents of a bill might use to slow down procedures and obstruct a vote.

Legislative intent

THE REPORTS that committees produce when they send a bill to the floor, as well as the speeches that the bill's supporters make, help to establish the bill's legislative intent—the reasons why Congress passed the legislation. Laws will often include specific language telling executive departments how they should be administered. When questions arise, the courts often consider legislative intent when they interpret those laws and how they have been administered.

Legislative Reorganization Acts (1946 and 1970)

IN ORDER to modernize and streamline the way it handles legislative business, Congress has twice conducted a major reexamination and reorganization of its internal operations. During World War II many senators and representatives became concerned about the slow and often cumbersome ways that Congress was doing business. The Legislative Reorganization Act of 1946 reduced the number of committees, recommended establishment of joint committees, increased the personal staffs of members, and established the first professional, nonpartisan committee staffs.

The Legislative Reorganization Act of 1970 increased the number of committee staff members, permitting the hiring of minority-party staff members. The act called for committees to open their doors and do more business in public (later specified in the "sunshine" rules of the Senate and House) and set the month of August as a regular recess period for Congress (except during times of war). It also upgraded the Legislative Reference Service into the Congressional Research Service to provide expanded research, reference, and information services to members and committees.

Legislative veto

BECAUSE THE Constitution permits the President to veto, or reject, legislation passed by Congress, Congress has tried to create its own legislative veto. The legislative veto began as a way to give the President an opportunity to create policies that would stand unless either the House or the Senate (or both) voted against them. In 1932, Congress enacted legislation that permitted President Herbert Hoover to reorganize the executive branch. His reorganization plans would automatically go into effect after 60 days if neither house disapproved. After Hoover was defeated for reelection, he issued executive orders to consolidate government activities. The Democratic majority in the House rejected all of his plans.

During the 1970s Congress considerably expanded its use of the legislative veto over many executive agency regulations. In the case of *Immigration and Naturalization Service v. Chadha* (1983), the Supreme Court ruled that a one-house legislative veto was an unconstitutional violation of the separation of powers. In cases where people's legal rights are at stake, the Court declared, both houses of Congress must enact legislation or pass a joint resolution to be signed by the President. Although the Supreme Court's ruling undermined the legislative veto's legal standing, Congress has not been willing to abandon the practice completely in its attempt to restrain the executive branch. Future court challenges will likely follow.

SEE ALSO
Judicial review; Veto

FURTHER READING
Fisher, Louis. *Constitutional Conflicts between Congress and the President.* Princeton, N.J.: Princeton University Press, 1985.

Library of Congress

ALWAYS IN need of information, Congress established its own library, which eventually became a national library. In April 1800, while preparing to move from Philadelphia to the then-wilderness of the District of Columbia, Congress realized that it would no longer be able to depend upon Philadelphia's libraries. So members appropriated $5,000 to purchase books for "the use of Congress." This was the beginning of the Library of Congress.

In 1802, Clerk of the House John Beckley became the first librarian of Congress, at a time when its catalog consisted of 740 volumes. These books were destroyed when British troops burned down the Capitol in 1814. Former President Thomas Jefferson then offered as a replacement his personal library, which Congress purchased. The old collection had consisted largely of law books and other reference materials. But Jefferson's library ranged more broadly over history, philosophy, and the arts and sciences. As new volumes were added in these fields, the Library of Congress grew into one of the world's most diverse research centers.

From 1824 until 1897 the Library of Congress occupied three stories along the West Front of the Capitol, an equal

The first catalog of the Library of Congress's collection, which included 152 items.

The impressive main reading room of the Library of Congress.

distance between the House and Senate wings. When its collection outgrew this space, Congress authorized the construction of a separate library building across the plaza from the Capitol. This magnificently decorated building with its high-domed central reading room has been named the Thomas Jefferson Building. Two additional buildings, named for John Adams and James Madison, were later constructed nearby.

Funded mostly by Congress but also through some private donations, the library has become an unparalleled research collection. In 1990 the library held an estimated 12 million books, newspapers, and magazines; 4 million maps; 16 million photographs, prints, and motion pictures; and 39 million manuscript documents (including the papers of many prominent senators and representatives of the past). The Library of Congress also operates the Congres-

sional Research Service, which provides nonpartisan research assistance to committees and members of Congress. Its services to the general public include a national library of braille, large-print, and recorded materials for the blind and physically handicapped.

SEE ALSO

Congressional Research Service; Legislative agencies

FURTHER READING

Goodrum, Charles A. *Treasures of the Library of Congress.* New York: Abrams, 1991.
Simpson, Andrew L. *The Library of Congress.* New York: Chelsea House, 1989.

Line-item veto

UNLIKE MOST state governors, the President does not have the line-item veto. This means that the President must approve or veto an entire appropriations bill and may not veto any single line or part of the bill. Presidents Ronald Reagan and George Bush both called for a constitutional amendment to give them such a partial veto as a means of controlling federal spending and reducing the deficit (the difference between what the federal government spends and what it receives in tax revenue, when the revenues do not cover the expenses). With this power they could disapprove of what they considered wasteful "pork barrel" spending without having to reject the many more worthy projects in the rest of an appropriations bill. Congressional opponents responded that the line-item veto would shift the constitutional "power of the purse" from Congress to the President. Senator Robert C. Byrd (Democrat–West Virginia) led the opposition to the line-item veto, saying that it would "turn an elected President into a king" and would disrupt the system of checks and balances by giving the President too much power over federal spending.

SEE ALSO

Pork barrel politics; Veto

Lobbying

LOBBYISTS ARE people hired by groups or organizations with particular interests to convince members of Congress to pass or defeat legislation. They may work for business corporations, labor unions, executive branch agencies, foreign governments, or private or public interest groups. Although lobbyists were present during the 1st Congress—and in the British Parliament before that—the term did not come into use until the 1820s. As the name suggests, lobbyists often work the lobbies and corridors surrounding the House and Senate chamber, intercepting members and arguing their client's case. Maurice Rosenblatt, a lobbyist for many causes, described the job as "one man, one buttonhole. It is that personal eye-to-eye contact that has the maximum effect."

Because of scandals in which lobbyists employed questionable tactics to win legislation for special interests, they acquired a sinister image. Senator Norris Cotton (Republican–New Hampshire) considered this image unjust because most lobbyists perform a legitimate and necessary function by "presenting diverse social and economic viewpoints to Congress" and by providing legal knowledge and technical skills to help frame legislation. Since 1876 Congress has enacted increasingly tighter requirements for lobbyists to register and to identify their clients and fees. Many

loopholes remain in these regulations, but Congress has been concerned that further limitations on lobbying might also restrict the constitutional rights of free speech and freedom to petition.

Rather than return to their home state, some former members of Congress stay in Washington as lobbyists, making use of their experience on Capitol Hill—and their floor privileges in the House and Senate chambers and access to the cloakrooms and dining rooms. George Smathers (Democrat–Florida) explained that as a former senator he could "get in to see senators a lot more quickly than you can if you're just a normal lobbyist." Over time, however, former members often find that their advantages as lobbyists diminish as fewer of their old colleagues remain in office.

SEE ALSO

Floor privileges

FURTHER READING

Byrd, Robert C. "Lobbyists." In *The Senate, 1789–1989: Addresses on the History of the United States Senate.* Vol. 2. Washington, D.C.: Government Printing Office, 1991.
Thompson, Margaret Susan. *The "Spider's Web": Congress and Lobbying in the Age of Grant.* Ithaca, N.Y.: Cornell University Press, 1985.

Lodge, Henry Cabot, Sr.

☆ *Born: May 12, 1850, Boston, Mass.*
☆ *Political party: Republican*
☆ *Representative from Massachusetts: 1887–93*
☆ *Senator from Massachusetts: 1893–1924*
☆ *President pro tempore: 1911–13*
☆ *Senate majority leader: 1919–24*
☆ *Died: Nov. 9, 1924, Cambridge, Mass.*

A SCHOLAR in politics, Henry Cabot Lodge taught history at Harvard before he was elected to Congress. Known to be

strong in his dislikes, Lodge displayed a deep antagonism toward another scholar in politics, Woodrow Wilson, who became President in 1913. Recognizing that a split in the Republican party in the 1912 election had put a Democrat in the White House, Lodge worked to reunite his party and defeat Wilson. When the Republicans regained the majority in the Senate in the 1918 elections, Lodge, as majority leader and chairman of the Foreign Relations Committee, was determined to deny Wilson and the Democratic party the triumph of writing the treaty that ended World War I. Lodge added a series of Republican reservations to Wilson's Treaty of Versailles. Such reservations could alter the interpretation of the treaty and could affect whether the other parties to the treaty would still accept it. Wilson, an equally stubborn man, refused to compromise and took his case directly to the people.

Without the compromise offered by the Republican reservations, the Senate twice defeated the Treaty of Versailles. Republicans triumphed in the elections of 1920, but victory also brought disappointment. Despite Lodge's objections to the treaty, he wanted the United States to play a strong role in international affairs. Instead, his policies resulted in the United States's embrace of isolationism during the decades between the world wars.

SEE ALSO

Treaty of Versailles

FURTHER READING

Garraty, John A. *Henry Cabot Lodge: A Biography.* New York: Knopf, 1968.
Widenor, William C. "Henry Cabot Lodge: The Astute Parliamentarian." In *First among Equals: Outstanding Senate Leaders of the Twentieth Century,* edited by Richard A. Baker and Roger H. Davidson. Washington, D.C.: Congressional Quarterly, 1991.

Long, Huey P.

☆ *Born: Aug. 30, 1893, Winnfield, La.*
☆ *Political party: Democrat*
☆ *Senator from Louisiana: 1931–35*
☆ *Died: Sept. 10, 1935, Baton Rouge, La.*

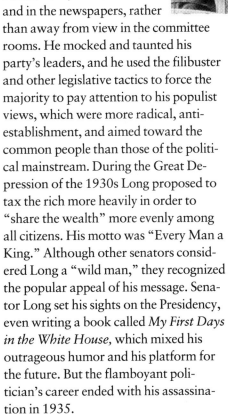

HUEY LONG served less than a single term in the Senate and never chaired a committee—in fact, he resigned from the committees to which he was appointed. Within Congress he was more of a gadfly than an effective legislator. Yet he held great influence because of his strong political base in Louisiana, his unpredictability, and his ability to sway the public. Long preferred to do his work out in public on the Senate floor, or on the radio and in the newspapers, rather than away from view in the committee rooms. He mocked and taunted his party's leaders, and he used the filibuster and other legislative tactics to force the majority to pay attention to his populist views, which were more radical, anti-establishment, and aimed toward the common people than those of the political mainstream. During the Great Depression of the 1930s Long proposed to tax the rich more heavily in order to "share the wealth" more evenly among all citizens. His motto was "Every Man a King." Although other senators considered Long a "wild man," they recognized the popular appeal of his message. Senator Long set his sights on the Presidency, even writing a book called *My First Days in the White House,* which mixed his outrageous humor and his platform for the future. But the flamboyant politician's career ended with his assassination in 1935.

FURTHER READING

Williams, T. Harry. *Huey Long.* New York: Knopf, 1969.

Longworth, Nicholas

☆ *Born: Nov. 5, 1869, Cincinnati, Ohio*
☆ *Political party: Republican*
☆ *Representative from Ohio: 1903–13, 1915–31*
☆ *House majority leader: 1923–25*
☆ *Speaker of the House: 1925–31*
☆ *Died: Apr. 9, 1931, Aiken, S.C.*

THE ARISTOCRATIC Nicholas Longworth seemed too much a dandy to be an effective politician. He played the violin, dressed impeccably, and loved fine food, card playing, and dancing. But Nick Longworth could also be a tough politician who knew how to bargain and compromise and when to hold the line and fight. As Speaker of the House, he ruled his party and the House firmly. He ordered that progressive Republicans who had bolted their party during the election of 1924 be barred from the Republican conference, removed from their committee assignments, and denied their seniority. He won changes in the House rules to strengthen majority control by making it more difficult to discharge a bill from committee against the wishes of the leadership. Although he demanded discipline within his party, Longworth worked closely with the minority leader, John Nance Garner, to make the House work as efficiently as possible. Republicans sometimes protested that the Speaker was *too* fair to the Democrats. As a testament to Longworth's popularity among members of both parties, the House later named one of its office buildings in his honor.

FURTHER READING

Cheney, Richard B., and Lynne V. Cheney. *Kings of the Hill: Power and Personality in the House of Representatives.* New York: Continuum, 1983.

Louisiana Purchase (1803)

FRANCE'S OFFER to sell the vast Louisiana Territory to the United States in 1803 sparked a constitutional dilemma. President Thomas Jefferson wanted to purchase the territory, which would double the size of the United States. But Jefferson also favored a narrow interpretation of the Constitution—and nowhere did it provide for acquiring additional territory. Because of the need to act quickly on the deal, there was no time to amend the Constitution. Instead, the Jeffersonian Democratic-Republicans in Congress passed legislation that gave the President permission to sign a treaty to receive the territory, and Congress appropriated the money to pay for it. Congress acted under the provision of the Constitution (Article 5, Section 3) that gave Congress the power to regulate the territories, arguing that that power included the right to purchase new territories. Congress and the President therefore stretched the Constitution to fit new circumstances and solve their dilemma.

The House mace was made in 1841.

FURTHER READING

Smelser, Marshall. *The Democratic Republic, 1801–1815.* New York: Harper & Row, 1968.

Mace of the House of Representatives

THE SYMBOL of authority of the House sergeant at arms is a 46-inch silver mace decorated with lashed rods and axes that are topped by a flying eagle. The House first adopted a mace, modeled after the mace of ancient Roman officials, in 1789. At the beginning of each day's session of the House, an assistant sergeant at arms brings the mace from its cabinet and sets it to the right of the Speaker's chair. There the mace stands upright on a marble pedestal for as long as the House remains in session. During moments of extreme turmoil in the House, the sergeant at arms will hold up the mace to restore order in the chamber. The Senate does not use a mace, but the symbol of the mace appears frequently in the decoration around the Senate and House chambers and office buildings.

SEE ALSO
Sergeant at arms

William Maclay, Senate diarist

Maclay, William

☆ *Born: July 20, 1737, New Garden, Pa.*
☆ *Political party: Anti-Federalist*
☆ *Senator from Pennsylvania: 1789–91*
☆ *Died: Apr. 16, 1804, Harrisburg, Pa.*

THE DIARY of Senator William Maclay gives a rare glimpse of the Senate during the 1st Congress, when the Senate met entirely behind closed doors. The official records of its earliest debates and activi-

ties are thin and unrevealing. But Maclay kept a lively and highly opinionated diary of his personal observations. An Anti-Federalist who believed in simplicity of manners, Maclay was sharply critical and suspicious of the Senate's first president, John Adams, and other Federalists. His diary described in detail President Washington's first inauguration in the Senate chamber and the President's personal visit to receive the Senate's advice and consent on a treaty with the Indian nations. The diary also gives modern readers a glimpse into the first Senate committees, the earliest lobbyists, and the hectic last-minute business before the Senate adjourned. The first senators drew lots to see whether they would serve a full six-year term, a four-year term, or a two-year term, so that one-third of the Senate would stand for election every two years thereafter. Since Maclay drew a two-year term, his Senate service ended with the 1st Congress, and so did his diary.

FURTHER READING

Bowling, Kenneth R., and Helen E. Veit, eds. *The Diary of William Maclay and Other Notes on Senate Debates.* Baltimore, Md.: Johns Hopkins University Press, 1988.

Madison, James

☆ *Born: Mar. 16, 1751, Port Conway, Va.*
☆ *Political party: Democratic-Republican*
☆ *Member of the Continental Congress: 1780–83, 1787–88*
☆ *Delegate to the Constitutional Convention: 1787*
☆ *Representative from Virginia: 1789–97*
☆ *President: 1809–17*
☆ *Died: June 28, 1836, Orange County, Va.*

ALTHOUGH JAMES Madison had been one of the principal authors of the Constitution, he had a hard time getting elected to the government it created. In

Representative James Madison

1788 Virginia state legislators declined to elect him to the Senate because they doubted that he would "obey instructions" on how to vote in the Senate. When he ran for a seat in the House of Representatives in 1789, Madison again faced strong opposition. Recognizing Virginians' deep concerns about the newly formed federal government, Madison promised voters that he would support constitutional amendments to protect their rights and liberties.

Once elected, Madison remained true to his word. He introduced and managed to secure passage of a series of amendments, which became the Constitution's Bill of Rights. Although he held no official title, Madison served as floor leader of the House for President George Washington's administration during the 1st Congress. However, he soon came to oppose the financial programs of Treasury Secretary Alexander Hamilton. During the 1790s Madison broke with the Federalists and became one of the chief organizers of the Democratic-Republican party.

SEE ALSO
Constitution; Instruction of senators

FURTHER READING
Rakove, Jack N. *James Madison and the Creation of the American Republic.* Glenview, Ill.: Scott, Foresman, 1990.
Rutland, Robert A. *James Madison: The Founding Father.* New York: Macmillan, 1987.

Majority leader

MEMBERS OF the majority party in both the House and Senate elect a leader to represent them in floor proceedings and to serve as a spokesperson for their party's position on the issues. The majority leader schedules business on the floor, plans party strategy, and attempts to keep the majority party as united as possible when casting roll call votes. Majority leaders receive a higher salary than other members, a car and driver, and a separate leadership office and staff within the Capitol.

The Constitution provides for presiding officers for the House and Senate but says nothing about party floor leadership. This was because the framers of the Constitution hoped that the United States might avoid parties—or factions, as they called them. But within a few years after the federal government had started, such controversial issues as the Jay Treaty divided Americans, and their congressional representatives, into opposing political parties. Early Presidents turned to certain members of the House and Senate to act as their spokesmen, to promote their programs, and to make sure other members of their party voted with them. Formal party leadership positions, such as majority and minority leaders and whips, evolved over time.

House majority leaders

Because of the House's larger size, its parties were first to require active floor leadership to keep their members informed and in line. The Speaker would designate one member to act as his spokesman on the floor, often choosing the chairman of the powerful Ways and Means Committee or the Appropriations Committee. By the Civil War the press was using the terms *majority* and *minority leader* to describe the top party officials in the House.

After progressive House members revolted against the dictatorial leadership of Speaker Joseph G. Cannon in 1910, Speakers lost the power to name the floor leader. Instead, the party conferences elected the leader. These leaders devoted their attention to floor business and no longer chaired committees. Ma-

MAJORITY LEADERS OF THE HOUSE[†]

Sereno E. Payne (Republican–New York), 1899–1911

Oscar W. Underwood (Democrat–Alabama), 1911–15

Claude Kitchin (Democrat–North Carolina), 1915–19

Franklin W. Mondell (Republican–Wyoming), 1919–23

Nicholas Longworth (Republican–Ohio), 1923–25

John Q. Tilson (Republican–Connecticut), 1925–31

Henry T. Rainey (Democrat–Illinois), 1931–33

Joseph W. Byrns (Democrat–Tennessee), 1933–35

William Bankhead (Democrat–Alabama), 1935–36

Sam Rayburn (Democrat–Texas), 1937–40

John W. McCormack (Democrat–Massachusetts), 1940–47, 1949–53, 1955–61

Charles A. Halleck (Republican–Indiana), 1947–49, 1953–55

Carl Albert (Democrat–Oklahoma), 1961–69

Hale Boggs (Democrat–Louisiana), 1969–72

Thomas P. ("Tip") O'Neill, Jr. (Democrat–Massachusetts), 1973–77

Jim Wright (Democrat–Texas), 1977–87

Thomas S. Foley (Democrat–Washington), 1987–89

Richard A. Gephardt (Democrat–Missouri), 1989–

[†]*Identification of majority leaders in the 19th century was unofficial, and a comprehensive list is unavailable.*

MAJORITY LEADERS OF THE SENATE

John Worth Kern (Democrat–Indiana), 1913–17*

Thomas S. Martin (Democrat–Virginia), 1917–19*

Henry Cabot Lodge, Sr. (Republican–Massachusetts), 1919–24*

Charles Curtis (Republican–Kansas), 1925–29

James S. Watson (Republican–Indiana), 1929–33

Joseph T. Robinson (Democrat–Arkansas), 1933–37

Alben W. Barkley (Democrat–Kentucky), 1937–47

Wallace H. White, Jr. (Republican–Maine), 1947–49

Scott Lucas (Democrat–Illinois), 1949–51

Ernest McFarland (Democrat–Arizona), 1951–53

Robert A. Taft, Sr. (Republican–Ohio), 1953

William F. Knowland (Republican–California), 1953–55

Lyndon B. Johnson (Democrat–Texas), 1955–61

Mike Mansfield (Democrat–Montana), 1961–77

Robert C. Byrd (Democrat–West Virginia), 1977–81, 1987–89

Howard Baker (Republican–Tennessee), 1981–85

Robert Dole (Republican–Kansas), 1985–87

George S. Mitchell (Democrat–Maine), 1989–

conference chairman; not officially designated majority leader

jority leaders also became the prime candidates to move up to the Speakership.

Senate majority leaders

During the 19th century, leadership in the Senate was divided among the majority party caucus (or conference) leader and the most powerful committee chairmen. "No one is *the* Senator, no one may speak for his party as well as himself," Woodrow Wilson wrote in his study of Congress in 1885. By the time Wilson became President in 1913, Senate party leaders began to emerge. Democratic conference chairman John Worth Kern and later Republican conference chairman Henry Cabot Lodge performed all the functions of modern majority lead-

Senate majority leader Mike Mansfield and minority leader Everett Dirksen in 1964.

ers, although neither formally held the title. The Democrats first designated a floor leader in 1921. They elected Oscar W. Underwood (Democrat–Alabama), who had previously served as House majority leader from 1911 to 1915. In 1925 the Republicans designated Charles Curtis (Republican–Kansas) as their first official majority leader.

House rules favor the majority party and limit the role of the minority—as long as the majority stays united. Senate rules give more authority to individual members of both the majority and minority parties and provide few specific powers for the leaders. Senate rules require that the presiding officer must recognize the majority and minority leaders before other senators seeking recognition to speak. This procedure gives the leadership increased control over the proceedings. The floor leaders also chair their party steering committees, which determine committee assignments. But otherwise the job carries few specific powers. The power of the majority leader depends instead on the skill, intelligence, and personality of the person who holds the post.

SEE ALSO

Leadership; Minority leader

Mansfield, Mike

☆ *Born: Mar. 19, 1903, New York, N.Y.*
☆ *Political party: Democrat*
☆ *Representative from Montana:*
    1943–53
☆ *Senator from Montana: 1953–77*
☆ *Senate majority whip: 1957–61*
☆ *Senate majority leader: 1961–77*

IT WAS not easy following Lyndon B. Johnson as Senate majority leader. Although many senators were glad to see the domineering Johnson leave, others wanted Johnson's strong style of leadership to continue. Mansfield believed that all senators should be equal and should act out of a sense of their own responsibility rather than be driven by a powerful leader. Explaining his leadership style, Mansfield said, "I am neither a circus ringmaster, the master of ceremonies of a Senate night club, a tamer of Senate lions, or a wheeler and dealer." Instead, he argued that senators needed to work out their own agreements and accommodations through mutual respect for each other. Although some people, including President Lyndon B. Johnson, grumbled over Mansfield's permissive style, it helped promote a burst of legislative activity in the 1960s and made Mansfield the longest-serving majority leader in Senate history.

SEE ALSO

Johnson, Lyndon B.; Leadership; Majority leader

FURTHER READING

Baker, Ross K. "Mike Mansfield and the Birth of the Modern Senate." In *First among Equals: Outstanding Senate Leaders of the Twentieth Century,* edited by Richard A. Baker and Roger Davidson. Washington, D.C.: Congressional Quarterly, 1991.

Markup sessions

AFTER HEARINGS have been held on a bill, the members of the subcommittee or full committee will meet to "mark up" the bill. This means that they will make final changes, adding and removing words and provisions, revising the amounts of money authorized, and otherwise polishing and perfecting the text before reporting it to the floor. The name dates back to the time when committee members and clerks literally "marked up" bills by writing the new amendments on the original text. Until the 1970s, markup sessions were held behind closed doors and were the occasion for much last-minute compromising and deal making. But "sunshine" rules adopted by the House in 1973 and the Senate in 1975 required that committees hold their markups in public session.

S E E A L S O
Committees; Hearings; "Sunshine" rules

Mavericks

ALTHOUGH MOST members of Congress still follow the advice of Speaker Sam Rayburn (Democrat–Texas) that "to get along you have to go along," a few senators and representatives made their career not by "going along" but by becoming legislative mavericks. Mavericks tend to represent a minority viewpoint within their own party and tend to refuse to bend their principles to prevailing attitudes. Mavericks are often showmen who enjoy the spotlight of publicity. They will employ disruptive tactics to stop or slow down action on a bill, trying to make the majority agree with their demands. They may show contempt for the rules, courtesies, and elaborate forms of politeness that other legislators adopt with each other.

Robert La Follette, Sr. (Republican–Wisconsin) would rather lose a legislative battle than to accept "half a loaf." George Norris (Republican–Nebraska) challenged powerful Speaker of the House Joseph G. Cannon and was successful in reducing the Speaker's powers. Huey P. Long (Democrat–Louisiana) resigned from his committee assignments and devoted his attention to flamboyant speeches on the Senate floor, often mimicking and mocking other senators. Joseph R. McCarthy (Republican–Wisconsin) flaunted the Senate's rules and decorum until he was censured. Mavericks generally work outside of their party's official leadership. By contrast, Representative Newt Gingrich (Republican–Georgia) gained enough notoriety from his maverick stands to be elected one of his party's leaders in the House.

S E E A L S O
Independents

McCarthy, Joseph R.

☆ *Born: Nov. 14, 1908, Grand Chute, Wis.*
☆ *Political party: Republican*
☆ *Senator from Wisconsin: 1947–57*
☆ *Died: May 2, 1957, Bethesda, Md.*

AS A RELATIVELY obscure freshman senator, Joe McCarthy made himself a household name when he declared at a political rally in Wheeling, West Virginia, in 1950 that he held in his hand a list of 205 known communists within the State Department. McCarthy exploited the tense cold war atmosphere of the time to shock his audience—and the nation as well. In fact, he had no hard evi-

Senator Joseph R. McCarthy (right) confronts Senator Millard Tydings at a hearing.

dence of communists in government, but people willingly believed him just the same. McCarthy's influence increased in 1953 when he used his chairmanship of the Permanent Subcommittee on Investigations to hold a series of dramatic hearings, bullying witnesses and intimidating senators who opposed him. Justifying his actions as necessary to combat communist subversion, McCarthy disrupted the Senate's normal rules, customs, and decorum. Eventually, his charges and behavior became too outrageous. Following the Army-McCarthy hearings in 1954, when McCarthy recklessly accused the U.S. Army of harboring communists, public opinion shifted away from McCarthy, and the Senate censured him by a vote of 67 to 22 for conduct "contrary to senatorial traditions."

SEE ALSO
Army-McCarthy hearings (1954); Censure; Investigations

FURTHER READING
Oshinsky, David. *A Conspiracy So Immense: The World of Joseph McCarthy.* New York: Free Press, 1983.

McNary, Charles L.

☆ *Born: June 12, 1874, Salem, Oreg.*
☆ *Political party: Republican*
☆ *Senator from Oregon: 1917–44*
☆ *Senate minority leader: 1933–44*
☆ *Died: Feb. 25, 1944, Fort Lauderdale, Fla.*

NO MINORITY leader ever commanded so few members as effectively as Charles McNary did. After the 1936 election the number of Senate Republicans shrank to 16, against 76 Democrats and 4 independents. But McNary led his party by coaxing and accommodation, rather than by confrontation, and he was a shrewd judge of legislative behavior. In 1937 when President Franklin D. Roosevelt announced his plan to "pack" the Supreme Court with liberal justices (to prevent conservative justices from ruling New Deal programs unconstitutional), Republican senators wanted to lead the fight against the plan. McNary cautioned restraint, urging them to let

Democrats take the lead against the plan instead. He reasoned that if the Republicans remained quiet, the Democrats would fight among themselves and split their swollen majority. McNary's strategy worked, the Court plan was defeated, the Democrats became divided, and the small band of Republicans was able to form an effective coalition with the Democratic conservatives to dominate the Senate for many years.

SEE ALSO

Court-packing plan (1937); Minority leader

FURTHER READING

Neal, Steve. *McNary of Oregon: A Political Biography*. Portland, Oreg.: Western Imprints, 1983.

Media coverage of Congress

OF THE THREE branches of the federal government, Congress traditionally has been the most open to newspaper and broadcast journalists. While the executive and judicial branches do much of their work in private, Congress holds hearings, debates, and votes in public. Representing both parties and a wide range of ideologies, members of Congress are usually willing to give interviews and information to the press.

In 1789 the popularly elected House opened its floor debates and voting to the public and the press. Senators, still elected by state legislatures, debated in closed session until 1794. The first reporters to cover Congress were really stenographers paid by private newspapers to record the debates. From their notes evolved the *Congressional Record*. By the 1820s "letter writers," or correspondents, sat in the congressional galleries gathering information for more interpretive reporting.

When the number of these correspondents increased, the Senate set aside the first press gallery in 1841, and the House did so soon afterward. These press galleries guaranteed accredited reporters regular seats in the Senate and

Press photographers covered the Senate Judiciary Committee hearings on the nomination of Robert Bork (far left) to the Supreme Court.

House chambers and also provided them a room behind the galleries in which to write their stories. By the 1850s telegraph facilities were set up within the press galleries to decrease the time it took correspondents to wire the news to their papers. In the 20th century Congress established separate radio-television galleries as well as recording studios where members could prepare taped remarks for broadcast.

The press, President, and Congress

Despite Congress's openness, press attention has shifted steadily toward the White House since the 1930s. A single President is easier to visualize and portray than 535 voting members of Congress. Presidents have gained easier access to the media than to individual members of Congress, and they can use television to appeal directly to public opinion.

Yet there are some 5,000 reporters who hold passes to the House and Senate press galleries. To become accredited and receive a congressional press pass, reporters must show that they work full-time as journalists, have no affiliation with any government agency, and are not involved in lobbying Congress for any private interests. Gallery space could never accommodate these thousands of reporters, but only a small number is present regularly at the Capitol to cover committee hearings and floor proceedings. A larger number of reporters appears only occasionally, in search of some specific information or to interview members and staff about the issues of the day.

Regional reporting

Some journalists report for national news networks, magazines, and major metropolitan newspapers. But most on Capitol Hill are "regional reporters" who report for smaller papers or chains of papers located in a particular state or region. Regional reporters seek news that will be of special interest to local or regional readers and viewers. They generally form mutual working relationships with the members of Congress from their region, who are their best sources of news. In return, the members of Congress seek favorable publicity to keep their name and their activities before the voters back home.

FURTHER READING

Ritchie, Donald A. *Press Gallery: Congress and the Washington Correspondents.* Cambridge: Harvard University Press, 1991.

Michel, Robert H.

☆ *Born: Mar. 2, 1923, Peoria, Ill.*
☆ *Political party: Republican*
☆ *Representative from Illinois: 1957–*
☆ *House minority whip: 1975–81*
☆ *House minority leader: 1981–*

BOB MICHEL set the record for having spent the longest time in the minority of any member of Congress. He was first elected to the House in 1956, shortly after Democrats regained the majority. Michel gained a seat on the powerful House Appropriations Committee but noted that it took three terms before the "crusty old chairman named Clarence Cannon" (Democrat–Missouri) seemed to recognize that the freshman Republican was a member of his committee. After more than 30 years of service, Michel remained a member of the minority, although by then he had become the Republican floor leader and one of the best-known members of the House. During his years in the minority, Michel often worked closely with the leaders of the majority. By understanding when to accommodate the majority and when to stand up against it, he offered effective support for Republican Presidents Ronald Reagan and George Bush despite the lack of a Republican majority in the House.

"Millionaires' club"

BY THE END of the 19th century, so many rich men had been elected to the Senate that critics dubbed it a "millionaires' club." Reformers charged that wealthy senators were neither representative of average citizens nor sensitive to their needs. The image of the "millionaires' club" was a contributing factor to the movement toward direct election of senators. Even after direct election, however, the great expense of running for national office continued to favor wealthy candidates.

Minority leader

ELECTED BY the members of the minority party in each house, minority leaders represent the interests of their party on the Senate and House floors—but with fewer votes to count on than majority leaders do. Minority leaders work to keep their party united and to attract enough votes from the majority party to affect legislation. Like majority leaders, minority leaders receive a higher salary than regular members, a car and driver, and a separate leadership office in the Capitol.

Minority leaders work with majority leaders on scheduling, but they lack the majority leaders' control over calling up legislation. House rules generally favor the majority, but in the Senate, where

much of the business is done by unanimous consent, the minority leader's cooperation is more crucial. That is because the minority leader, or any other minority member, can stop an action by objecting, thereby requiring time-consuming legislative procedures and voting. Senator Robert C. Byrd (Democrat–West Virginia) noted the need for cooperation between the leaders: "An element of compromise and forbearance [tolerance] is crucial if the Senate is to function properly—or if, indeed, it is to function at all."

When the President's party holds the majority in Congress, the minority leaders become the chief voices of opposition to administration programs. They are featured prominently in the media and are often given television time to respond to the President's broadcast speeches. When the President's party is in the minority in Congress, the minority leaders serve as his spokesmen. Representative Robert Michel (Republican–Illinois) has described this as a "dual role" that requires a leader to look at issues from two perspectives, "your own district's and the President's."

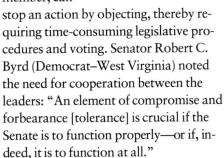

Senate minority leader Hugh Scott (right) with majority leader Mike Mansfield.

SEE ALSO

Majority leader; Michel, Robert H.

FURTHER READING

Baker, Richard A., and Roger H. Davidson, eds. *First among Equals: Outstanding Senate Leaders of the Twentieth Century.* Washington, D.C.: Congressional Quarterly, 1991.

Byrd, Robert C. "Party Floor Leaders." In *The Senate, 1789–1989: Addresses on the History of the United States Senate.* Vol. 2. Washington, D.C.: Government Printing Office, 1991.

Missouri Compromise (1821)

THE FIRST great legislative compromise designed to quiet and settle the slavery issue was the Missouri Compromise, which drew a line on the map that slavery was not to spread across. Having acquired the vast territory of the Louisiana Purchase in 1803, the United States faced the question of whether slave owners could take slaves into the new territories. In 1818, when Missouri asked to join the Union, Northern members of Congress supported an amendment requiring emancipation of any slaves in Missouri. Slave owners, however, objected to any limit on their right to own slaves. At the time, the Senate was evenly divided between slaveholding and non-slaveholding states. Neither the North nor the South wanted to become the minority. After dramatic and heated debates, Congress agreed to admit Missouri as a slaveholding state and Maine, at the same time, as a free state, preserving the balance of political power between the sections in the Senate. Congress also set the 36th parallel as the boundary above which slavery could not spread. The Missouri Compromise held until Congress repealed its dividing line with the Kansas-Nebraska Act of 1854.

Mitchell, George J.

☆ Born: Aug. 20, 1933, Waterville, Maine
☆ Political party: Democrat
☆ Senator from Maine: 1980–
☆ Majority leader: 1989–

WHAT QUALITIES lift senators into their party's leadership? Candidates are judged by their fellow senators on how articulate they will be in presenting their party's programs in the Senate and to the national media. They are chosen for their skills as legislative strategists. And they are often measured by their success in raising campaign funds for their colleagues. All of these qualities helped George Mitchell become Democratic majority leader in 1989.

Mitchell first learned the legislative process when he served on the Senate staff from 1962 to 1965 as executive assistant to Edmund Muskie (Democrat–Maine). In 1980 he was appointed to succeed Muskie (who had resigned to become secretary of state). Mitchell chaired the Democratic Senatorial Campaign Committee in 1986, raising funds that helped the Democrats win back the majority in the Senate. He campaigned for the position of majority leader with a promise to improve the "quality of life" for the members by scheduling Senate business to avoid late-night sessions and to allow members to return home over long weekends. Mitchell's eloquence and persistence as a member of the committee investigating the Iran-Contra scandal also convinced Democratic senators of his ability to serve as their spokesman.

SEE ALSO

Iran-Contra investigation (1986); Majority leader

Morning business

THE FIRST thing that the House and Senate do each legislative day is to set aside a period called the Morning Hour for introducing bills, resolutions, memorials, committee reports, and messages from the President, department heads, or the other body. These activities are known as morning business. On each new legislative day, morning business follows the reading of the journal and comes at the beginning of the Morning Hour.

SEE ALSO

Legislative day; Morning Hour

Morning Hour

AT THE BEGINNING of a new legislative day, the House and Senate have a period called the Morning Hour when morning business is conducted and during which members may make brief speeches on any subject. In the House Morning Hour speeches are limited to one minute per member. The Senate sets aside the first two hours of a new legislative day as Morning Hour, and members speak briefly, although without set time limitations. Morning Hour gives members the opportunity to speak on the current issues of the day, even if there is no pending legislation dealing with those issues.

SEE ALSO

Legislative day; Morning business

Morrill, Justin S.

☆ Born: Apr. 14, 1810, Strafford, Vt.
☆ Political party: Whig, Republican
☆ Representative from Maine: 1855–67
☆ Senator from Maine: 1867–98
☆ Died: Dec. 28, 1898, Washington, D.C.

WHEN THE Southern Democrats left Congress as their states seceded in 1860 and 1861, they opened the way for the new Republican majority to enact its domestic legislation. Even as the Civil War was being fought, Congress still had to deal with nonmilitary measures. One of the most important of these was the Morrill Land Grant College Act, sponsored by Representative Justin Morrill of Maine. The Morrill Act set aside public land that could be sold to establish and operate state agricultural and mechanical arts (A&M) colleges. Many state universities today owe their origins to this act, passed in 1862. Justin Morrill remained in the House and Senate for 43 years of continuous service as a powerful committee chairman (of the House Ways and Means and Senate Finance Committees) and a productive legislator. He turned down repeated requests to join Presidential cabinets, noting that there was no appointed office that would cause him to resign from Congress, which he considered "the highest honor" and "the highest function that I could perform."

The Morrill Act established the land grant colleges in 1862.

Motions

WHEN LEGISLATORS seek some action, whether in committee or on the floor, they make a motion. To make a motion, members first must be recognized, or called upon, by the chair or presiding officer. The member then announces, for example, "Mr. Chairman, I move that we report the bill as amended." Or "Madam President, I move that the yeas and nays be called." Or "Mr. Speaker, I move that the reading of the journal be dispensed with." The motion must be seconded (that is, at least one other member must indicate support) and be voted upon by voice or roll call vote. Motions trigger different types of parliamentary actions, and the rules of the Senate and House establish the priority of motions (that is, which ones must be taken up first and in what order).

Frederick A. Muhlenberg, first Speaker of the House

Muhlenberg, Frederick Augustus

☆ Born: Jan. 1, 1750, Trappe, Pa.
☆ Political party: Federalist, Democratic-Republican
☆ Delegate to the Continental Congress: 1779–80
☆ Representative from Pennsylvania: 1789–97
☆ Speaker of the House: 1789–91, 1793–95
☆ Died: June 4, 1801, Lancaster, Pa.

THE FIRST Speaker of the House of Representatives, Frederick Muhlenberg, was a Lutheran minister who had previously served as a member of the Continental Congress, speaker of the Pennsylvania Assembly, and president of the Pennsylvania State Convention that ratified the Constitution. His experience in government and his representation of a middle state (whereas President George Washington was a Southerner and Vice President John Adams came from New England) led to Muhlenberg's election as Speaker. A portly, distinguished-looking man, he brought honesty, integrity, and dignity to his office. However, because he attempted to rule with impartiality, following the model of the speakers of the British House of Commons, Muhlenberg displeased members of the Federalist party. They removed him as Speaker in favor of a more ardent champion of Federalist policies. Muhlenberg later switched to the Democratic-Republican party.

FURTHER READING

Peters, Ronald M., Jr. *The American Speakership: The Office in Historical Perspective.* Baltimore, Md.: Johns Hopkins University Press, 1990.

Native Americans in Congress

ALTHOUGH CONGRESS has long had committees and subcommittees that deal with issues related to American Indians, few Native Americans have served in the House or Senate. Originally, the Constitution treated the Indian tribes as separate nations. Indians were not citizens and were not counted for purposes of taxes or for determining a state's representation in the House (Article 1, Section 2). Not until the Dawes Act of 1887 did Congress grant U.S. citizenship to the Indians.

Native American Ben Nighthorse Campbell served in the House and Senate.

The first member of Congress to claim Native American ancestry was Charles Curtis (Republican–Kansas), who was one-eighth Kaw-Osage. His mother died when he was three, and Curtis was for a while raised by his Indian grandmother. He often visited the Kaw reservation in Oklahoma. Even after he was elected to the House in 1892 and to the Senate in 1906, Curtis was listed on the rolls of the Interior Department as an Indian ward of the government. A few other members, largely from Oklahoma, were also part Indian.

Benjamin Reifel (Republican–South Dakota), a Sioux born on the Rosebud Indian Reservation, served in the House from 1961 to 1971. Ben Nighthorse Campbell (Democrat–Colorado), a Cheyenne who designs Indian jewelry and dresses and wears his hair in Indian style, was elected to the House in 1986 and to the Senate in 1992. Senator Daniel Akaka (Democrat–Hawaii) notes that his Polynesian heritage also makes him a Native American.

FURTHER READING
Unrau, William E. *Mixed-Bloods and Tribal Dissolution: Charles Curtis and the Quest for Indian Identity*. Lawrence: University Press of Kansas, 1989.

Richard Nixon during his first term in the House of Representatives.

Nixon, Richard M.

☆ *Born: Jan. 9, 1913, Yorba Linda, Calif.*
☆ *Political party: Republican*
☆ *Representative from California: 1947–51*
☆ *Senator from California: 1951–53*
☆ *Vice President: 1953–61*
☆ *President: 1969–74*

RICHARD NIXON'S national political career was launched by one congressional investigation and destroyed by another. As a freshman representative in 1948, Nixon won national notice during the House Un-American Activities Committee's investigation of charges by Whittaker Chambers that former State Department official Alger Hiss had been a communist. Hiss vigorously denied the charges and many high-ranking officials who had worked with him doubted these charges, but Nixon's support of Chambers was considered vindicated when a jury found Hiss guilty of perjury, or lying under oath. The notoriety of the Hiss-Chambers investigation propelled Nixon into the Senate in 1950, and he became Vice President in 1952, while he was still in his thirties.

In 1968 Nixon was elected President, and he was reelected by a landslide four years later. But allegations of improper campaign activity in 1972, including a break-in at Democratic headquarters at the Watergate office building, led a special Senate committee chaired by Senator Sam Ervin (Democrat–North Carolina) to investigate. Testimony from White House aides, the revelation that Nixon had secretly tape-recorded his con-

versations, and other evidence unearthed by the Senate investigation caused Nixon to resign the Presidency in 1974.

SEE ALSO
Investigations; Watergate investigation (1973)

FURTHER READING
Nixon, Richard M. *RN: The Memoirs of Richard Nixon*. New York: Grosset & Dunlap, 1978.
Parmet, Herbert S. *Richard Nixon and His America*. Boston: Little, Brown, 1990.
Pious, Richard M. *Richard M. Nixon: A Political Life*. Englewood Cliffs, N.J.: Julian Messner, 1991.

Nominations, confirmation of

ACCORDING TO the Constitution (Article 2, Section 2), the Senate alone has the authority to advise and consent on nominations made by the President. These nominations include those of members of the cabinet, executive agency heads, diplomats, judges, federal attorneys, and military officers. This power is critically important to the federal system of checks and balances. Along with the development of "senatorial courtesy"—by which senators usually will not vote to confirm nominees opposed by their home-state senators—the confirmation power has given the Senate great influence over certain types of appointments. For instance, Presidents generally nominate federal judges and U.S. marshals from lists provided by senators and key House members.

Both the executive branch and the Senate committees handling the nominations carefully screen the nominees. Often, the Federal Bureau of Investiga-

President George Washington nominated Alexander Hamilton to be secretary of the Treasury.

tion (FBI) conducts an investigation of the nominee's life. The staff of the Senate committee to which the nomination is referred also compiles information, and witnesses testify at committee hearings about the nominee's qualifications. For instance, the Senate agriculture committee holds nomination hearings for the secretary of agriculture, and the Foreign Relations Committee handles the nomination of the secretary of state.

The Senate defeated the nomination of former senator John Tower for secretary of defense.

Cabinet versus Court nominations

Out of the many hundreds of cabinet nominations made since 1789, the Senate has rejected only nine (another six were withdrawn because they would probably not have been confirmed). The low number of rejections suggests that the Senate believes that Presidents should have the right to name their own cabinets, as long as those nominees appear fully fit for office. By contrast, the Senate has rejected 26 Supreme Court nominees, about 20 percent of the total number of nominations. This considerably larger percentage of rejections suggests that the Senate seeks a larger role in the choice of members of the independent judicial branch.

Some critics have argued that in dealing with judicial nominations, the Senate should confine itself to examining each nominee's personal integrity and legal qualifications. But the Senate has also considered the political and ideological positions of judicial nominations. For instance, in 1930 the Senate rejected the Supreme Court nomination of John J. Parker because of opposition from labor unions and civil rights groups. In 1987 the Senate rejected the conservative Judge Robert Bork as too rigidly ideological—that is, rather than having an open mind, he would be influenced by his personal philosophy in how he viewed issues that came before the court.

SEE ALSO

Advice and consent; Checks and balances; Senatorial courtesy

FURTHER READING

Byrd, Robert C. "Nominations." In *The Senate, 1789–1989: Addresses on the History of the United States Senate.* Vol. 2. Washington, D.C.: Government Printing Office, 1991.

Nonvoting delegates

SEE Delegates

Norris, George W.

☆ *Born: July 11, 1861, Clyde, Ohio*
☆ *Political party: Republican*
☆ *Representative from Nebraska: 1903–13*
☆ *Senator from Nebraska: 1913–43*
☆ *Died: Sept. 2, 1944, McCook, Nebr.*

HAILED AS a "Great Insurgent" in Congress, George Norris devoted his long career to reforming government and improving the nation's general welfare. In 1910 he led the revolt against House Speaker Joseph G. Cannon to reduce the power of the conservative Speaker and make it easier to enact reform legislation. Norris was a persistent

Senator George Norris sponsored legislation that built the TVA dams.

man, willing to devote years to a good fight. From 1918 to 1933 he advocated that the federal government build dams in the Tennessee River Valley to provide low-cost electricity to an impoverished area and to create a model for public power programs elsewhere. Although Presidents Calvin Coolidge and Herbert Hoover vetoed his bills, Norris fought on. Finally, as part of the first hundred days of the New Deal, Congress again enacted the bill, and President Franklin D. Roosevelt signed the Tennessee Valley Authority (TVA) into law. Under TVA, the government built dams and powerhouses, replanted forests, and brought electricity to remote areas. "Changed times change attitudes," Norris explained. He owed his success to standing firmly by his principles until national attitudes changed to support him.

SEE ALSO
Cannon, Joseph G.; First hundred days of the New Deal; Insurgents

FURTHER READING
Lowitt, Richard. *George W. Norris: The Making of a Progressive, 1861–1912.* 1963. Reprint. Westport, Conn.: Greenwood, 1980.
Lowitt, Richard. *George W. Norris: The Persistence of a Progressive, 1913–1933.* Urbana: University of Illinois Press, 1971.
Lowitt, Richard. *George W. Norris: The Triumph of a Progressive: 1933–1944.* Urbana: University of Illinois Press, 1978.

Oath of office

ALL MEMBERS of Congress take the same oath of office when they begin a new term. The Vice President usually administers the oath to senators, and the Speaker of the House administers the oath to representatives:

> I, [member's name], do solemnly swear (or affirm) that I will support and defend the Constitution of the United States against all enemies, foreign and domestic; that I will bear true faith and allegiance to the same; that I take this obligation freely, without any mental reservation or purpose of evasion; and that I will well and faithfully discharge the duties of the office on which I am about to enter: So help me God.

Office buildings

SEE Capitol building

Officers of the House and Senate

THE VICE PRESIDENT of the United States, various elected members of Congress, and elected staff members are the officers of the House and Senate. The Constitution assigns the Vice President to serve as presiding officer of the Senate (or president of the Senate), with the power to cast tiebreaking votes. Article 1, Section 3, of the Constitution instructs the Senate to elect a president pro tempore (temporary president) to preside in the absence of the Vice President. In recent years, the president pro tempore has been the longest-serving member of the majority party. Article 1, Section 2, of the Constitution instructs the House to elect a Speaker as its presiding officer. The Vice President, the Speaker of the House, and the president pro tempore are therefore the three constitutional officers of Congress, and they stand in that order in the line of Presidential succession (that is, the order in which they would move up to the Presidency in the case of a vacancy).

Each house also elects its own ad-

Nineteenth-century senators took the oath of office on this Bible.

ministrative officers. The Senate elects the secretary of the Senate, sergeant at arms, chaplain, and secretaries for the majority and minority parties. None of these officers are senators. The House elects the clerk of the House, sergeant at arms, doorkeeper, and chaplain, none of whom are representatives.

The political parties represented in Congress also elect officers, including majority and minority leaders, conference (caucus) chairs, and party secretaries.

SEE ALSO

Chaplain; Clerk of the House; Constitution; President pro tempore of the Senate; Sergeant at arms; Speaker of the House; Vice President

O'Neill, Thomas P. ("Tip"), Jr.

☆ Born: Dec. 9, 1912, Cambridge, Mass.
☆ Political party: Democrat
☆ Representative from Massachusetts: 1953–87
☆ House majority whip: 1971–73
☆ House majority leader: 1973–77
☆ Speaker of the House: 1977–87

WHEN HE first ran for public office, Tip O'Neill received some shrewd advice from his father, who said: "All politics is local." During his long career in the House of Representatives, O'Neill would repeat that advice to new members. What he meant was that regardless of the issue, representatives must consider the interests, needs, and opinions of their own local district. "You can be the most important congressman in the country, but you had better not forget the people back home," he would tell them. When members become so involved in national issues that they lose connection with their own constituents, then the next election might send them packing. Keeping his father's advice in mind, O'Neill

won reelection repeatedly. He served for 34 years in the House, becoming Democratic whip, majority leader, and Speaker of the House. From 1981 through 1986, when the Republicans held the majority in the Senate and Ronald Reagan was President, Speaker O'Neill found himself the highest-ranking Democrat in the federal government. Although O'Neill had little success in opposing Reagan's conservative economic program, he was able to marshal House Democrats to prevent the dismantling of federal health, education, and social welfare programs.

FURTHER READING

O'Neill, Thomas P., Jr., and William Novak. *Man of the House: The Life and Political Memoirs of Speaker Tip O'Neill.* New York: Random House, 1987.

Oratory

THE ERA before the Civil War was known as the golden age of debate, when oratory, the art of public speaking, flourished in Congress. But the quality of oratory in Congress declined substantially in later years. Modern visitors to the galleries who expect to hear great speech making or dramatic debates are often disappointed to find someone reading a dry and technical speech to a largely empty chamber. Regardless of the empty chairs, members speak to establish a record of support for or disapproval of some legislation, as their words are recorded in the *Congressional Record* and broadcast on television.

By contrast, the speeches of many 19th-century senators and representatives could pack the chambers and the galleries. Daniel Webster (Whig–Massachusetts), for instance, used oratory to sway public opinion and influence his colleagues' votes. Such speeches carried great moral and intellectual authority and were reprinted widely in newspapers and pamphlets. Students memorized the most stirring passages. Eloquence and the skillful use of rhetoric helped establish a member's reputation as a wise statesman. By the 20th century, members known for oratory, such as Everett M. Dirksen (Republican–Illinois), seemed amusingly eccentric.

Many factors eroded the use of oratory as a legislative tool. To speed business, in 1847 the House, with its many members, established a five-minute rule limiting how long its members could speak on amendments. When the new House and Senate chambers were opened in the late 1850s, poor acoustics made it more difficult for speakers to be heard; one representative called the House chamber "the worst place in America for a man to speak." Not for another century would microphones be installed for amplification.

Styles of political campaigning also changed. Stump speaking (addressing a crowd usually from an elevated area or impromptu stage) required strong lungs, a loud voice, and colorful language to reach and hold audiences. But the introduction of television required members of Congress to tone down their voices and their rhetoric for the new "cool" medium. Long, thoughtful speeches might establish a record, but only a few seconds would ever be carried on an evening news broadcast. So politicians learned to use catchy phrases, and sound bites replaced oratory.

Effective legislators also suspect that most floor speeches are aimed more at attracting attention from the media and constituents at home than at persuading colleagues. Senator Warren Magnuson (Democrat–Washington) summed up this attitude: "If you've got the votes, you don't need a speech. If you need the speech, you don't have the votes."

SEE ALSO
Debate; Webster, Daniel

FURTHER READING
Cmiel, Kenneth. *Democratic Eloquence: The Fight over Popular Speech in Nineteenth-Century America*. New York: Morrow, 1990.

Organized crime investigation (1950)

THE FIRST nationally televised congressional investigation looked into the underworld of organized crime in the United States. The hearings drew a large audience and made the special investigating committee's chairman, Estes Kefauver (Democrat–Tennessee), a major contender for his party's Presidential nomination. A notable moment occurred when mobster Frank Costello refused to allow the television cameras to film his face while he testified. Instead, the cameras followed Costello's hands,

Senator Estes Kefauver (second from left) chaired a 1960 investigation into organized crime.

whose nervous gestures betrayed his otherwise cool appearance. Although the Kefauver hearings had little impact on legislation, they provided the first indication of the power that the new medium of television would have in future investigations.

SEE ALSO

Investigations; Media coverage of Congress

FURTHER READING

Gorman, Joseph Bruce. *Kefauver: A Political Biography*. New York: Oxford, 1971.

"Other body"

WHEN VICE PRESIDENT Thomas Jefferson wrote his manual of parliamentary procedure, he observed that it was poor form for members of one house of Congress to refer to the debates or actions of the other house. "The opinion of each house should be left to its own independency," Jefferson wrote, "not to be influenced by the proceedings of the other." In this spirit of independence, and in an effort to avoid misunderstanding and ill will between the two bodies, members of the House generally do not mention the Senate by name and simply call it the "other body." Senators, who no longer use Jefferson's manual as part of their rules, are more likely to refer to the House by name, although by tradition they do not speak critically of the House or question the motives of its members. House members find "other body" preferable to "upper body" when referring to the Senate and consider the phrase more in keeping with the equality of the two chambers.

SEE ALSO

Jefferson's manual; "Upper house"

Oversight

IN GENERAL usage, *oversight* usually means something that has been forgotten or overlooked. But in Congress it means just the opposite. When Congress performs its oversight functions, it is supervising, or looking over, the business of executive branch departments. The Legislative Reorganization Act of 1946 assigned to each committee or subcommittee with jurisdiction over legislation relating to a particular agency, or with the power to appropriate its funds, the power to exercise "continuous watchfulness" over that agency. Through their oversight functions, congressional committees monitor how well agencies are administering the laws and if they are spending federal money properly. The General Accounting Office conducts regular audits of agency finances. Committees also call agency heads to testify during oversight hearings. By contrast to investigations, which are usually special hearings concerned with a single issue or event, oversight is a regular, year-to-year, ongoing procedure. Consequently, Congress's oversight functions get less attention from the media than do splashier investigations.

SEE ALSO

General Accounting Office (GAO); Investigations; Legislative Reorganization Acts (1946 and 1970)

FURTHER READING

Oleszek, Walter J. "Legislative Oversight." In *Congressional Procedures and Policy Process*. Washington, D.C.: Congressional Quarterly, 1989.
Ripley, Randall B. *Congress: Process and Policy*. New York: Norton, 1988.

Pages

DURING EACH session of Congress, high school juniors from every state work as pages for the House and Senate. Dressed in blue uniforms, they sit on either side of the presiding officers in the chambers, ready to run errands, set up podiums for speakers, and generally help out in the chambers and cloakrooms. From 6:15 A.M. to 10:30 A.M. they attend high school classes at a special page school before beginning their daily duties for Congress.

The term *page* dates back to the medieval European practice of having youths serve as attendants to knights and other nobles. In 1827 the House appointed its first pages, Charles B. Chalmers, Edward Dunn, and John C. Burch. Shortly afterward, Senator Daniel Webster employed 9-year-old Grafton Dulany Hanson and 12-year-old Isaac Bassett as the Senate's first two pages. Bassett devoted the next 64 years of his life to Senate service, working as a messenger and doorkeeper. John Burch similarly spent a long career on Capitol Hill and was eventually elected secretary of the Senate. Other pages grew up to win election as senators and representatives, including Senator David Pryor (Democrat–Arkansas) and Representative John Dingell, Jr. (Democrat–Michigan).

Before the Capitol was wired for electricity and signal bells were installed, pages raced from room to room summoning members to vote. Before telephones, pages rode horseback to the White House and executive depart-

Pages carry boxes of electoral ballots to be counted at a joint session of Congress.

Senator George Wharton Pepper played baseball with the pages outside the Capitol during the 1920s.

ments, delivering bills and correspondence. Pages also worked as the first telephone operators in the Capitol. Although technology replaced these functions, pages can still be seen darting through the Capitol carrying messages for the members.

Initially, only boys served as pages. The first female page, Gene Cox, the 13-year-old daughter of Representative Eugene Cox (Democrat–Georgia), served for a single day in 1939. Not until the 1970s were girls as well as boys regularly appointed congressional pages. One page described her experiences as "a chance to watch [Congress] day by day. . . . When you look at one piece—one day—it means nothing, but after a while you discover how it all fits and locks together."

FURTHER READING

Severn, Bill. *Democracy's Messengers: The Capitol Pages.* New York: Hawthorn, 1975.

Pair voting

A SENATOR or representative who expects to be absent during a recorded vote (in which a member's name will be listed as voting yea or nay) can arrange to be paired with another member who plans to vote the opposite way and is also going to be absent. With this voluntary agreement the two absent members show how they would have voted and that their votes would not have changed the final result. If one of the pair is present for the vote, it is called a "live pair." In a live pair the member votes "present" and announces how the pair of them would have voted on that issue. Paired votes appear in the *Congressional Record* at the end of the recorded vote tally.

Parliamentarian

THE RULES of the Senate and House are few in number, but the precedents— the previous actions of the two bodies and the rulings of their presiding officers—are voluminous. The accumulated precedents serve as guides for future actions. In order to operate properly within the boundaries of these precedents, and to plan strategies for passing or defeating legislation, the Senate and House each appoint staff members to serve as parliamentarians.

Before the 1920s various clerks kept track of the rules and precedents and offered advice to the presiding officers. In 1928 Speaker Nicholas Longworth appointed Lewis Deschler as the first House parliamentarian. It was a tribute to Deschler's nonpartisanship that he continued in the job until 1974, through both Republican and Democratic majorities. In 1937 Charles Watkins became the Senate's first official parliamentarian, and he, too, remained in his post under both parties until his retirement in 1964.

"Ventriloquists"

The parliamentarian sits at the front desk, immediately below the presiding officer. When a question about some matter of parliamentary procedure arises from the floor, the presiding officer leans over and consults the parliamentarian. Because the presiding officers invariably announce aloud exactly what the parliamentarians have just whispered, the parliamentarians have been called the "ventriloquists" of the House and Senate. But presiding officers have learned the wisdom of following the parliamentarian's advice. Those who ignore the parliamentarian and rule differently face being overridden by a majority vote of the House or Senate. Some members of Congress rely entirely on the parliamentarian for advice, while others study the rules and precedents independently and win recognition on Capitol Hill for their mastery of parliamentary procedure. These members are often members of the minority who can be especially effective in using their knowledge of the rules to block passage of legislation that the majority favors.

The parliamentarians are responsible for publishing the collected precedents of their chamber so that members and staff can become aware of them. Recently, the precedents have also been compiled in computers, and terminals have been installed at the front desks, giving the parliamentarians much faster access. Parliamentarians try to avoid taking sides in parliamentary disputes, and they offer advice to the leaders and members of both parties.

SEE ALSO

Parliamentary procedure; Precedents; Rules, House and Senate

FURTHER READING

Riddick, Floyd M., and Alan S. Frumin. *Riddick's Senate Procedure: Precedents and Practices*. Washington, D.C.: Government Printing Office, 1992.

Parliamentary government

MOST NATIONAL legislatures around the world operate under parliamentary systems that are very different from the U.S. government under which Congress operates. Parliamentary governments separate the ceremonial head of state (the king, queen, or president) from the political head of government (the prime minister or premier). Though most parliaments have two chambers, the upper body, such as the British House of Lords, may be hereditary (members inherit their seat from family members) rather than elected and is usually very limited in its powers. The popularly elected lower house, such as the British House of Commons, holds the real legislative power.

In the British House of Commons, the parties sit facing each other.

The majority party in the lower house elects the prime minister, who appoints cabinet secretaries from among other members of the parliamentary majority. The leader of the opposition party appoints a "shadow" cabinet as a counterpart to promote the minority party's interests. If the prime minister's party loses its majority through the death, resignation, or defection of some of its members, or if it loses on a major issue, then new parliamentary elections are held. The British Parliament also developed the "vote of confidence" procedure by which members of the majority party are called to stand in a new election with their prime minister. A prime minister who loses a vote of confidence will call for a new election. Party loyalty and regularity are therefore essential in parliamentary governments. In parliamentary systems where the major parties are unable to win a clear majority, they must enter into coalitions with one or more minor parties or hold new elections.

The legislative chambers of parliamentary governments even look unlike the Congress. U.S. senators and representatives sit in semicircular rows facing the presiding officer, with the center aisle separating the parties. By contrast, in the British House of Commons and many other similar legislatures, members of Parliament (MPs) sit with opposing parties facing each other. On key issues, MPs line up to vote (a procedure called a division). Those who choose not to vote with their party must walk to the other side, a physical act that requires considerable political courage. Party defections are therefore much more rare in a parliamentary government than in Congress, where members feel free to vote according to their conscience and are not bound to follow their party's leaders.

Parliamentary governments usually feature a question period when members may address questions directly to the prime minister and cabinet secretaries, who appear personally in the chamber to respond. The U.S. Congress cannot call the President to answer such questions, but congressional committees regularly call upon cabinet secretaries to testify.

Parliamentary systems offer efficient and effective leadership under majority rule, but they also diminish minority rights. In nations where one party holds the overwhelming majority, this situation can foster a "tyranny of the majority" and "constitutional dictatorship." The U.S. system of separation of powers and of checks and balances is less efficient, but it is deliberately so, to prevent the development of arbitrary power.

FURTHER READING

Pious, Richard M., "A Prime Minister for America?" *Constitution* 4 (Fall 1992): 4-12.

Parliamentary procedure

"SO MUCH of what we do around here [in Congress]," House Republican leader Robert Michel observed, "is determined by how we do it." Parliamentary procedure is the "how" by which Congress operates. It is the collected rules and precedents—the previous actions of the Senate and House and rulings of their presiding officers. It is also the customs, courtesies, and accepted behavior of Congress. Parliamentary procedure establishes the daily routines of the House and Senate. It sets the ways in which members seek recognition on the floor, address the chair and each other, introduce bills and resolutions, and seek to win the passage of legislation

The gavel used by the Senate's presiding officer.

or to block it through objections, amendments, filibusters, and other tactics within the rules of order.

The United States inherited its basic parliamentary procedures from the British Parliament during the colonial era. New England town meetings and colonial legislatures followed these traditional methods of operating, as did the Continental Congress, the Congress under the Articles of Confederation, the Constitutional Convention, and the U.S. Congress. In 1801 President Thomas Jefferson published the first volume of parliamentary procedure in the United States, known as Jefferson's manual, which is still part of the House rules.

The House and Senate adopt their own rules and set precedents by their actions. Parliamentarians on the staff of both houses compile and study these rules and precedents in order to advise the presiding officers on how to keep the floor proceedings moving fairly and properly.

To casual visitors in the galleries, the procedures on the House and Senate floor may seem excessively formal. But the parliamentary procedure that they are witnessing evolved over 200 years of legislative activity to enable the Senate and House to function in ways that are reasonably fair and efficient. The procedures prevent presiding officers from ruling arbitrarily, and they ensure that both sides have an opportunity to be heard and to offer their own bills and amendments. Although their emotions often rise over the immediate issues before them, members of Congress have adopted parliamentary procedures that enable them to operate in a rational and orderly manner.

SEE ALSO

Jefferson's manual; Precedents; Rules, House and Senate

The first recorded meeting of the Republican party took place in this Ripon, Wisconsin, schoolhouse on March 20, 1854.

Party organizations

DEMOCRATIC AND Republican party organizations in the Senate and House help the members of the two parties formulate and defend their programs and get enough members elected to enact them. The basic party organization is the conference or caucus, made up of all the members of one party in that house, such as all the Democrats in the House of Representatives or all the Republicans in the Senate. The conference elects its own chairman (the Democratic floor leader also chairs the Senate Democratic Conference, and the other conferences or caucuses elect separate floor leaders and chairs) and secretary. The conferences also elect the Speaker of the House, the president pro tempore of the Senate, and the majority and minority floor leaders and whips for each chamber. The party conferences also appoint steering committees to assign members of that party to congressional committees.

Although the parties are essentially private organizations, the Legislative Reorganization Act of 1946 acknowledged their legitimate role in the operations of the Congress by enabling each major party to establish a Policy Committee and by funding their staffs. Congress also funds the operations of the majority and minority party secretaries, elected staff members who assist the floor leaders.

Republican and Democratic Senatorial Campaign Committees and Congressional Campaign Committees are appointed by the party conferences to raise funds and otherwise assist party candidates for election to Congress.

SEE ALSO
Caucuses; Majority leader; Minority leader

Patronage

THE AWARDING of government jobs on the basis of political ties or favors is known as patronage—that is, a patron or official sponsor arranged the job. During the first century of the federal government, almost all nonelected posts went by patronage to elected officials' supporters and fellow party members. After each election, the patronage jobholders from the losing party found themselves out of work. "To the victor belongs the spoils," explained Secretary of State William L. Marcy. (Patronage was also called the "spoils system.")

Patronage helped build political party organizations, but many patronage appointees were poorly qualified for their jobs. Election turnovers disrupted agency operations and removed experienced staff. Office seekers besieged members of Congress and new Presidents, demanding high government jobs in return for their party service. After a disappointed job seeker shot and killed President James Garfield in 1881, Congress enacted the first civil service law in 1883. It required the executive branch to assign most jobs according to merit rather than political influence. To obtain a civil service position, an applicant must take a qualifying examination or demonstrate sufficient professional training and experience. Once appointed, civil servants cannot be fired for political reasons. The Office of Personnel Management now enforces all rules relating to civil service hiring. Even after establishing a civil service system for the executive branch, however, Congress continued to assign most of its own jobs according to patronage. At first this was because Congress met for only half the year and hired a small staff for only those months. Only a few committees, such as Finance, Ways and Means, Printing, and Claims, which received correspondence and other documents even after Congress had adjourned, were authorized to employ a year-round staff. Members of the House and Senate appointed their own office staffs. Sometimes members appointed their wives, children, and other relatives as their secretaries, messengers, or committee clerks, a practice known as nepotism. New ethics laws eventually outlawed nepotism, but members continued to appoint their campaign supporters to posts in their own offices and committees and to other jobs around the Capitol. Both parties had patronage commit-

A 19th-century member of Congress presents constituents who were seeking federal jobs.

tees to assign clerks, elevator operators, and Capitol police to their members for patronage appointments.

Patronage began to decline after World War II, as Congress began to meet on a year-round basis and as the growth in members' personal staffs relieved the pressure of making patronage appointments elsewhere. But outside of members' own offices (where staffs generally reflect the member's political leaning), the trend in the general operations of Congress has continued toward a permanent, professional, and nonpartisan staff.

Perks

ELECTED OFFICIALS enjoy many benefits of office, known as perquisites, or "perks." Members of Congress send mail free of charge, park in special lots at Washington airports, and are reimbursed for trips they make to their home state and abroad. At the Capitol they have special subways, elevators, restaurants, low-cost gymnasiums, shops that offer discount-price supplies, and free plants from the Botanical Gardens to decorate their offices. Some congressional leaders are also assigned cars and drivers.

Critics of perks argue that the people's representatives should not receive special privileges at the taxpayers' expense. But questions arise about what privileges are necessary for the performance of congressional duties. Members need to keep in close contact with their constituents, which requires extensive communication and travel. They maintain homes in Washington and in their home state and have to decide where to raise their family. They must get to the floor quickly to vote, and their crowded daily schedules give them little time to shop, dine, or even get their hair trimmed away from

the Capitol. They exercise in the Capitol gyms to keep fit and to relieve the stress of their job.

Over the years, members have viewed perks in different ways. In the 1st Congress James Madison declined to accept the free stationery supplies provided to each representative but noted that he was "the sole exception." In the 1920s a reporter tried to question Senator William E. Borah (Republican–Idaho) about the then-free haircuts for members. Borah grumbled, "You tell that reporter to go to the devil. I want the same service that was received here by Henry Clay and John C. Calhoun." But periodic criticism by the press and by constituents has caused Congress to abandon such perks as free haircuts and shaving mugs and to raise the costs of other services so that they are more in line with costs elsewhere. In 1992 the House abolished its 150-year-old bank after published reports revealed that members had been able to bounce checks—that is, write checks for more money than they had deposited—without penalty. Although no public funds were involved, voters saw the House bank scandal as just another example of a perk that allowed members of Congress to operate under different rules than did average citizens.

S E E   A L S O
House bank scandal (1992)

Persian Gulf debate (1991)

AFTER IRAQ invaded Kuwait in August 1990, threatening the world's oil supplies, President George Bush sent American troops to the Persian Gulf. Claiming this was a defensive action—and calling it Operation Desert Shield—to protect neighboring Saudi Arabia, the President did not initially ask for congressional approval. But in January 1991 the President sought congressional approval to use military force—Operation Desert Storm—in support of United Nations resolutions that set a deadline for Iraq to withdraw from Kuwait.

Recalling that in 1964 the Gulf of Tonkin Resolution had led to the Vietnam War, senators and representatives recognized that their approval would be the equivalent of a declaration of war. With a large national audience watching on television, Congress held a dramatic debate over the Persian Gulf Resolution. Most Republicans supported the President, while most Democrats favored continuing the use of economic sanctions against Iraq. But enough Democrats joined Republicans to pass the Persian Gulf Resolution by a vote of 52 to 47 in the Senate and 250 to 183 in the House. Combat began four days later, and U.S.-led forces drove Iraq out of Kuwait. Notable in this incident was Congress's failure to invoke the War Powers Act, which raised serious doubts about that act's effectiveness. Under the War Powers Act, military troops must be withdrawn from combat after 60 days unless Congress has declared war or otherwise authorized the use of military force. The President's supporters in Congress believed that applying the War Powers Act would limit his ability to act.

Opponents of the war feared that triggering the War Powers Act would actually sanction the use of the military in combat for 60 days. Therefore, neither side called for enforcement of the War Powers Act.

SEE ALSO
Gulf of Tonkin Resolution (1964); War powers

Petition, citizens' right to

THE 1ST Amendment to the Constitution guarantees citizens the right "to petition the Government for a redress of grievances." People have readily exercised this right, sending Congress petitions on any number of issues. A petitioner can be a single individual or a long list of signatures. In the early 19th century, reformers petitioned Congress to ban alcohol, abolish slavery, and give the vote to women. After the Civil War, many individuals (known as claimants)

Lobbyists and citizens petitioning their senator in an 1882 cartoon.

petitioned the government for military pensions or for compensation for property destroyed during the war. During the depression of the late 1920s and 1930s, Congress received petitions to improve roads, censor the movies, and provide economic relief.

When citizens write to their senators and representatives for help with their Social Security payments, veterans' pensions, and other problems with the bureaucracy, they are utilizing their right to petition.

Pocket veto

S E E Veto

Point of order

S E E Precedents

Political action committees (PACs)

S E E Campaign financing

Political parties in Congress

THE AUTHORS of the U.S. Constitution hoped that the federal government could avoid political parties. They wanted a government run by independent-minded people who served out of a sense of civic virtue. They envisioned parties ("factions") as the tool of the politically ambitious and as a source of corruption. However, not long after the new government began, many of those who opposed parties became the founders and leaders of political parties. They discovered that a two-party system could contribute to the constitutional system of checks and balances. The competing parties would help keep any one group from becoming powerful enough to threaten citizens' rights.

First parties in Congress

Although they were not as organized as modern political parties, identifiable parties first emerged in the 1790s. The Federalist party consolidated those who supported the policies of the Washington administration, particularly the financial program of Treasury Secretary Alexander Hamilton. In 1792 James Madison and Thomas Jefferson launched an opposition Democratic-Republican party, which gained the majority in the House of Representatives that year. Opposing a strong, activist central government, Democratic-Republicans rallied against Hamilton's programs. Their strength in Congress came largely from Southern and Western districts, while the Federalists were strongest in New England. By 1800 political caucuses in Congress were selecting their party's Presidential candidates. The Federalist party shrank steadily until it expired in the essentially one-party Era of Good Feelings after the War of 1812.

The second party system

During the 1820s the political system split apart again. Denouncing "King Caucus"—the congressionally dominated system of nominating Presidential candidates—Andrew Jackson won the Presidency in 1828. Behind the scenes, New York Senator Martin Van Buren built a new political instrument, the Democratic party, to support Jackson's policies. Jackson's veto of a bill renewing the charter of the Bank of the United

THE BALANCE OF POWER.
The Political Complexion of the next Senate.

In 1881, when the Senate was evenly divided, both parties courted Senators David Davis (below) and William Mahone (above) to switch sides and break the tie.

States in 1832 led to the rise of the opposition Whig party. Kentucky Senator Henry Clay served as the Whigs' leader in Congress. By the 1840s the two parties had become such permanent fixtures on Capitol Hill that they took over the assignment of senators and representatives to committees and shaped much of the daily operations of Congress. Party leaders began to emerge in the House, while senators continued to insist that because they were all equal, they needed no formal leadership. The Democrats and Whigs were both national parties—that is, they elected members from every region of the country. Then, in the 1850s, agitation over the slavery issue disrupted these national coalitions. New parties such as the Free Soil and American (Know-Nothing) parties emerged but did not attract a majority of the voters. By 1856 the new Republican party had absorbed these smaller parties and supplanted the Whigs as the chief opposition to the Democrats.

Republicans versus Democrats

The election of 1860, followed by the secession of the Southern states, gave the Republicans control of the White House and the majority in both houses of Congress. The Republicans remained the majority party for the rest of the 19th century, although after the last of the Southern states had been readmitted to the Union in 1870, Democrats often controlled one of the houses of Congress. The "solid South," consisting of the 11 former Confederate states, remained overwhelmingly Democratic. The North, with the exception of such major cities as New York and Boston, remained overwhelmingly Republican. Border states and some Midwestern and Western states swung back and forth, changing the majorities in Congress. When the Republican party's conservative and progressive wings split apart in 1912 (with Theodore Roosevelt leading the progressives in a campaign for greater social, economic, and political reform), Woodrow Wilson won the Presidency and Democrats captured the House and Senate. Six years later the Republicans regained their congressional majorities, which they held until the stock market crash of 1929 and the Great Depression that followed. It was during the 1920s that the two parties formally elected majority and minority leaders in the Senate.

The long Democratic majority

In the 1930s New Deal programs to combat the depression won widespread popular approval, and Democratic majorities in Congress grew to enormous proportions. At their peak, after the 1936 election, there were 76 Democrats in the Senate (opposed to 16 Republicans and 4 independents) and 334 Democrats in the House (opposed to 88 Republicans and 13 independents). For the next six decades, with only rare exceptions, the

Democrats retained their majorities in Congress, even when they lost the White House to the Republicans.

Third parties

Although a two-party system has prevailed through most of American history, many third parties have appeared and have elected members to Congress. Third parties generally have had more success in winning election in smaller House districts than in statewide Senate races. In the 19th century, the Anti-Masonic, Nullifiers, American (Know-Nothing), Free Soil, States' Rightists, Unionists, Constitutional Union, Liberal Republican, National (Greenback), People's (Populist), and Silver Republican parties all sent members to Congress. Third parties in the 20th century have included the Socialist, Progressive (Bull Moose), Prohibition, and Conservative parties.

If a third party is large enough, its members can form their own caucus, as the Progressives did after the 1912 election. But usually they are too few in number and choose to join either the Republican or Democratic caucus, which will give them their committee assignments. The major parties are not always tolerant of third parties, however. Victor Berger of Wisconsin became the first Socialist elected to Congress, serving in the House from 1911 to 1913. Although he was elected again in 1918 and 1920, the House refused to let him take his seat because of his opposition to U.S. participation in World War I.

SEE ALSO

Caucuses

FURTHER READING

Martis, Kenneth C. *The Historical Atlas of Political Parties in the United States Congress, 1789–1989.* New York: Macmillan, 1989.

Pork barrel politics

WHEN MEMBERS of Congress try to gain federal funds for projects in their district or state, they are often accused of playing "pork barrel politics." This curious expression dates back to the days of plantation slavery before the Civil War, when field hands dipped into large barrels of salt pork for their food. Similarly, those senators and representatives who win special projects for their constituents are "bringing home the bacon."

Legislation authorizing improvements in rivers and harbors, flood control and dams, construction of federal buildings, and highway construction traditionally caused members to scramble to get something in for their state or district. More recently, energy and defense appropriations bills have attracted pork barrel amendments. Members of Congress defend their pork barrel efforts as a way of more evenly distributing federal money throughout the nation. But critics charge that Congress often diverts funds to projects and places not out of national need but to enhance members' chances of reelection. Senator Norris Cotton (Republican–New Hampshire), who served on the Appropriations Committee, spoke for many when he called pork barrel politics "one of the worst features of the whole system of federal grants and subsidies."

Pork barrel politics has become associated with a variety of colorful legislative terms. When members seize upon a bill that the President is likely to sign into law and then add pork barrel amendments, it is called a "Christmas tree" bill. Special projects are hung upon the bill the way ornaments adorn a Christmas tree. When Congress specifies exactly where and how federal money should be spent—for example, specifying the awarding of a grant to a certain university to conduct weapons research—it is "earmarking" the funds, just as some farm animals are marked on the ear to identify who owns them. And when members trade their votes for each other's pork barrel projects, the practice is called "logrolling." This expression dates back to the frontier practice of neighbors working together to clear their farmland and gather logs for building their homes, barns, and fences. Whoever helped his neighbors in logrolling would receive their help in return.

FURTHER READING

Cotton, Norris. *In the Senate: Amidst the Conflict and the Turmoil.* New York: Dodd, Mead, 1978.

Powell, Adam Clayton, Jr.

☆ *Born: Nov. 29, 1908, New Haven, Conn.*
☆ *Political party: Democrat*
☆ *Representative from New York: 1945–67, 1969–71*
☆ *Died: Apr. 4, 1972, Miami, Fla.*

ADAM CLAYTON Powell excelled in the politics of confrontation. An African American, he won election to Congress in 1944, when racial segregation existed in much of the country and when Southerners who advocated white supremacy chaired most of the congressional committees. Instead of acting deferentially and seeking compromise, Powell ridiculed segregation, attacked discrimination, and promoted equality and civil rights at every opportunity. He set out to be an "irritant," believing that "whenever a person keeps prodding, keeps them squirming . . . it serves a purpose." Between 1950 and 1960, he repeatedly

attached a "Powell Amendment" to other bills, seeking to ban federal funds for segregated facilities.

Seniority eventually made him chairman of the House Committee on Education and Labor, where he managed many important bills. But Powell's antagonistic style worked better when he was an "outsider" rather than an "insider." Friends and enemies alike found him increasingly unreliable, and he was frequently absent from the House. In 1967, after much criticism of his behavior, the House removed Powell as committee chairman and voted not to seat him as a member. The Supreme Court ruled 7 to 1 that Powell's exclusion had been unconstitutional. He won his seat back in a special election. But by 1970 Powell's constituents had lost patience, and they defeated him in the Democratic primary when he ran for renomination.

SEE ALSO

African Americans in Congress; Insurgents

FURTHER READING

Hamilton, Charles. *Adam Clayton Powell, Jr.: The Political Biography of an American Dilemma.* New York: Macmillan, 1991.
Powell, Adam Clayton. *Adam by Adam.* New York: Dial, 1971.

Precedents

THE RULES of the House and Senate are relatively few in number, but each time that either body interprets those rules, it establishes a precedent, or guide to future behavior. Senate and House precedents number in the thousands. A member who objects to some procedural action on the floor will rise to make a point of order. The presiding officer will then rule on the point of order, based on the parliamentarian's reading of the rules and precedents. If no one appeals the ruling, then it becomes a new precedent. If members object to the chair's ruling, they can vote by a simple majority to overturn the ruling—and in their own way set a precedent. Precedents established by a vote carry the greatest weight in future actions. However, a different majority voting at a different time can reverse an earlier precedent.

For instance, the rules of the Senate prohibit a senator from making more than two speeches on the same subject in a single day. In 1935 the presiding officer ruled that if a senator made a motion to suggest the absence of a quorum (that not enough members were present to conduct business), the motion counted as a "speech." Over the next 50 years that precedent was rarely applied, but in 1986 one senator objected that another senator had spoken twice against a bill—including suggesting the absence of a quorum—and should not speak again. Citing the 1935 precedent, the presiding officer agreed. A heated debate followed, and by a vote of 92 to 5 the senators overturned the chair's ruling, voided the 1935 precedent, and thereby set a new precedent for the future.

Those involved in planning legislative strategy must know the precedents as well as the rules. Because there are so many precedents, the House and Senate parliamentarians from time to time publish volumes of the precedents, arranged by subject. Computer programs have also compiled

precedents for the parliamentarians' ready access during debate.

SEE ALSO
Parliamentarian; Parliamentary procedure; Rules, House and Senate

Presidential relations with Congress

THE PRESIDENT and Congress both share and compete for power. The Constitution suggests Presidential involvement in legislation in two ways: First, in the annual State of the Union message the President may recommend for Congress's consideration "such measures as he shall judge necessary" (Article 2, Section 3). Second, the President can veto measures he disapproves of (though the veto is subject to being overridden by a two-thirds vote of both the House and Senate) (Article 1, Section 7). Though 19th-century Presidents often

President Dwight D. Eisenhower (right) shared a laugh with House Speaker Sam Rayburn (left) and other members of Congress.

adopted a passive role, limiting themselves to administering the laws that Congress enacted, modern Presidents have defined their role as "chief legislator" as well as "chief executive" and have attempted to exert strong influence over Congress.

As the leader of his political party, the President tends to work through his party in Congress. When a President's party holds the majority in Congress, the likelihood of passing the President's legislative program is great. When a President's party is in the minority, stalemate can occur, a situation that has been called the "deadlock of democracy." When such a "divided government" occurs, Presidents can seek to build bipartisan policies, as Democratic President Harry S. Truman did in promoting a bipartisan foreign policy during the Republican 80th Congress (1947–49). Alternatively, they can lambast Congress for opposing their policies and being a "do nothing" Congress, as Truman did effectively during the election of 1948.

Mandates to lead

Popular Presidents who have won election by a large margin assert that they have a mandate to lead. Under these circumstances, Congress will often follow the President's lead on the assumption that his program represents the popular will. But members of Congress also feel they have a mandate from their constituents, and they will often remain fiercely independent from Presidential leadership. Franklin D. Roosevelt won reelection by one of the largest margins in history in 1936, but the next year Congress blocked his plan to "pack" the Supreme Court, feeling he had overstepped himself. House Speaker Sam Rayburn, whose service in Congress extended from the Presidency of Woodrow Wilson to John F. Kennedy, insisted that he served *under* no President, "but I have

served *with* eight of them."

Since a President's success is often judged by his ability to win passage of legislation, he spends much time trying to convince Congress to support him. In addition to personal addresses to Congress, Presidents assign certain staff members to act as liaisons with the Senate and House, lobbying for the administration's proposals and finding out what members of Congress want from the administration in return. Presidents will telephone members to solicit their votes, invite them to the White House, and otherwise twist arms, appeal to patriotism, and offer favors in return for congressional support. When all else fails, Presidents can use the threat of vetoing legislation as a means to force at least a compromise.

Disputes over foreign policy

In dealing with military and foreign policies, Presidents have often acted independently of Congress. Although Congress has the constitutional power to declare war, and the Senate ratifies treaties and confirms diplomatic nominations, Presidents often take action without consulting first with Congress. Congressional leaders complain that they are called in for briefings only after the major decisions have been made and that Presidents seek their consent rather than their advice. Members of Congress expressed a desire to be consulted during the takeoff as well as during the crash landing. They enacted the War Powers Act in 1973 to require the President to notify them whenever he sent troops into a combat situation.

FURTHER READING

Bond, John R., and Richard Fleisher. *The President in the Legislative Arena.* Chicago: University of Chicago Press, 1990.

Burns, James McGregor. *The Deadlock of Democracy: Four-Party Politics in America.* Englewood Cliffs, N.J.: Prentice-Hall, 1963.

Presidential succession, congressional role in

IF A PRESIDENT dies or resigns, the Constitution provides for the Vice President to succeed to the office. But if the Vice President for some reason cannot assume the Presidency, then by law the Congress determines who will become President. In the 19th century, the president pro tempore of the Senate, who replaced the Vice President as presiding officer of the Senate, stood next in line. Had the Senate removed President Andrew Johnson from office in 1868, President pro tempore Benjamin Wade would have become president. After the death of Vice President Thomas Hendricks in November 1885, Senator George F. Hoar (Republican–Massachusetts) pointed out the absence of both a Speaker of the House and a president pro tempore of the Senate during the long break between the Congress that ended its term on March 3 after an election and the next Congress that began on the first Monday in December, as speci-

Vice President Harry Truman took the Presidential oath of office after the death of President Franklin D. Roosevelt in 1945.

fied by the Constitution (Article 1, Section 4). In 1886 Congress changed the law to put members of the cabinet next in line of succession, beginning with the secretary of state. But when Harry S. Truman became President following the death of Franklin D. Roosevelt in 1945, Truman thought it wrong to elevate nonelected officials to the Presidency. At Truman's urging, Congress changed the Act of Presidential Succession to put the Speaker of the House and president pro tempore of the Senate (both offices described in the Constitution) ahead of the cabinet members in the line of succession.

The 25th Amendment to the Constitution, ratified in 1967, further affected Presidential succession by allowing the President to appoint—with the advice and consent of Congress—someone to fill a vacancy in the Vice Presidency. Even so, when the President delivers the annual State of the Union message, in the presence of the Vice President, Speaker, president pro tempore, the cabinet, and the Congress, one member of the cabinet always remains absent. This assures that one person in the line of succession will be able to assume the Presidency in case some tragedy befalls all the others.

SEE ALSO
President pro tempore of the Senate; Speaker of the House; Vice President

President pro tempore of the Senate

THE CONSTITUTION (Article 1, Section 3) requires the Senate to elect a president pro tempore (*pro tempore* is a Latin phrase meaning "for the time being") to serve as presiding officer when the Vice President is absent. The president pro tempore can preside over the Senate, swear in senators, and sign legislation. Originally, when Vice Presidents presided daily over the Senate, presidents pro tempore were elected to serve only during a particular absence of the Vice President or for the duration of the term of a Vice President who died in office or succeeded to the Presidency. In the 5th Congress (1797–99), for instance, the Senate elected five different presidents pro tem. To give the office more continuity, in 1890 the Senate changed the term of president pro tempore to last until another was elected, so the term might last for several Congresses. During the 20th century the Senate began electing the senior member of the majority party as president pro tem, to hold the office until he retired or his party lost the majority.

The seal of the Senate president pro tempore

Since modern Vice Presidents generally appear in the Senate only for ceremonial occasions or to break tie votes, the president pro tem opens each session and then assigns junior senators in the majority party to take rotating turns presiding during the day's session. The president pro tempore also stands third in line, behind the Vice President and Speaker of the House, in the order of Presidential succession.

SEE ALSO

Officers of the House and Senate; Vice President

FURTHER READING

Byrd, Robert C. "The President Pro Tempore." In *The Senate, 1789–1989: Addresses on the History of the United States Senate*. Vol. 2. Washington, D.C.: Government Printing Office, 1991.

Press

SEE Media coverage of Congress

Previous question

THE PREVIOUS question is a procedural device used in the House of Representatives to limit debate and avoid potentially damaging amendments by a bill's opponents. Managers of a bill can make a motion calling for the previous question —"question" in this case meaning the bill being debated. If the motion passes, no further amendments can be introduced and the House must vote on the original bill. Although the House permits this parliamentary tactic, the Senate has resisted it. Senate rules have traditionally been more tolerant of the minority and make it more difficult to cut off debate. Rather than needing a majority vote (51 percent) for the previous question, the Senate must achieve a three-fifths vote (60 percent) to invoke cloture and cut off debate.

SEE ALSO

Cloture; Motions; Parliamentary procedure

Private laws

WHEN CONGRESS acts to aid a specific individual, family, or other small group, it passes a private law. Public laws, by comparison, deal with society as a whole. The first private bill, which was passed in September 1789, awarded 17 months' back pay to a military officer. Many other private bills that followed dealt with military pensions or claims of citizens whose property was damaged during wartime. Other private bills permitted specifically named foreigners to immigrate and become naturalized citizens of the United States. By 1900 private bills far outnumbered the public bills that Congress considered. Later, Congress turned settlement of most private claims over to the executive departments and enacted more comprehensive veterans' pensions and immigration laws that reduced the need to address them case by case. Legislation has also more narrowly defined the circumstances in which Congress will consider private claims. However, Congress continues to enact private laws to aid citizens who have been injured by government programs or who have appealed an executive agency ruling, such as one requiring the deportation of a noncitizen. Private laws are numbered separately from public laws. During the 102nd Congress, for example, they were numbered Private Law 102-1 and up.

SEE ALSO
Acts

Pro forma sessions

VISITORS TO the galleries sometimes are puzzled to see the Senate or House come into session and then adjourn within a few seconds. Why does Congress bother with these short pro forma (a Latin phrase meaning "as a matter of form") sessions? The Constitution says that neither the Senate nor the House may adjourn for more than three days without the other's consent (Article 1, Section 5). This requirement prevents either house from trying to delay legislation by refusing to meet. Rather than always having to ask the other body's permission not to meet, the Senate or House simply holds a pro forma session in which one member gavels the chamber to order and then immediately declares it adjourned. Regardless of how briefly this session lasts, it counts as a day's session. Pro

forma sessions allow senators or representatives more time to spend in committee hearings or other business off the floor.

Protest

ON ANY day, you might observe a rally or demonstration on the Capitol grounds. Concerned citizens, labor unions, women's rights organizations, civil rights activists, environmentalists, and advocates of special interests of every kind assemble at the Capitol, unfurl their banners, listen to their speakers, and then seek out their senators and representatives to lobby for their cause.

The 1st Amendment to the Constitution protects the "right of the people peaceably to assemble," and the Capitol

Protesters gather at the U.S. Capitol on Earth Day.

has often provided the backdrop for citizens' peaceful assembly. In 1894, during a severe economic depression, Ohio business executive Jacob Coxey led an army of unemployed men and women to Washington to demand federal job programs. "General" Coxey's army reached the Capitol but was prohibited from walking on the grass or displaying any banners or signs. When Coxey stepped forward to speak, he was arrested for walking on the grass. During another great depression, in 1932, an army of Bonus Marchers appeared on the Capitol grounds. World War I army veterans assembled outside the Capitol while the Senate debated making an early bonus payment to help them through the hard times. Although many people expected trouble when the Senate voted down the Bonus Bill, the marchers sang "America" and dispersed. Later, regular army troops forced the veterans out of Washington.

During the Vietnam War in the 1960s, antiwar protestors regularly picketed and protested at the Capitol. Every January on the anniversary of the Supreme Court's 1972 ruling in *Roe v. Wade,* which legalized abortion, antiabortion protestors have marched on the Capitol. Smaller groups often gather on the Capitol steps to protest political oppression and human rights violations in their native land. Regardless of the issues, these groups can receive a permit to assemble peacefully at the Capitol to exercise their constitutional rights.

SEE ALSO
Bonus Marchers; Coxey's army

Proxy voting

WHEN MEMBERS expect to be absent from a committee meeting, they will ar-

range for a colleague to cast their vote by proxy (from a Latin word meaning "to take care of"), or written permission. The chair usually holds proxies for absent members of the majority, and at times a sole member will cast proxies for all the members of the minority. Critics call this procedure "ghost voting" and accuse absent members of not performing their job. However, those who vote by proxy may be at another committee hearing, participating in a floor debate, or conducting some other legislative business. Because of the competing demands on members' time, committees would find it difficult to carry on business without proxy voting. No proxies are allowed in roll call votes on the floor of either the House or Senate, but absent members may "pair" their vote—that is, couple it with that of another member who would have voted the opposite way to show that these two votes would not have changed the outcome.

SEE ALSO
Pair voting

Public opinion

SHOULD CONGRESS respond to public opinion, or should it try to lead it? James Madison observed that "public opinion sets bounds to every government, and is the real sovereign [ruler] in every free one." Edmund Burke, a member of the British Parliament in the 18th century, expressed a different attitude when he told his constituents, "Your representative owes you, not his industry only, but his judgment; and he betrays, instead of serving you, if he sacrifices it to your opinion."

Members of Congress generally win election because they reflect the views of

ANOTHER OLD WOMAN TRIES TO SWEEP BACK THE SEA.

President William McKinley could not sweep back the tides of public opinion demanding war with Spain.

the majority in their home state or districts. Once in office, senators and representatives keep in constant contact with their constituents. They travel home regularly, hold public meetings, circulate questionnaires in their newsletters, and read public opinion polls. Members of Congress remain keenly interested in the mail and telephone responses of their constituents to current issues, and they take these into consideration when casting their votes. "Without public opinion on its side," commented Representative Dante Fascell (Democrat–Florida), "Congress can't move very much one way or the other." Yet polls constantly change, reflecting the public's shifting moods and attitudes and indicating that effective leadership can alter public opinion.

Presidents are also aware of the pressure that public opinion can bring on Congress. Presidents often appeal their cases directly to the people through the media, encouraging citizens to write to their senators and representatives on behalf of legislation that the President wants. During his battles with Congress over Reconstruction, Andrew Johnson became the first President to give an interview for publication to a reporter. "I want to give these fellows hell," Johnson said, gesturing toward the Capitol, "and

I think I can do it better through your paper than through a message [to Congress], because the people read the papers more than they do messages." President Franklin D. Roosevelt effectively used his "fireside chats" over the radio to build public support for New Deal legislation, just as later Presidents used television to promote their programs.

SEE ALSO

Media coverage of Congress; Presidential relations with Congress

FURTHER READING

Israel, Fred L. "The Public Looks at Congress." In *Understanding Congress: Research Perspectives,* edited by Roger H. Davidson and Richard C. Sachs. Washington, D.C.: Government Printing Office, 1991.

Qualifications for membership

THE CONSTITUTION specifically lists the qualifications necessary to become a member of the House or Senate. A representative must be at least 25 years old, have been a U.S. citizen for seven years, and be a resident of the state (although not necessarily the district) from which he or she is chosen (Article 1, Section 2). A senator must be at least 30 years old, have been a citizen for nine years, and be a resident of his or her state (Article 1, Section 3).

When the House refused to seat Adam Clayton Powell, Jr., in 1967, citing his prolonged absences and other objectionable behavior, the Supreme Court ruled the action uncon-

The House denied Adam Clayton Powell, Jr., his seat in 1967.

stitutional. The Court said that no requirements besides age, citizenship, and residence could be considered in seating a member. In the earlier years, a few members served while younger than the minimum age specified by the Constitution, but no action was taken against them. Henry Clay, for instance, was only 29 when he first took his seat as a senator. When another senator questioned this, Clay responded, "I hope my colleague will propound that question to my constituents." By this Clay meant that the voters should decide who is eligible. In later years, however, Congress insisted that those elected while still too young to serve must wait until they have reached the required age before they can take the oath of office and become a member of Congress.

SEE ALSO

Clay, Henry; Powell, Adam Clayton, Jr.

Quorum

A QUORUM is the minimum attendance—half the members plus one—necessary for either the Senate or House to conduct business. If a quorum is not present, no business can be transacted. Normally, far fewer than half the senators and representatives are present on the floor. However, a quorum is assumed to be present until any member suggests its absence. When that happens, bells ring to summon absent members to the floor.

In the House, members respond to quorum calls by going to the chamber and answering when their name is called. During the 19th century, members of the minority could stall House business simply by not answering quorum calls. But in 1890 House Speaker Thomas B. Reed stopped this practice by counting anyone he saw, even if they had not responded when their name was called.

Senators use quorum calls as a delaying tactic to suspend floor activity between speeches or while working out some legislative compromise off the floor. The clerk slowly calls the roll, but senators do not need to respond. As soon as they are ready to proceed, a senator will ask unanimous consent to suspend the quorum call, and business will pick up where it left off. Only for "live" quorums (three bells rather than two) must senators respond to a quorum call. Those trying to filibuster will often use quorum calls to delay or stop business altogether. The leadership will also use "live" quorum calls to bring as many members as possible to the floor to be present for some important business.

SEE ALSO

Bells; Filibuster; Reed, Thomas B.; Unanimous consent agreements

During the 1st Congress, the Senate and House failed for more than a month to achieve a quorum.

Rankin, Jeannette

☆ *Born: June 11, 1880, Missoula, Mont.*
☆ *Political party: Republican*
☆ *Representative from Montana: 1917–19, 1941–43*
☆ *Died: May 18, 1973, Carmel, Calif.*

A LEADER in the campaign to give women the right to vote in Montana, Jeannette Rankin in 1916 became the first woman elected to Congress. In the House of Representatives, she initially

Representative Jeannette Rankin was the first woman elected to Congress.

devoted herself to winning national suffrage (voting rights) for women, but her attentions were soon diverted to the war in Europe. A pacifist, Rankin joined 49 other antiwar members of the House to vote against U.S. entry into World War I in 1917. The following year she lost a bid to be elected to the Senate. Ironically, in 1940 Rankin again won a seat in the House, and she was there when the Japanese bombed Pearl Harbor on December 7, 1941. Standing firm for her beliefs against enormous pressure, she became the only member of Congress to vote against war with Japan.

Rankin never again ran for Congress but resumed her private activities on behalf of peace and women's rights. At 90, she was protesting the Vietnam War. After her death, the state of Montana sent a statue of Jeannette Rankin to the U.S. Capitol, bearing the motto "I cannot vote for war."

SEE ALSO
Women in Congress

FURTHER READING
Josephson, Hannah. *Jeannette Rankin, First Lady in Congress.* Indianapolis: Bobbs-Merrill, 1974.

Ranking members

AT THE BEGINNING of each Congress, minority party members of each committee elect their ranking member, usually the person with the most seniority on that committee. However, party rules limit the number of committees and subcommittees on which someone may be the ranking member. In cases where the most senior member is already the ranking member of another committee, the next most senior member generally moves up to the ranking position.

The ranking member appoints and supervises the minority staff of a committee or subcommittee and looks out for the minority party's interests in all committee business. A committee chairman will try to work closely with the ranking member in order to maintain goodwill and to keep their committee as united as possible when reporting legislation out to the full House or Senate.

SEE ALSO
Chairs of committees; Seniority

Rayburn, Sam

☆ *Born: Jan. 6, 1882, Kingston, Tenn.*
☆ *Political party: Democrat*
☆ *Representative from Texas: 1913–61*
☆ *House majority leader: 1937–40*
☆ *Speaker of the House: 1940–47, 1949–53, 1955–61*
☆ *Died: Nov. 16, 1961, Bonham, Tex.*

"TO GET along, go along," Sam Rayburn would advise new members of the House of Representatives. An extremely effective legislator himself, "Mr. Sam" was famous for hard work, fair play, and keeping his word to other members. "He's so damned sincere and dedicated to a cause and he knows his country and his job inside out so well," said another representative, "that I would feel pretty dirty to turn him down and not trust him." Except for two Republican Congresses, Rayburn served as Speaker of the House from 1940 to 1961. Democratic Presidents depended upon him to get the votes in the House for their programs. But despite the Democratic majorities, Rayburn had to contend with a coalition between conservative Democrats and Republicans. They especially dominated the House Rules Committee, chaired by former judge Howard Smith of Virginia. As one of his last acts as Speaker, Rayburn threw his prestige behind a plan to enlarge the Rules Committee and break the conservatives' control. "Boys, are you with me or with Judge Smith?" he asked House members. Rayburn won the vote by 217 to 212, clearing the way for the liberal legislation of the administrations of John F. Kennedy and Lyndon B. Johnson in the 1960s. In 1965 the Rayburn House Office Building opened, named in honor of the House's longest-serving Speaker.

SEE ALSO

Speaker of the House

FURTHER READING

Cheney, Richard B., and Lynne V. Cheney. *Kings of the Hill: Power and Personality in the House of Representatives.* New York: Continuum, 1983.
Hardeman, D. B., and Donald C. Bacon. *Rayburn: A Biography.* Austin: Texas Monthly Press, 1987.

Reapportionment

EVERY TEN years the United States conducts a census of its population, after which the House of Representatives is reapportioned—that is, the seats are reallocated in proportion to the states' populations. Some states gain congressional districts, some lose districts, and some keep the same number.

By statute, Congress sets the total number of representatives in the House. At first, the House simply enlarged its membership to accommodate new states and a growing population. After the 1790 census the House expanded from 65 to 105 members. The numbers increased steadily until 1911, when House membership reached 435. Since then, that number has remained the ceiling.

The 1990 census determined the current apportionment of representatives.

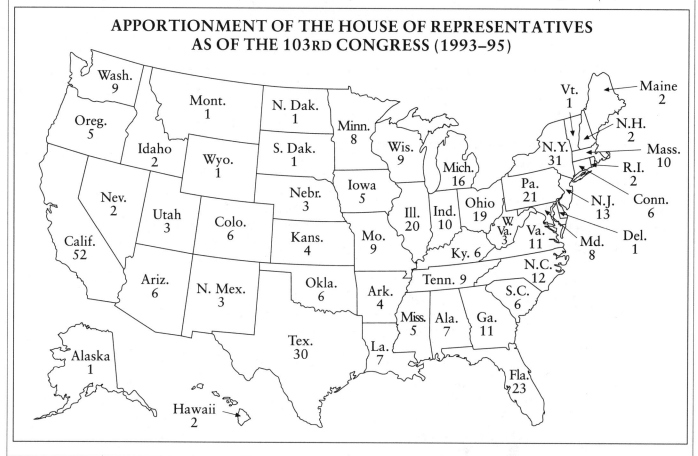

APPORTIONMENT OF THE HOUSE OF REPRESENTATIVES AS OF THE 103RD CONGRESS (1993–95)

Wash. 9
Oreg. 5
Mont. 1
N. Dak. 1
Minn. 8
Vt. 1
Maine 2
N.H. 2
N.Y. 31
Mass. 10
Idaho 2
Wyo. 1
S. Dak. 1
Wis. 9
R.I. 2
Nev. 2
Utah 3
Colo. 6
Nebr. 3
Iowa 5
Mich. 16
Pa. 21
N.J. 13
Conn. 6
Calif. 52
Ill. 20
Ind. 10
Ohio 19
W. Va. 3
Va. 11
Del. 1
Ariz. 6
N. Mex. 3
Kans. 4
Mo. 9
Ky. 6
Md. 8
N.C. 12
Okla. 6
Ark. 4
Tenn. 9
S.C. 6
Alaska 1
Tex. 30
La. 7
Miss. 5
Ala. 7
Ga. 11
Hawaii 2
Fla. 23

After each census the states redraw the lines of their congressional districts to conform to any changes in the population. (In addition to the 435 voting members, the House also has various delegates who represent U.S. territories.)

In the 1790s each member of the House represented about 33,000 people. By the 1990s each member represented nearly 600,000 people. However, at times the population size of congressional districts has varied widely. For many years the state legislatures that drew the boundaries for their state's congressional districts favored less-populated rural areas over cities by giving the rural areas greater proportional representation. In the 1964 case of *Wesberry v. Sanders,* the Supreme Court ruled such inequalities unconstitutional. The Court ordered that congressional districts be drawn to provide "one person, one vote."

The majority party in the state legislature invariably tries to draw the reapportionment lines to favor its own candidates in elections. Sometimes they resort to gerrymandering—drawing oddly shaped districts to combine areas where their party registration is the strongest. The Voting Rights Act of 1982 encouraged states not to divide up districts in such a way that minority groups cannot elect their own candidates. In the redistricting that followed the 1990 census, this led to the creation of many more districts where African-American and Hispanic-American candidates stood a better chance of election.

Recent censuses have shown a steady shift of the population toward the South and West. After the 1990 census, California increased to 52 districts, the largest number of seats that any state delegation has held in the House. By contrast, 13 states, primarily in the East and Midwest, lost seats in the House.

SEE ALSO
Gerrymandering

Recess

BETWEEN THE opening of a session and its final adjournment, or closing, Congress calls the time it takes off "recesses." During the 19th century, Congress took few long recesses because it generally met for only half the year and then adjourned so that members could spend the other half back home. But in recent years, the first session of a two-year Congress begins on January 3 and runs to the middle of December, averaging more than 300 days. The second session begins the following January 3 and adjourns in October, a month before the November election, averaging more than 250 days. Congress does not meet every day during these sessions. The Senate and House often do not meet on either Friday or Monday, recessing to give members long weekends to return to their home state.

Congress will also recess for a week corresponding with major federal holidays. And some members of the House call these recesses "district work periods" because instead of taking vacations, many members spend the time working directly with their constituents in their home district. Other members use recesses for international travel or simply to spend time with their families. The Legislative Reorganization Act of 1970 also provided that Congress take a 30-day recess each August, except in time of war.

Whenever Congress is in recess, Presidents gain some additional leeway. During longer congressional recesses, the President can kill a bill with a pocket veto—in a sense, putting the bill unsigned in his pocket—which Congress cannot override. Presidents also make recess appointments, giving the individual named some time in the post before the Senate returns to begin the confirmation process. This gives the nominee the chance to demonstrate an ability to perform the duties of the office. However, the Senate can still reject a recess appointee.

SEE ALSO

Adjournment; Legislative Reorganization Acts (1946 and 1970); Nominations, confirmation of; Veto

Recision bills

THE CONGRESSIONAL Budget and Impoundment Control Act of 1974 forbade Presidents from impounding, or withholding, money that Congress had appropriated for federal projects. But it permitted the President to ask Congress for a recision, a cancellation or cutback, of any appropriation that was no longer needed. Because of the soaring federal deficits, proposals before Congress have suggested giving the President an "enhanced recision" power. The President could then cut back appropriated funds unless a majority in both houses voted to restore those funds.

SEE ALSO

Appropriations; Budget and Impoundment Control Act, Congressional (1974)

Reconstruction, congressional

CONGRESS AND President Andrew Johnson fought bitterly over the Reconstruction of the South after the Civil War. Johnson believed he was following the wishes of the assassinated Abraham Lincoln by pursuing a quick and lenient

African Americans gained the right to vote during Reconstruction.

return of the South into the Union. Radical Republicans, led by Representative Thaddeus Stevens, argued that these former Confederate states had committed "state suicide" and reverted to the status of territories. Radicals wanted to readmit the Southern states only if they ensured the civil rights and liberties of the freedmen (the term used for former slaves). Moderates in Congress hoped to work with Johnson but were dismayed when he vetoed the Freedmen's Bureau Bill, which provided funds to build and run schools for the freedmen. The bill's sponsor, Senator William Fessenden (Republican–Maine) declared that Johnson had "broken the faith, betrayed his trust, and must sink from detestation to contempt." Johnson's veto drove moderate and radical Republicans together in support of tough Reconstruction measures, and it eventually led to the failed effort to impeach and remove the President.

Congress took control of Reconstruction policies away from the President, drafting the 14th and 15th Amendments to the Constitution to protect the civil liberties and voting rights of African Americans. In 1866 and 1875 Congress also enacted civil rights bills to guarantee all citizens equal rights in hotels, restaurants, trains, and other public accommodations and transportation facilities. Federal troops occupied many Southern states during Reconstruction, enabling the freedmen to vote and to elect Republican candidates—both black and white— to Congress. When these federal troops left, following the election of 1876, Congressional Reconstruction collapsed. The Supreme Court later ruled the civil rights acts unconstitutional. In the following decades African Americans lost the right to vote, and racial segregation became the law throughout the South.

SEE ALSO

African Americans in Congress; Civil rights legislation; Impeachment of Andrew Johnson (1868); Stevens, Thaddeus

FURTHER READING

Foner, Eric. *Reconstruction: America's Unfinished Revolution, 1863–1877.* New York: Harper & Row, 1988.

Records of Congress

AFTER THE hearings and debates end and Congress has adopted or rejected a piece of legislation, a nomination, or a treaty, the official records go to the National Archives and Records Administration in Washington, D.C. There, archivists catalog, box, and open the records for research, subject to the rules of the Senate and House. Although congressional records are not included under the Freedom of Information Act (which sets the terms for access to executive branch records), most Senate records open automatically after 20 years, and House records after 30 years. Records involving national security and personal privacy are closed for as much as 50 years. Official records are those of the committees and support staff. Senators' and representatives' papers are considered their personal property. Although in the past many members of Congress destroyed their papers, today most members send their papers to home-state libraries and historical societies.

Before the National Archives opened in 1936, the records of Congress were stored haphazardly throughout the Capitol building. Conditions were often so bad that the documents deteriorated or were destroyed. Congressional documents include copies of bills and resolutions, transcripts of hearings, nominations, treaties, correspondence, and petitions that range from individual postcards to great rolls containing thousands of signatures.

Nineteenth-century clerks of Congress folded documents in thirds to fit within the pigeonholes of their desks and tied bundles of documents with red tape. "Cutting through the red tape" referred to removing the tape to find needed documents—and the expression is still used for getting something done in the bureaucracy. In recent years many records have been microfilmed, or they exist only in computers. Such technological advances both facilitate and complicate the jobs of those archivists who preserve, catalog, and make available for research the records of Congress.

FURTHER READING

Viola, Herman J. *The National Archives of the United States.* New York: Abrams, 1984.

Records of Congress are stored in the National Archives building in Washington.

Recruitment

WHO RUNS for Congress? The kind of candidate has changed significantly over time. When political parties were strong institutions, they chose candidates based on party loyalty. Local party bosses and political "machines" in the larger cities determined all local and congressional candidates. For instance, in 1934 the Democratic machine in Kansas City, Missouri, picked Harry S. Truman for the Senate. A political machine is a tightly run political organization based on patronage. Many machine politicians who became candidates were far less talented and honest than Truman. Party endorsements were particularly important to senatorial candidates when senators were chosen by state legislatures rather than by popular vote. Since Senate candidates had to have strong support within the state legislature, most 19th-century senators served first in a state legislature or as governor of their state. Because they identified strongly with their party, they tended to vote with other members of their party in Congress.

After the 17th Amendment established direct election of senators in 1913, and after many states provided for primaries where voters could choose party candidates, the influence of party organizations declined and reform candidates often successfully challenged the machines.

Self-selected candidates

Congressional candidates became increasingly self-selected rather than party-selected. Fewer candidates for federal office had any experience in local or state government. Many congressional candidates had never run for public office before but had gained their experience in law, business, or universities.

Some gained public attention as astronauts, athletes, or actors: Senator John Glenn (Democrat–Ohio) won fame as the first American astronaut to orbit the earth. Senator Bill Bradley (Democrat–New Jersey) played professional basketball for the New York Knicks. And Representative Fred Grandy (Republican–Iowa) had a featured role in a television series called "The Love Boat."

Instead of state legislators and governors running for the Senate, many members of the House became Senate candidates. Congressional staff members also began to run for office themselves. In the 102nd Congress, both Speaker of the House Thomas Foley and Senate majority leader George Mitchell were former members of the congressional staff.

The chances of self-selected candidates winning election improved with the growth of broadcast news. In the 19th century, newspapers identified strongly with one political party or the other and strongly endorsed that party's candidates. Candidates could address only limited audiences during a campaign, and they had to rely on party organizations to organize rallies, put up posters, and get party members out to vote. But the development of radio, and more important, of television, allowed candidates to talk directly to the voters. With enough money, and with effective advertisements, an individual unknown to 99 percent of the voters at the beginning of a race can become known well enough to upset the incumbent, the person currently serving in the office.

Before his election to the Senate, Bill Bradley played basketball for the New York Knicks.

The value of a family name

Having a prominent family name has always been an asset in winning party nomination and election to Congress. At age 30, Russell Long (Democrat–Louisiana) followed his famous father, Huey P. Long, to the Senate. Also at age 30, Edward M. Kennedy (Democrat–Massachusetts) won the Senate seat once held by his brother John F. Kennedy. His Republican opponent, George Cabot Lodge, was the son of another former Massachusetts senator, Henry Cabot Lodge, Jr. Similarly, in 1990 Representative Susan Molinari (Republican–New York) took the House seat that her father, Guy Molinari, had held for a decade.

Republican and Democratic campaign committees in both the House and Senate try to recruit strong candidates to run against incumbents from the opposition party. Campaign committees promise to raise funds for these candidates and to help them gain name recognition. Other candidates draw their support and financial base from their past connections with chambers of commerce, labor unions, consumer and environmental organizations, the civil rights and women's rights movements, antiabortion activists, and other single- and multi-issue groups.

SEE ALSO
Campaign committees; Families in Congress

FURTHER READING
Cannon, David T. *Actors, Athletes, and Astronauts: Political Amateurs in the United States Congress.* Chicago: University of Chicago Press, 1990.

Reed, Thomas B.

☆ *Born: Oct. 18, 1839, Portland, Maine*
☆ *Political party: Republican*
☆ *Representative from Maine: 1877–99*
☆ *Speaker of the House: 1889–91, 1895–99*
☆ *Died: Dec. 7, 1902, Washington, D.C.*

SIX FEET, three inches tall and weighing nearly 300 pounds, Speaker Thomas B. Reed ruled the House of Representatives so firmly that people called him "Czar" Reed. After years of weak leadership, Reed was unwilling to sit helplessly in the Speaker's chair and watch the majority become powerless to pass legislation. The minority Democrats had been disrupting House business by making motions to adjourn and then demanding roll call votes. Reed declared these motions "dilatory," or deliberately delay-

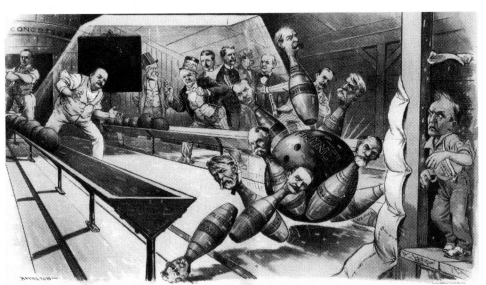

In this cartoon, House Speaker Tom Reed bowled over his opponents.

ing, and ruled them out of order. The minority also tried to stall House business by not answering quorum calls—a practice known as the "disappearing quorum." Reed simply took it upon himself to count anyone he saw, even if they had not answered "present." One furious Kentucky Democrat shouted, "I deny your right, Mr. Speaker, to count me present." Reed calmly responded, "The Chair is making a statement of fact that the gentleman from Kentucky is present. Does he wish to deny it?"

Reed got his way, and the rules of the House were changed to recognize the Speaker's right to count a quorum and to declare delaying motions out of order. The rules of the House, he insisted, were designed not to protect the minority but "to promote the orderly conduct of business." Reed used his power as Speaker to promote the Republican party's conservative financial programs. But even Reed could not stop the House stampede to vote for war with Spain in 1898. After the war he strongly opposed the taking of Puerto Rico and the Philippines as U.S. territories. He retired as Speaker when he failed to persuade his party to abandon its expansionist foreign policies.

SEE ALSO

Quorum; Rules, House and Senate; Speaker of the House

FURTHER READING

Cheney, Richard B., and Lynne V. Cheney. *Kings of the Hill: Power and Personality in the House of Representatives.* New York: Continuum, 1983.

Referrals to committee

ONCE A BILL or resolution is introduced, the parliamentarian, acting for the presiding officer, refers it to the appropriate committee. The rules of the Senate and House spell out which committees should handle what types of legislation. For instance, bills dealing with the federal courts would be referred to the Judiciary Committees, whereas bills dealing with education would go to the education and labor committees. Sometimes, however, one bill covers issues over which more than one committee has jurisdiction. In these cases the parliamentarian makes multiple referrals. In the Senate, a bill setting clean air standards for automobile exhaust systems might be referred to both the Committee on Energy and Natural Resources and the Committee on Environment and Public Works. An entire bill could be referred to two or more committees, or the individual sections of the bill might be separated and distributed to the committees that deal with such issues. Authors therefore try to draft bills in such a way as to increase the likelihood that they will be referred to the most sympathetic committees.

SEE ALSO

Committees; Parliamentarian

Regulation of commerce

ONE OF the Constitution's most important delegations of power to Congress is to "regulate commerce with foreign nations and among the several states" (Article 1, Section 8). Since practically all business crosses state lines, Congress has increasingly used the commerce clause to regulate railroads and other interstate transportation; to pass antitrust laws to prevent monopoly (the control of entire industries by a few large corporations); to set up independent regulatory commissions such as the Federal Trade Commission, the Securities and Exchange Commission, and the Environmental Protection Agency; and to prohibit racial discrimination in hotels, restaurants, buses, or any other form of public accommodation or transportation. The commerce clause also permits Congress to set tariffs, or taxes, on imported goods to protect U.S. industries and farm products and to impose economic sanctions, or penalties, on other nations to support U.S. foreign policy. Commerce issues are handled primarily by the House Energy and Commerce Committee and the Senate Commerce, Science, and Transportation Committee.

Reporters of debate

DURING DEBATES in the Senate and House chamber, a reporter of debate takes down whatever the members say or do. The next morning, the entire debate, floor statements, and votes will be published in the daily *Congressional Record*. There are many steps in this amazingly fast process.

Since the 1840s the Senate and House have each employed teams of reporters of debate. (Prior to 1840 these reporters—or stenographers—were employees of the newspapers that published the debates.) When the chamber is in session, reporters go on the floor in 10-minute rotations, taking down what they hear before returning to transcribe their notes. Since speakers are not always clear, and reporters make mistakes, members of Congress (or their staffs) are permitted to review the reporters' notes and make corrections before the *Record* is published. Some members also correct grammatical errors and otherwise polish their remarks. Occasionally, when tem-

pers flare, members will say things that they regret, perhaps insulting a colleague. They may delete such offending remarks entirely from the transcript.

More often, the *Record* tells more than what happened, rather than less. Instead of reading an entire speech, a speaker might read just the opening paragraphs and ask for unanimous consent to "revise and extend" these remarks for the *Record*. The speaker then hands the reporter a copy of the unread text. Congress grants these unanimous consent requests to speed up the proceedings and to avoid having to listen to endless speeches.

Modern reporters of debate take shorthand notes on a device similar to a court reporting machine. The machine enters their notes immediately into a computer system that converts the text into standard English. The computer system facilitates editing, speeds typesetting, and reduces costs and printing errors. Even with such assistance, however, reporters still provide a human touch to editing the daily proceedings of Congress—and members appreciate their help in making their remarks present-

Official reporters of debate in 1908, reviewing their transcripts for publication in the Congressional Record.

able. As Senator Everett Dirksen (Republican–Illinois) once observed, "Congress is really the home of the split infinitive . . . ; this is the place where the dangling participle is certainly nourished; this is the home of the broken sentence; and if there were no dashes I do not know what the distinguished reporters of debate would do . . . and yet, somehow, out of this great funnel it all comes out all right, and it is always readable."

SEE ALSO
Congressional Record

Representation

AS A RESULT of the Great Compromise of 1787, the Constitution provided for fundamentally different types of representation in the House and Senate. Membership in the House is proportional to the population of the state. The number of representatives to which each state is entitled is determined every 10 years after a national census, or head count, has been taken. In the 1st Congress each member of the House represented about 30,000 constituents. By the 103rd Congress the average House member represented nearly 600,000 constituents. At first the number of representatives grew with each census, from 105 after the 1790 census to 435 after the 1910 census. Then Congress froze the number at 435 to keep the House at a manageable size.

The membership of the Senate grows by two each time a new state joins the Union. Every state is entitled to two senators, regardless of the size of its population. Before the ratification of the 17th Amendment in 1913, when senators were still elected by state legislatures, senators were compared to ambas-

sadors, representing their state's political establishment in the national legislature. With direct election of senators, however, senators see themselves as representing the people of their state, who voted them into office.

SEE ALSO
Bicameral; Great Compromise (1787); Reapportionment

Resolutions

TO STATE its decisions or declare its opinions, Congress uses three different types of resolutions. A single house can pass a simple resolution for such internal business as adopting rules, creating special committees, or printing documents. Simple resolutions also express the sense of one house on a matter, such as a Senate resolution congratulating the Washington Redskins on their victory in the Super Bowl. Because only one house enacts such a resolution, and the President does not sign it, the resolution does not become law. Resolutions are identified as H. Res. or S. Res., and they are numbered consecutively during a Congress.

Concurrent resolutions

When both houses express the opinion of Congress on some issue, set the date of adjournment, or deal with some other internal matter affecting both houses, they adopt a concurrent resolution. For instance, in 1992 Congress by concurrent resolution declared that the 27th Amendment to the Constitution, proposed 202 years earlier to regulate increases in congressional salaries, had

Page one of a Senate resolution

finally been ratified by three-quarters of the states and had become part of the Constitution. Presidents do not sign concurrent resolutions. Concurrent resolutions are numbered, with the prefix H. Con. Res. when introduced in the House and S. Con. Res. when introduced in the Senate.

Joint resolutions

Unlike simple and concurrent resolutions, joint resolutions become law if the President signs them. Congress proposes amendments to the Constitution, creates joint committees, and expresses the joint opinion of Congress on specific issues using joint resolutions. Joint resolutions are numbered, with the prefix H. J. Res. when introduced in the House and S. J. Res. when introduced in the Senate.

SEE ALSO

Bills; Concurrent resolutions; Joint resolutions; Legislation

---

Revels, Hiram R.

☆ *Born: Sept. 27, 1827, Fayetteville, N.C.*
☆ *Political party: Republican*
☆ *Senator from Mississippi: 1870–71*
☆ *Died: Jan. 16, 1901, Aberdeen, Miss.*

THE FIRST African American elected to the Senate was Hiram Revels. Although born in North Carolina during slavery, Revels's parents had been free and he was never a slave. He attended Knox College in Illinois and became a minister in the African Methodist Episcopal Church in Baltimore, Maryland. During the Civil War, Revels raised two black regiments to fight for the Union and served as a chaplain in a black regiment at Vicksburg, Mississippi. He remained in Mississippi after the war and became active in Reconstruction politics. In 1870

Hiram Rhodes Revels was the first African-American senator.

the state legislature chose Revels to fill a seat in the Senate that had been vacant since the start of the Civil War. Although he served only a brief term, Revels established a significant precedent just by taking his seat, against the objection of white Southerners. As a senator, Revels won notice for speaking out against racial segregation.

SEE ALSO

African Americans in Congress; Reconstruction, congressional

FURTHER READING

Thompson, Julius. *Hiram R. Revels, 1827–1901: A Biography.* New York: Arno Press, 1982.

Revenue bills

IN ORDER for the federal government to function, it must be able to raise revenue, or money. A chief limitation of the Continental Congress and the Congress under the Articles of Confederation was their reliance on the states for all funds. Because the states were slow to act, Congress was always short of funds, even to pay troops during and after the revolutionary war. The Constitution (Article 1, Section 8) therefore gave Congress the power to "lay [set] and collect taxes, duties, imposts and excises, to pay the debts and provide for the common defense and general welfare of the United States." The framers of the Constitution regarded the "power of the purse" to be so important that they decided that the House of Representatives—at that time the only members of Congress directly elected by the people—should be able to originate any revenue bill. However, according to the Constitution (Article 1, Section 7), the Senate could amend these bills just as it could any other legislation.

At first Congress raised revenues

chiefly through tariffs, which are duties or taxes set on imported goods. During the Civil War, and after enactment of the 16th Amendment to the Constitution in 1913, Congress also levied income taxes on individuals and corporations. Revenue bills are handled by the House Ways and Means Committee and the Senate Finance Committee, a responsibility that has traditionally made them two of the most powerful committees of Congress. Not until 1944 did a President—Franklin D. Roosevelt—veto a revenue bill. Congress, always jealous of its power of the purse, immediately voted to override his veto.

SEE ALSO
Appropriations

Riders

LIKE A HITCHHIKER thumbing a ride, a "rider" is an amendment looking for a vehicle to take it where it wants to go. Members with a bill that cannot attract enough votes on its own will add it as an amendment to a popular bill that is likely to pass. Riders usually are not germane to the bill—that is, they have little or nothing in common with the bill on which they are riding. House rules prohibit non-germane amendments, so riders are used in the Senate, with the hope that the House will accept them in the conference committee that hammers out the differences between the House and Senate versions of the bill. Appropriations bills, which provide for payment of federal money for many different projects, are favorite vehicles for these legislative riders.

SEE ALSO
Appropriations; Conference committees; Germaneness

Robinson, Joseph T.

☆ *Born: Aug. 26, 1872, Lonoke, Ark.*
☆ *Political party: Democrat*
☆ *Representative from Arkansas: 1903–13*
☆ *Senator from Arkansas: 1913–37*
☆ *Senate minority leader: 1923–33*
☆ *Senate majority leader: 1933–37*
☆ *Died: July 14, 1937, Washington, D.C.*

AS DEMOCRATIC majority leader during the first years of the New Deal, Joe Robinson got the Senate's usually slow machinery to work with amazing speed. He personally served as floor manager of President Franklin D. Roosevelt's emergency banking bill and drove it through the Senate in one afternoon. Robinson similarly volunteered to manage other New Deal bills. Many committee chairmen were happy to give up this responsibility because they were conservative Southern Democrats who felt uncomfortable with liberal New Deal proposals but did not want to stand in the way of ending the depression. Most senators liked and trusted Robinson and willingly followed his lead. But if they crossed him, Robinson would bellow and bang his fist on his desk until he whipped the Senate into line. A big, bluff, tough man, he gave the impression of "brute animal strength," said one reporter, "and a willingness to use it."

When President Roosevelt proposed expanding the Supreme Court in 1937, in order to add more liberal justices, Robinson reluctantly went along. Against strong opposition from members of his own party, he put together a slim majority in favor of the bill. But during an intense fight Robinson died of a heart attack. Without his leadership, the court plan collapsed and the Democratic majority split badly for the remainder of the New Deal years.

SEE ALSO

Court-packing plan (1937); First hundred days of the New Deal; Majority leader

FURTHER READING

Bacon, Donald C. "Joseph Taylor Robinson: The Good Soldier." In *First among Equals: Outstanding Senate Leaders of the Twentieth Century*, edited by Richard A. Baker and Roger H. Davidson. Washington, D.C.: Congressional Quarterly, 1991.

Rules committees

LIKE THE rules of the two bodies, the House and Senate rules committees operate very differently. The House Rules Committee plays a powerful role in all House proceedings. When bills are reported out of committee, but before they are debated by the full House, the House Rules Committee determines the rules under which the bill will be debated, setting time limits and other conditions for the debate.

The House Rules Committee can adopt an open rule, a closed rule, or a modified rule. If it adopts no rule at all, the bill will not get to the House floor. Under an open rule, members can debate and amend a bill as much as they want. Under a closed rule, members may not introduce amendments from the floor, and they can debate the bill only for a limited time, with the time divided equally between the opposing sides. A modified rule is not as restrictive as a closed rule but spells out how many and what types of amendments may be introduced from the floor.

By the type of rule it adopts, the Rules Committee can therefore make it much easier for the House majority to get its way, or it can block the passage of a bill or at least make it more difficult. Before 1910, when progressives led a revolt against the conservative Speaker Joseph G. Cannon for blocking their reform legislation, Speakers of the House appointed the chairman of the Rules Committee and served on the committee themselves, which increased the Speaker's control over legislation. After 1910 the chairmanship went to the committee member from the majority party who had the most seniority. In the 1950s a conservative coalition of Republicans and Democrats controlled the Rules Committee under chairman Howard Smith (Democrat–Virginia). Because this conservative coalition frustrated many liberal initiatives, Speaker Sam Rayburn led the movement to enlarge the Rules Committee and make it more representative of the majority party as a whole rather than just its conservative wing. Legislative reforms in the 1970s also increased the influence of the Speaker and the majority party leadership over the Rules Committee.

Although the House has separate committees for rules and administration, the Senate has combined these functions into a single Rules and Administration Committee. Time limits and other stipulations on debate and amendment of Senate bills are arranged by unanimous consent agreements worked out by the leadership and the bill's sponsors. Because bills do not go to the Senate Rules Committee for specific rules, and because the Senate revises its general rules very infrequently, the Rules and Administration Committee devotes more of its attention to such administrative duties as assigning office and parking space and overseeing the Senate's general operations.

SEE ALSO

Cannon, Joseph G.; Committees; Rayburn, Sam; Rules, House and Senate; Smith, Howard W.; Unanimous consent agreements

FURTHER READING

Oleszek, Walter J. *Congressional Procedures and the Policy Process*. Washington, D.C.: Congressional Quarterly, 1989.

Rules, House and Senate

IN ORDER to get business done and to operate as fairly as possible, each house of Congress has established rules of procedure. The Constitution (Article 1, Section 4) allows the House and Senate to establish their own separate rules. In the 1st Congress, both houses appointed special committees to propose rules. From the beginning, the rules of the House favored majority rule, while the rules of the Senate protected the rights of the minority. The difference between the two has acted as an additional check and balance on the powers of the federal government.

The first rules of the House dealt with the Speaker's powers, the proper behavior of members, the procedures of debate, the handling of bills, and the operations of the House as a committee of the whole (a device to enable the whole House to act as a committee, in order to limit debate and speed its procedures). Two hundred years later, despite periodic revision, the basic rules of the House still address these issues. House Speaker

Thomas B. Reed argued that the rules of the House were designed to promote order and prevent "pandemonium." Although the smaller Senate had the luxury of allowing every member to have a say, the larger House needed tighter rules to get things accomplished. Beginning in the 1840s, the House adopted rules limiting how much time members could speak on any issue—to prevent filibustering (talking a bill to death) or other obstructive tactics by the minority. Regardless of which party has held the majority, its members have promoted rules to give the majority power to act.

From the beginning, Senate rules differed from House rules. For instance, the Senate does not operate as a committee of the whole, and it had no other means of limiting debate until it adopted its first cloture rule in 1917. Although various revisions of the rules have strengthened the majority's ability to act, the Senate has remained a body of equals. Even the most junior member of the minority may speak at length on any Senate bill and therefore has a chance to affect the bill's final shape.

The rules of both the House and Senate remain few in number. A few outmoded rules have been dropped, and a

In 1953 Senators Herbert Lehman, Hubert Humphrey, Irving Ives, and James Duff planned strategy to tighten the Senate's rules against filibusters.

few new rules added. But whenever either body applies or interprets a rule, it establishes a precedent, or model, and the precedents are so numerous that they fill thick volumes. These accumulating precedents have enabled Congress to function and to meet the ever-changing needs of the nation without having to constantly change its rules.

SEE ALSO

Checks and balances; Cloture; Committee of the whole; Filibuster; Precedents; Rules committees

FURTHER READING

Byrd, Robert C. "Rules." In *The Senate, 1789–1989: Addresses on the History of the United States Senate.* Vol. 2. Washington, D.C.: Government Printing Office, 1991.
McNeil, Neil. *Forge of Democracy: The House of Representatives.* New York: David McKay, 1963.

Russell, Richard B., Jr.

☆ *Born: Nov. 2, 1897, Winder, Ga.*
☆ *Political party: Democrat*
☆ *Senator from Georgia: 1933–71*
☆ *Died: Jan. 21, 1971, Washington, D.C.*

A "SENATOR'S senator," through seniority Richard Russell chaired such powerful committees as Armed Services and Appropriations, and through personal integrity he earned a deep respect from his colleagues. Senator Norris Cotton (Republican–North Carolina) noted that Russell "engaged in debate only on rare occasions. When he did so, he spoke quietly, but a silence fell upon the Senate and every member listened attentively, which is about the highest tribute a senator can receive." Russell became an authority on a range of issues from agriculture to military policy. But he also led the Southern caucus in the Senate and devoted his great parliamentary skills to defending racial segregation and opposing civil rights legislation. Some called him the last general of the Confederacy. Russell paid dearly for this stand. Despite the prestige he earned in the Senate, his unbending defense of segregation prevented him from becoming a national leader and achieving the Democratic nomination for President that he sought. After Russell's death, the Senate named its first office building in his honor.

SEE ALSO

Civil rights legislation

FURTHER READING

Fite, Gilbert C. *Richard B. Russell, Jr., Senator from Georgia.* Chapel Hill: University of North Carolina Press, 1991.

Salaries

CONGRESS SETS the salaries of the President, Supreme Court justices, and other members of the executive and judicial branches. To prevent salaries from being used as a weapon, the Constitution (Article 2, Section 1, and Article 3, Section 1) prohibits Congress from raising or lowering a President's salary during that President's term or from lowering the salaries of federal judges who serve lifetime terms.

Congress also sets the salaries of its own members, a power that has caused it no end of trouble. Members of the Continental Congress had been paid by their states. To give the U.S. Congress more independence, the Constitution provided that the federal government would pay their salaries. Representative James Madison highly disapproved of legislative bodies increasing their own salaries. While serving in the Virginia legislature, he declined a raise that had been voted on while he was a member. In the 1st Congress, Madison proposed 12 amendments to the Constitution, 10 of

An editorial
cartoon attacked
the congressional
"salary grab" in
1873, contrasting
congressmen's
salaries with the
low pay of their
clerks.

which became the Bill of Rights. But to
Madison's disappointment, the states
failed to ratify his amendment to prohibit Congress from receiving any pay
raise until after the next general House
election.

From six dollars a day to annual salaries

During the 1st Congress, senators
and representatives set their pay at six
dollars per diem (a day) for every day
that Congress met. The sum came to less
than $1,000 a year, but that was still
higher than the average citizen's income.
Some members accused their colleagues
of dragging out business just so they
could collect more days' pay. To correct
this tendency, Congress adopted an annual salary of $1,500 in 1816. However,
voters angrily disapproved and defeated
many members for reelection. The next
Congress returned to a per diem salary,
at eight dollars a day. Not until 1856 did
Congress manage to set an annual salary
of $3,000. Civil War inflation pushed
this up to $5,000 in 1866.

At the end of the 42nd Congress, in
1873, Congress increased its members'
salaries to $7,500, but made the pay in-
crease retroactive (effective backward in
time, taking effect at the beginning of the
Congress two years earlier, in 1871). In
effect, members voted themselves a
$5,000 bonus. Newspapers so strongly
denounced this "salary grab" that the
43rd Congress repealed the salary increase. Congressional salaries remained
at $5,000 for the rest of the 19th century.
During the 20th century, salaries steadily
increased along with the cost of living, so
that by 1989 members were receiving
$89,000 a year.

Limits on outside income

Critics have complained that elected
representatives should not earn higher
salaries than their average constituents
do. Members of Congress respond by
pointing to the expense of maintaining a
family and home in both Washington
and their home state. Ethics laws have
also limited their outside incomes.
Whereas Daniel Webster had carried on

an active law practice as a senator, arguing many cases before the Supreme Court, modern senators and representatives are restricted in the amount of private business they can conduct while serving in office. An ethics code adopted in 1977 prohibited members from earning more than 15 percent of their congressional salaries in outside income. The code did permit members to supplement their income by giving speeches for fees, called honoraria. But honoraria often came from special interest groups that hoped to shape legislation. In 1989 the House voted to raise members' salaries over the next two years to $125,100 and to ban honoraria. The Senate chose a smaller pay increase, to $101,900, but allowed senators to earn the difference in honoraria. In 1991 after continued public criticism, the Senate abandoned honoraria and raised its salaries to equal those paid to House members. Congress also established automatic cost-of-living increases for its members in the future, which by 1993 raised salaries to $133,600.

Once again the pay raise caused a storm of public protest. The states responded by voting for the still-pending amendment on congressional salaries, which was finally ratified in 1992, 202 years after James Madison had proposed it. The 27th Amendment to the Constitution requires that in the future, members of Congress must stand for reelection before any new pay raise can take effect.

SEE ALSO

Ethics

FURTHER READING

Byrd, Robert C. "Congressional Salaries." In *The Senate, 1789–1989: Address on the History of the United States Senate.* Vol. 2. Washington, D.C.: Government Printing Office, 1991.

Scandals, congressional

AS COLLECTIVE bodies, the Senate and House have had their share of heroes and scoundrels. Honorable men and women, concerned about the national issues of their day, have occupied the chambers alongside colleagues more interested in personal gain. With critical issues and multimillion-dollar appropriations at stake, lobbyists have at times resorted to unscrupulous methods, including bribery and other special favors, in return for members' votes. Media exposure of these scandals and outraged public opinion have spurred Congress to revise some of its rules and ethical standards to prevent further abuses of power and position.

Railroad scandals

Beginning in the 1850s, Congress voted large grants of land and money to stimulate railroad construction. Competing railroad entrepreneurs offered shares of stock to key members of Congress to win support for their projects. In 1857 a freshman representative revealed that he had been offered $1,500 to vote to aid a Minnesota railroad. The House committee investigating these charges recommended that four members be expelled, but they resigned from office. In 1873 Congress was shaken by a larger railroad scandal known as Credit Mobilier (the name of a construction company involved in building the first transcontinental railroad). Representative Oakes Ames (Republican–Massachusetts) acted as a lobbyist for Credit Mobilier and distributed stock to powerful senators and representatives "where it will do the most good for us." The *New York Sun* broke the story with the headline "How the Credit Mobilier

The business dealings of former Senate Democratic Secretary Bobby Baker (second from left) were the subject of investigation in 1964.

Bought Its Way through Congress." Senate and House investigations led to the censure of two representatives and the tarnishing of the reputation of many others.

"The Treason of the Senate"

During the Progressive Era at the start of the 20th century, muckraking magazine writers attacked the Senate as a "millionaires' club" composed of wealthy men or those indebted to wealthy business interests. In 1906 David Graham Phillips published a series of nine articles in *Cosmopolitan* magazine entitled "The Treason of the Senate." By "treason," Phillips meant that some senators were working for big business rather than for the public interest. The "Treason of the Senate" and other muckraking articles led to the defeat or retirement of several powerful senators and gave a boost to the progressive goal of direct election of senators, which the 17th Amendment achieved in 1913.

Campaign financing scandals

As the cost of campaigning for Congress escalated, members running for re-election sought campaign funds from a variety of sources, some of which raised questions about conflict of interest. In 1963 when the Senate investigated the business activities of the secretary to the Senate Democratic majority, Bobby Baker, he told of arranging unreported gifts and contributions from business interests to senators. The Senate responded by requiring senators to file more complete statements about their campaign financing and fund-raising. In the 1970s the House investigated a Korean-American businessman, Tongsun Park, accused of making illegal gifts to members of the House. The press labeled this incident "Koreagate," after the recent Watergate scandal. Even more shocking was the Federal Bureau of Investigation's Abscam (short for "Arab scam") operation, in which an FBI agent masqueraded as an Arab sheikh and offered money to various members of Congress in return for favorable legislation. As a result of Abscam, the House expelled one member, two other representatives and a senator resigned, and several others were defeated for reelection.

In 1991 the Senate Ethics Committee investigated the Keating Five—five senators who had intervened with federal bank regulators on behalf of savings and loan banker Charles Keating. Since Keating had made large campaign contributions to these senators, the question arose about whether they had exceeded the efforts they would normally have made for a constituent. The committee criticized their judgment, and the Senate reprimanded one senator for his involvement. The Keating scandal renewed calls for campaign financing reform.

SEE ALSO

Campaign financing; Censure; Credit Mobilier scandal (1872–73); Ethics; Expulsion; House bank scandal (1992); Salaries

FURTHER READING

Baker, Bobby. *Wheeling and Dealing: Confessions of a Capitol Hill Operator.* New York: Norton, 1978.
Mowry, George E., and Judson Grenier, eds. *The Treason of the Senate.* Chicago: University of Chicago Press, 1964.
Wilbur, W. Allan. "The Credit Mobilier Scandal." In *Congress Investigates: A Documented History, 1792–1974,* edited by Arthur M. Schlesinger, Jr., and Roger Bruns. New York: Bowker, 1975.

The Teapot Dome scandal captured public attention during the 1920s.

Seating in the chambers

THE CENTER aisle in both the Senate and House chambers divides the political parties. As the presiding officer looks into the chamber, Republicans sit to the left of the center aisle, Democrats to the right. Each senator has a desk, and the more senior senators tend to sit along the center aisle and toward the front, where it is easier to catch the presiding officer's attention to gain recognition to speak. Junior senators occupy seats in the rear and far ends of the chamber, and they move forward and inward with seniority. Some senators prefer to remain in back-row seats or to occupy a specific desk for sentimental purposes, because it belonged to a relative or to a famous predecessor. Senators find it prestigious to sit at the desks of Henry Clay, John C. Calhoun, or Daniel Webster. Modern senators carve their name into the desk drawers, alongside the names of their predecessors. The majority and minority leaders occupy the front desks on either side of the center aisle.

In 1914, after House membership had increased to 435, desks in the chamber were replaced with rows of leather-covered chairs. House members simply take a vacant chair on their party's side of the chamber. When members wish to address the House, they must speak from lecterns in the "well" of the chamber— the lower level at the foot of the Speaker's desk. Managers of legislation may also speak from two long tables on each side of the aisle.

Nineteenth-century representatives drew numbered marbles to determine their seating in the House chamber.

Secrecy

CONGRESS HAS always been the most open branch of the federal government. Yet Congress has also done much of its work in secret and has expended much energy trying to plug "leaks" of secrets to the media.

The Continental Congress and the Congress under the Articles of Confederation debated entirely in closed session, and the Constitution was also written in secret session. The Constitution did not require Congress to conduct its business in public. It specified only that each house keep a journal of its proceedings "and from time to time publish the same, excepting such parts as may in their judgment require secrecy" (Article 1, Section 5). This was the only mention of secrecy in the Constitution. Because House members would stand for direct election by the people in just two years, however, they wanted their constituents to know what they were doing. The House immediately opened its doors and debated and voted in public session. By contrast, the Senate, elected by state legislatures, met entirely in secret session from 1789 until 1794. Even after the Senate constructed a gallery, it opened its doors only for legislative sessions. Executive sessions, which dealt with treaties and nominations, remained secret until 1929. Similarly, many committees of both the House and Senate met in closed-door executive sessions, especially when "marking up" a bill (making final changes before reporting it from the committee).

Legislative bodies are not designed to keep secrets. For every person or group with a reason to keep a secret, there is usually someone else with a reason to publish it. Members of Congress,

The press turned the spotlight of publicity on a secret committee hearing in 1890.

staff, and the executive branch have all leaked secret information to provoke some legislative action or public response. Leaking is a mutual act between the person releasing the information and the journalist who receives it and publishes it. Each one benefits by getting the story out. Sometimes, however, no single individual leaks a story, but an enterprising journalist pieces it together by gathering observations from a large number of sources.

Angry reaction to leaks

Having done more of its business in secret, the Senate has often reacted angrily to leaks. In 1811 and 1841 the Senate censured senators accused of releasing secret information. In 1848 and 1871 the Senate held newspaper correspondents prisoner in Capitol committee rooms, in unsuccessful attempts to force them to reveal their sources. In 1892 the Senate fired its executive clerk when he was suspected of being the source of frequent leaks from executive sessions. But the next time that the Senate met in secret, reporters went out of their way to print even more details, thereby proving the fired clerk's innocence.

Events climaxed in 1929 when a United Press reporter published a nomination vote from a secret session. Until then the Senate had believed secrecy necessary to protect the privacy of nominees and the sensitivity of foreign nations with whom the United States had signed treaties. But in 1929 the Senate concluded that it could not suppress such important information. Senators voted to open all executive sessions except for the very few dealing with highly classified national security issues.

Although Congress now does much less business in secret, in 1992 it once again investigated a leak. During the Senate Judiciary Committee's hearings on the nomination of Clarence Thomas to the Supreme Court, two reporters learned that the committee had received charges that the nominee had sexually harassed a former member of his staff, Anita Hill. Hill had not wished to appear in public, but she agreed to testify after the story broke. The Senate appointed a special counsel to investigate the source of the leak, but he concluded that so many members of the committee and staff had the information that it was impossible to determine who had leaked it. The special counsel condemned the practice of leaking because it ran contrary to the atmosphere of mutual cooperation and respect needed to conduct legislative business.

SEE ALSO

Censure; Media coverage of Congress

FURTHER READING

Ritchie, Donald A. *Press Gallery: Congress and the Washington Correspondent.* Cambridge: Harvard University Press, 1991.

Secretary of the Senate

THE SENATE elects a secretary to serve as its chief administrative officer. Historically the equivalent of the clerk of the House of Representatives as well as the more recently created director of nonlegislative services for the House, the secretary of the Senate supervises the various clerks, parliamentarians, and other general staff members of the Senate, is responsible for the disbursement of salaries and payment of other expenses, oversees stationery supplies, registers all lobbyists, and handles numerous other duties to make sure that the Senate functions properly.

As one of its first items of business in 1789, the Senate elected Samuel Allyn Otis as the first secretary. Otis's chief

The first secretary of the Senate, Samuel A. Otis

function was to keep the legislative journal that the Constitution required, making rough notes during the proceedings and having clerks copy them in fine handwritten script into a "smooth journal." Otis purchased supplies for the Senate and began many of the practices that are continued today. In the absence of the Vice President or president pro tempore, the secretary can sign legislation and preside over the Senate, as Secretary of the Senate Leslie Biffle did for two days in 1947. The secretary (or one of the bill clerks working for the secretary) also delivers messages and bills from the Senate to the House.

SEE ALSO

Clerk of the House; Director of nonlegislative services; Officers of the House and Senate

FURTHER READING

Byrd, Robert C. "Secretary of the Senate." In *The Senate, 1789–1989: Addresses on the History of the United States Senate*. Vol. 2. Washington, D.C.: Government Printing Office, 1991.

Sectionalism

SECTIONAL, OR regional, loyalties were present in Congress from the beginning, but they became stronger during and after the 1820s. As the North grew industrial, it sought protective tariffs (taxes on foreign goods imported into the United States) to protect its products. Because the South remained agricultural, it opposed tariffs that would raise the prices of the manufactured goods it needed. Southerners defended slavery, while an antislavery movement grew in the North. The new Western states had their own demands for roads and other internal improvements. Moreover, when Southerners migrated West, they wanted to be able to bring their slaves, but Northerners objected to slavery in the Western territories.

Congress served as the battleground for sectional rivalries and alliances. Although both the Whig and Democratic parties were national organizations, electing members of Congress from all regions, increasingly members crossed party lines to stand together to defend their common sectional interests. John C. Calhoun (Democrat–South Carolina) articulated the Southern position in Congress, while Daniel Webster (Whig–Massachusetts) often spoke for New England. From the 1820s to the 1850s, Henry Clay (Whig–Kentucky) and other congressional leaders worked out one compromise after another to defuse sectional tensions. But as the differences between the sections grew more pronounced, particularly over slavery, compromise became impossible. When the new Republican party won the Presidential election of 1860, the Southern states seceded and the nation plunged into Civil War.

Sectional identities persisted after the Civil War, notably in the Democratic party's long control of the "solid South." But the war had so drained emotions that sectional tensions never again reached their earlier levels. In the modern Congress, various caucuses continue to bring together members from the same region who seek a common agenda to promote the interests of their region.

SEE ALSO

Calhoun, John C.; Clay, Henry; Compromise of 1850; "Solid South"; Webster, Daniel

FURTHER READING

Potter, David M. *The Impending Crisis, 1848–1861*. New York: Harper & Row, 1976.

Senate

ALL STATES are represented equally in the Senate by two senators (in contrast to the House, where a state's representation is in proportion to the size of the state's population). Senators serve six-year terms and are divided into three "classes," so that only one class, or one-third of the Senate, is up for election every two years. With two-thirds of its membership carrying over after each election, the Senate is a "continuing body." These longer terms (House members serve only two years) were intended to insulate the Senate—more than the House—from sudden shifts in public opinion.

The equality of the states' representation in the Senate, regardless of the size of the population, was designed to protect the smaller states. The Senate adopted rules that further enhanced minority rights. A small minority of senators, even a minority of one, can use the rules to delay or defeat objectionable legislation. The Senate's toleration of unlimited debate, in the form of the filibuster, has been its most notable difference from the House, whose rules favor the majority.

Although both houses of Congress share essentially the same powers, the Senate has the sole power of "advice and consent," to confirm the President's nominations and to ratify treaties. The Vice President serves as president (or presiding officer) of the Senate, and the senators elect their other officers. Like the House, the Senate determines its own rules and disciplines its own members. The Senate also sits as a court of impeachment once the House has voted to impeach, or formally accuse, a federal officer.

The first official photograph of the Senate in session, taken in 1963.

Initially, the Senate met in secret session, and even after it opened its doors in 1794 it operated for years in the shadow of the House. But during the 1830s the Senate emerged as a powerful counterforce to the strong Presidency of Andrew Jackson. Such rivals to Jackson as Henry Clay and Daniel Webster used the Senate as their forum, and a new political party, the Whigs, developed around them. Because senators were evenly divided between free and slave states, the Senate became the center of efforts to preserve the Union. Senators sought legislative compromise to calm popular passions, but decades of compromise could not prevent the Civil War.

The seal of the United States Senate

Senate leadership

The decades after the Civil War saw powerful committee chairmen exert strong party leadership over the Senate. By 1900 journalists were pointing to the Senate Four—Republicans Nelson Aldrich, William Allison, John C. Spooner, and Orville Platt—as being so influential that they could "block and defeat anything that the president or the House may desire." Press criticism of the Senate as a "millionaires' club," more responsive to powerful corporations than to public opinion, resulted in the 17th Amendment in 1913. It gave the privilege of electing senators to the voters rather than to state legislatures.

Throughout its first century, the Senate acted as a body of equals without official floor leaders. The position of majority leader emerged in 1913, when Democratic Caucus chairman John Worth Kern took on the role of directing his party's initiatives on the floor. The parties formalized the posts of majority and minority leader in the 1920s, and the leaders took the front-row seats on either side of the center aisle. Senate rules give the leaders the right of "first recognition," meaning that the presiding officer must recognize them to speak before any other senators.

A clublike atmosphere

The atmosphere of the Senate has been compared to that of an exclusive club. Within that club developed an "inner club" made up of powerful committee chairmen and ranking minority party members. The "inner club" drew its membership largely from conservative Southern Democratic committee chairmen and generally excluded junior members and Northern liberals. During the 1950s Majority Leader Lyndon B. Johnson (Democrat–Texas) began to change this structure by appointing freshmen senators to important committees rather than making them spend years in apprenticeships on lesser committees. Johnson's successor as majority leader, Mike Mansfield (Democrat–Missouri), furthered the trend by spreading power more equally among all senators.

While the upper houses of most parliaments (such as the British House of Lords) have declined in influence in the 20th century, the Senate remains a powerful legislative body. As the Constitution intended, the Senate serves to balance the House, just as the Congress as a whole checks and balances the executive and judiciary branches of the government.

SEE ALSO

Advice and consent; Bicameral; Committees; Filibuster; House-Senate Relations; "Inner club": Leadership; "Millionaires' club"; Nominations, confirmation of; Treaties

FURTHER READING

Baker, Richard A. *The United States Senate: A Bicentennial History*. Malabar, Fla.: Krieger, 1987.
Reedy, George E. *The U.S. Senate: Paralysis or a Search for Consensus?* New York: Crown, 1986.
Ritchie, Donald A. *The Senate*. New York: Chelsea House, 1988.

Senatorial courtesy

WHEN SENATORS vote against a nomination because the home-state senator objects to that nominee, they are showing "senatorial courtesy." They expect that other senators will reciprocate by voting against any objectionable nominee from their own state. The first instance of "senatorial courtesy" took place in 1789, when the Senate rejected the nomination of Benjamin Fishbourn to be a naval officer of the port of Savannah. The two senators from Georgia preferred another candidate and convinced their colleagues to vote against Fishbourn. President George Washington then submitted another nomination that was acceptable to the Georgia senators. "Senatorial courtesy" has given senators great influence over such appointments as federal judges and U.S. attorneys from their state.

Seniority

ADVANCEMENT IN Congress—increased power and privilege—generally comes through seniority. The longer that members serve, the more senior they become on their committees, leading to the chairmanship of important subcommittees and eventually to the chair of the full committee. Members also receive room assignments through seniority, gaining larger, better-placed offices with more impressive views the more often they are reelected and the more senior they become. Seniority is dated from the time that a member is sworn in. When groups of new members are sworn into the House together as a new "class," mem-

Representative Jamie Whitten

bers draw lots for office space and other privileges. The Senate, by contrast, uses a formula to determine each member's seniority ranking within that class. The formula includes, in order of importance: previous service in the Senate, service as Vice President, previous service in the House of Representatives, previous service as a state governor, and the size of the population of the senator's state. For a while some outgoing senators resigned just before the end of their term, to allow the governor to appoint their successor and give him a few days' lead in seniority over the rest of the class. But the parties changed their rules in 1980 to prohibit this practice by not recognizing the extra days toward seniority.

The seniority system favors smaller states and districts where one party predominates. When these states repeatedly reelect the same senators and representatives, they gain political power in Congress as those members advance in seniority to become committee chairs and ranking members. Arizona kept Carl Hayden (Democrat) in the House for 15 years and in the Senate for 41, where he became chairman of the Senate Appro-

TEN LONGEST-SERVING SENATORS AS OF THE START OF THE 103RD CONGRESS, 1993

1. **Carl Hayden** *(Democrat–Arizona),* 1927–69 = 41 years, 10 months (plus 15 years in the House)

2. **John Stennis** *(Democrat–Mississippi),* 1947–89 = 41 years, 2 months

3. **Russell Long** *(Democrat–Louisiana),* 1948–87 = 38 years

4. **Richard Russell** *(Democrat–Georgia),* 1933–71 = 38 years

5. **J. Strom Thurmond** *(Democrat until 1964/Republican since 1964–South Carolina),* 1954–present = 37 years, 4 months

6. **James Eastland** *(Democrat–Mississippi),* 1941, 1943–78 = 36 years, 3 months

7. **Francis Warren** *(Republican–Wyoming),* 1890–93, 1895–1929 = 36 years, 2 months

8. **Warren Magnuson** *(Democrat–Washington),* 1944–81 = 36 years (plus 8 years in the House)

9. **Kenneth McKellar** *(Democrat–Tennessee),* 1917–53 = 35 years, 10 months (plus 5 years in the House)

10. **Milton Young** *(Republican–North Carolina),* 1945–81 = 35 years, 9 months

TEN LONGEST-SERVING REPRESENTATIVES AS OF THE START OF THE 103RD CONGRESS, 1993

1. **Jamie Whitten** *(Democrat–Mississippi),* 1941–present = 51 years, 2 months

2. **Carl Vinson** *(Democrat–Georgia),* 1914–65 = 50 years, 2 months

3. **Emmanuel Celler** *(Democrat–New York),* 1923–73 = 49 years, 10 months

4. **Sam Rayburn** *(Democrat–Texas),* 1913–61 = 48 years, 10 months

5. **Wright Patman** *(Democrat–Texas),* 1929–76 = 47 years

6. **Joseph G. Cannon** *(Republican–Illinois),* 1873–91, 1893–1913, 1915–23 = 46 years

7. **Adolph Sabath** *(Democrat–Illinois),* 1907–52 = 45 years, 10 months

8. **George Mahon** *(Democrat–Texas),* 1935–79 = 44 years

9. **Melvin Price** *(Democrat–Illinois),* 1945–88 = 43 years, 3 months

10. **John McCormack** *(Democrat–Massachusetts),* 1928–71 = 42 years, 2 months

priations Committee. Mississippi returned Jamie Whitten (Democrat) regularly to the House for more than 50 years, and he chaired the House Appropriations Committee.

In 1975 House rules weakened the seniority system by providing that at the beginning of a Congress the members of the majority party could vote to remove a chairman, and could elect a new chair who was not necessarily the next most senior member. Several senior House members have lost their committee chairmanships under this rule, including Representative Whitten. In 1992, after Whitten's ill health limited his ability to lead his committee, the Democratic Caucus voted to remove him as chairman of the Appropriations Committee. In general, this reform made committee chairmen more accountable to other members. The reduction of seniority also decentralized power and diminished party leadership.

Separation of powers

SUSPICIOUS OF any concentration of power, the framers of the Constitution distributed power among the three branches of the federal government. The first three articles of the Constitution enumerate, or list, the specific powers of each of the branches. Essentially, Congress would enact laws, the executive branch would administer these laws, and the judiciary would interpret them. The framers expected that the three branches, with their different powers and responsibilities, would check and balance each other, preventing any one part of the government from becoming too strong or dictatorial.

The actual division of power was not clear-cut. For the Constitution also *implies* many overlapping powers, which each of the branches have claimed. Presidents have asserted the right to make foreign policy exclusively, without consulting Congress. Congress has attempted to "micromanage" the executive branch by enacting legislation that specifically defines how these laws must be administered. The courts have been accused of "legislating" by actively interpreting legislation in ways that Congress had not intended.

Although the Constitution distributed various powers among the three branches, it never constructed walls between them. Instead, the Constitution requires Congress and the President to share certain powers. In military policy, for instance, the President serves as commander in chief of the armed forces, but Congress is authorized to raise and fund an army and navy, and it votes to declare war. In foreign policy, Presidents appoint U.S. ambassadors and negotiate treaties, but the Senate confirms or rejects those nominations and treaties. Both the House and Senate vote to fund foreign aid and other U.S. diplomatic efforts. In determining fiscal policy, the President submits a budget for the federal government to Congress, but Congress enacts its own version of the budget, appropriates all money, and raises revenue to pay for federal spending. The President may veto, or reject, any revenue and appropriation bill, but by a two-thirds vote of both houses Congress can override that veto.

Presidents, Congress, and the general public have frequently grown impatient and frustrated with the slowness, inefficiency, and even deadlock of a government whose powers are divided. But as Supreme Court Justice Louis D. Brandeis noted in the case of *Myers v. United States* (1926), "The doctrine of separation of powers was adopted by the Constitution of 1787, not to promote efficiency but to preclude the exercise of arbitrary power."

SEE ALSO
Checks and balances; Constitution

FURTHER READING
Fisher, Louis. *Constitutional Conflicts between Congress and the President.* Princeton, N.J.: Princeton University Press, 1985.

Sergeant at arms

THE HOUSE and Senate each elect a sergeant at arms to enforce the rules and regulations and to oversee the protection of members, staff, and visitors. On April 7, 1789, the Senate elected James Mathers as its doorkeeper, to guard the doors of the chamber, which were kept closed and barred to the public during early debates. On May 12, 1789, the

The sergeant at arms carries the mace of the House as a warning to disorderly members.

House elected Joseph Wheaton as sergeant at arms, taking that title from the equivalent post in the British House of Commons. In 1798 the Senate, too, adopted the title of sergeant at arms.

The first sergeant at arms purchased firewood to heat the chambers in winter and guarded the chambers during the months when Congress was in recess. These functions have expanded over time. Today the Senate sergeant at arms supervises much of the maintenance of the Senate wing of the Capitol and office buildings and supervises a wide assortment of staff members, from computer specialists to janitors, carpenters, and barbers. The House assigns these functions differently, placing many of them under the clerk of the House, the doorkeeper, and the director of non-legislative services.

The House sergeant at arms carries the mace (silver rods lashed together and topped by a silver eagle), which is the symbol of the authority of the House. If debate grows heated and disorderly, the sergeant at arms lifts the mace high to remind members to restore order.

The House and Senate have also authorized their sergeants at arms to "arrest" absent members to bring them to the chambers to establish a quorum, the minimum number of members needed to conduct business. The sergeants at arms serve on the Capitol Police Board to oversee policing of the Capitol complex. They supervise parking, and they maintain crowd control during political demonstrations at the Capitol. The sergeants at arms have also become protocol officers who greet official visitors and lead processions of members at Presidential inaugurations, State of the Union messages, and other joint sessions and ceremonial meetings.

SEE ALSO

Capitol Police; Doorkeepers; Mace of the House of Representatives; Officers of the House and Senate; Quorum

FURTHER READING

Byrd, Robert C. "Sergeant at Arms." In *The Senate, 1789–1989: Addresses on the History of the United States Senate*. Vol. 2. Washington, D.C.: Government Printing Office, 1991.

Sessions

EACH CONGRESS is divided into at least two sessions. The first session takes place during the year following the election, and the second session follows the year after that. Originally, the Constitution provided that Congress would begin its sessions on the first Monday in December, more than a year after the election had been held. In 1933 the 20th Amendment moved the beginning of each session up to January 3. The 20th Amendment was designed to end the many lame-duck sessions that had occurred between an election and the start of the next Congress. These sessions were called lame-duck sessions because many of the members had retired or been defeated and were rapidly approaching the end of their term in office. Since the passage of the 20th Amendment, only a few lame-duck sessions have been held to take care of unfinished business. The last one, in 1982, addressed appropriations and budget issues.

Sessions generally run until the fall, although they may go right through December. If the Congress has adjourned, the President can call it back into a special session, which might be designated a third session of that Congress. The last such third session occurred during the 76th Congress (1939–41), when President Franklin D. Roosevelt called Congress back into session following the outbreak of war in Europe.

Legislation introduced but not acted upon during the first session remains alive and keeps the same number during the second session. But any unfinished business dies with the second session,

Assistant Door-keeper Isaac Bassett turned back the hands of the clock to give the Senate extra time at the end of a session.

and its sponsors must begin anew in the next Congress.

Representative Clem Miller (Democrat–California) compared the opening day of a new session to the first day of school, when everything seems brand-new and everyone seems hopeful:

Congressmen flood the tunnel that connects the offices with the Capitol. The hubbub is fierce. . . . Everywhere hands are grabbed. They set off smartly in platoons of four or six, waves of men and women proceeding along the gentle incline. Deep smiles of greeting, halloos, and backslapping. This may appear to outsiders as part of the ordinary political spectacle, the general overfriendliness of the trade; but it is much more than that. The emotions are real. The affection is a heartfelt display. It is the camaraderie of the shared experience. These people, these congressmen, have all been through the mill. They have returned from the indifferent cruelties of the political wars.

SEE ALSO
Lame-duck sessions

FURTHER READING
Miller, Clem. *Member of the House: Letters of a Congressman.* New York: Scribners, 1962.

Shadow senators

PEOPLE WHO live in territories that belong to the United States are represented in Congress by delegates in the House of Representatives and sometimes also by "shadow senators." The House provides all delegates with offices, staff, and committee assignments and permits them to speak in the House chamber. Shadow senators, by contrast, receive little offi-

Citizens of Washington, D.C., elected Jesse Jackson as their "shadow senator" to work for statehood.

cial recognition, serve on no committees, and do not participate in Senate debates. Rather than representing constituents, shadow senators devote most of their attention to lobbying efforts to turn their territory into a state. The first shadow senators were elected by the Tennessee legislature in 1796 to promote statehood. Michigan, California, Minnesota, Oregon, and Alaska also employed shadow senators. Following in this tradition, in 1990 the District of Columbia elected the Reverend Jesse Jackson as a shadow senator to advocate making Washington, D.C., a state.

SEE ALSO
Delegates

Shared powers

SEE Separation of powers

Sherman Antitrust Act (1890)

DURING THE 1880s Americans worried about the emergence of trusts, or combinations of businesses that tended to reduce competition. Trusts occurred whenever a single board of trustees controlled the management of many different companies. By consolidating these companies, trusts could monopolize, or dominate, production and set prices in a particular industry. Newspapers and magazines accused the Standard Oil Trust, the Sugar Trust, and other large-scale industries of improperly suppressing competition. Defenders of the trusts asserted that such consolidation allowed more efficient production and lower prices. Opponents argued that a lack of competition placed consumers, small

businesses, and farmers at the mercy of these monopolies, which could charge whatever prices they wanted.

In 1890 Congress responded to these public concerns by passing—almost unanimously—the Sherman Antitrust Act. Named for its chief sponsor, Senator John Sherman (Republican–Ohio), this act sought to end monopolies and make illegal any restriction on trade. However, the Sherman Act lacked any effective means of enforcement, and it failed to stop the growth of big business. During the 1890s the federal courts further weakened the Sherman Act by interpreting it to permit mergers and other forms of business consolidation. During the Progressive Era (1900–14), reformers continued the fight to "bust" the trusts. In 1914 Congress created the Federal Trade Commission in an effort to regulate business practices rather than try to abolish big business, as the Sherman Act had tried to do.

Smith, Howard W.

☆ *Born: Feb. 2, 1883, Broad Run, Va.*
☆ *Political party: Democrat*
☆ *Representative from Virginia: 1931–67*
☆ *Died: Oct. 3, 1976, Alexandria, Va.*

AS A MEMBER of the House Rules Committee for 32 years, including 12 as its chairman, Howard Smith fought for limited government and against nearly all federal programs for education, health, housing, or civil rights. Smith used the full powers of the Rules Committee, as well as his own command of the rules and precedents of the House, to frustrate his opponents. During the 1950s the Rules Committee was divided evenly between liberals and conservatives, and a tie vote could prevent legislation from reaching the floor. Sometimes, if Smith thought his side might lose a vote, he would simply go home, knowing that the committee could not meet without its chairman and that bills could not reach the House floor until the committee had acted. In 1961, fearing that the committee would block President John F. Kennedy's legislative programs, liberal Democrats led a revolt against Chairman Smith. They proposed to expand the size of the committee to add more liberal members. Speaker Sam Rayburn (Democrat–Texas) threw his support behind this effort, which won by a slim margin of 217 to 212. Smith continued to fight against social programs, but his power to obstruct had been greatly diminished.

SEE ALSO

Rayburn, Sam; Rules committees

FURTHER READING

Dierenfield, Bruce J. *Keeper of the Rules: Congressman Howard W. Smith of Virginia.* Charlottesville: University Press of Virginia, 1987.

Smith, Margaret Chase

☆ Born: Dec. 14, 1897, Skowhegan, Maine
☆ Political party: Republican
☆ Representative from Maine: 1940–49
☆ Senator from Maine: 1949–73

WHEN REPRESENTATIVE Clyde Smith (Republican–Maine) died in 1940, his wife, Margaret Chase Smith, ran for election to complete his term. She won four more terms in the House before being elected to the Senate. In an era when it was still uncommon for women to enter politics and serve in Congress, Smith avoided the more traditional "women's issues"—such as health and education—and joined the Senate Armed Services Committee, where she established her legislative reputation.

In 1950, when Senator Joseph R.

Senator Margaret Chase Smith with Lyndon B. Johnson

McCarthy began making reckless accusations about alleged communists in government, Senator Margaret Chase Smith asked what proof he had to back up his charges against government officials. McCarthy promised to produce evidence, but he never found anything that convinced her. When other senators seemed unwilling to confront McCarthy, Smith decided that someone had to speak out. On June 1, 1950, she rose in the Senate to deliver her "Declaration of Conscience." She called on the Senate to do some serious soul-searching about the abuse of its powers and privileges. She condemned the loose, unsupported charges that amounted to character assassination, and she defended as basic principles of American life "the right to criticize; the right to hold unpopular beliefs; the right to protest; the right of independent thought."

At the time, very few of Smith's colleagues rallied to her support. It took the Senate another four years before it censured McCarthy for the behavior that Margaret Chase Smith had first taken the floor to denounce.

SEE ALSO

McCarthy, Joseph R.; Women in Congress

FURTHER READING

Smith, Margaret Chase. *Declaration of Conscience.* Garden City, N.Y.: Doubleday, 1972.

Snuff

BEFORE THE Civil War, snuff (tobacco finely ground for inhaling) became so popular among senators that the Senate set a large silver urn, a vaselike container, of snuff on the Vice President's desk. But in 1850 Vice President Millard Fillmore complained, "I cannot understand what is going on in the Senate on

The Senate traditionally keeps snuffboxes in its chamber.

account of the conversation of Senators who come here to get a pinch of snuff." The urn was replaced with two small black-lacquered boxes, located on the ledges just behind and on either side of the Vice President's desk. If you look carefully from the gallery, you can still see these snuffboxes. For tradition's sake the boxes are kept filled, even though senators long ago stopped taking snuff.

FURTHER READING
Rienow, Robert, and Leona Train Rienow. *Snuff, Sin & the Senate.* Chicago: Follett, 1965.

"Solid South"

AFTER THE Civil War and Reconstruction, the Democratic party regained political control of the eleven former Confederate states. Denying the vote to African Americans and intimidating "carpetbaggers" (Southern Republicans, originally from the North, who got their nickname from their luggage made of carpet fabric), Democrats effectively eliminated the Republican party as a political force in the Southern states. For the next century, winning the Demo-

cratic primary in a Southern state meant winning the general election. Southerners also repeatedly reelected their senators and representatives, which enabled them to gain seniority in Congress. As a result, whenever the Democrats held the majority in the Senate or House, Southern Democrats tended to chair the most important committees. The "solid South" held its strongest grip on Congress between the 1930s and 1960s. Then the enactment of the Civil Rights Act of 1964 and the Voting Rights Act of 1965 alienated many white Southerners from the Democratic party. At the same time, Republicans adopted a "Southern strategy"—running candidates and making appointments that would appeal to the region's conservative sentiments. The strategy encouraged many Democrats to register or vote as Republicans. The "solid South" made way for a two-party South as Southern voters began electing Republicans as well as Democrats to Congress.

SEE ALSO
Boll Weevils; Carpetbaggers

FURTHER READING
Daniel, Pete. *Standing at the Crossroads: Southern Life since 1900.* New York: Hill & Wang, 1986.

Cartoonist Thomas Nast portrayed the "solid South" returning to Congress after the Civil War.

Joseph G. Cannon was a powerful Speaker of the House.

Speaker of the House

THE HOUSE elects a Speaker to serve as its presiding officer. At first the Speaker performed the role of moderator—modeled after the Speaker of the British House of Commons—directing the flow of legislative business and maintaining order. When Henry Clay became Speaker in 1811, he assumed the additional role of party leader, preserving his right to debate and vote like other members. (The Speaker must step down from the podium and speak from the floor if he wishes to address a specific issue.) Since Clay's time, most Speakers have combined the roles as leader both of the majority party and of the House as a whole.

As the number of members of the House grew, strong Speakers such as Thomas B. Reed, who served in the 1890s, interpreted and enforced the House rules to favor the majority and to block obstructionist tactics by the minority. In 1910, however, progressive re-formers protested against the "dictatorial" leadership of Speaker Joseph G. Cannon and stripped away many of his powers, including the authority to name all committee members and appoint the chairs of all committees. Today the Democratic Caucus and Republican Conference make committee assignments, and House committee members elect their own chairs. House reforms also prohibited the Speaker from serving on the Rules Committee.

A majority of votes is needed to elect a Speaker, and the position has often been hotly contested. The longest election took place between December 1855 and February 1856, when it took 133 ballots to elect Nathaniel Banks as Speaker. Since the 1930s it has become common for the majority leader to move up to become Speaker. Sam Rayburn (Democrat–Texas) holds the record of the longest service as Speaker: a total of 17 years, 2 months, and 2 days over three periods from 1940 to 1961.

When not presiding, the Speaker appoints a Speaker pro tem (a Latin phrase meaning "for the time being") to preside in his place. The Speaker, through the

SPEAKERS OF THE HOUSE

Frederick Augustus Muhlenberg (Federalist–Pennsylvania), 1789–91

Jonathan Trumbull (Federalist–Connecticut), 1791–93

Frederick Augustus Muhlenberg (Federalist–Pennsylvania), 1793–95

Jonathan Dayton (Democratic-Republican–New Jersey), 1795–99

Theodore Sedgwick (Federalist–Massachusetts), 1799–1801

Nathaniel Macon (Democratic-Republican–North Carolina), 1801–7

Joseph B. Varnum (Democratic-Republican–Massachusetts), 1807–11

Henry Clay (Democratic-Republican–Kentucky), 1811–14

Langdon Chives (Democratic-Republican–South Carolina), 1814–15

Henry Clay (Democratic-Republican–Kentucky), 1815–20

John W. Taylor (Democratic-Republican–New York), 1820–21

Philip P. Barbour (Democratic-Republican–Virginia), 1821–23

Henry Clay (Democratic-Republican–Kentucky), 1823–25

John W. Taylor (Democratic-Republican–New York), 1825–27

Andrew Stevenson (Democrat–Virginia), 1827–34

John Bell (Whig–Tennessee), 1834–35

James K. Polk (Democrat–Tennessee), 1835–39

Robert M. T. Hunter (Whig–Virginia), 1839–41

John White (Whig–Kentucky), 1841–43

John W. Jones (Democrat–Virginia), 1843–45

John Wesley Davis (Democrat–Indiana), 1845–47

Robert C. Winthrop (Whig–Massachusetts), 1847–49

Howell G. Cobb (Democrat–Georgia), 1849–51

Linn Boyd (Democrat–Kentucky), 1851–55

Nathaniel P. Banks (Republican–Massachusetts), 1856–57

James L. Orr (Democrat–South Carolina), 1857–59

William Pennington (Republican–New Jersey), 1860–61

Galusha A. Grow (Republican–Pennsylvania), 1861–63

Schuyler Colfax (Republican–Indiana), 1863–69

Theodore M. Pomeroy (Republican–New York), 1869

James G. Blaine (Republican–Maine), 1869–75

Michael C. Kerr (Democrat–Indiana), 1875–76

Samuel J. Randall (Democrat–Pennsylvania), 1876–81

J. Warren Keifer (Republican–Ohio), 1881–83

John G. Carlisle (Democrat–Kentucky), 1883–89

Thomas B. Reed (Republican–Maine), 1889–91

Charles F. Crisp (Democrat–Georgia), 1891–95

Thomas B. Reed (Republican–Maine), 1895–99

David B. Henderson (Republican–Iowa), 1899–1903

Joseph G. Cannon (Republican–Illinois), 1903–11

James Beauchamp ("Champ") Clark (Democrat–Missouri), 1911–19

Frederick H. Gillett (Republican–Massachusetts), 1919–25

Nicholas Longworth (Republican–Ohio), 1925–31

John Nance Garner (Democrat–Texas), 1931–33

Henry T. Rainey (Democrat–Illinois), 1933–34

Joseph W. Byrnes (Democrat–Tennessee), 1935–36

William Bankhead (Democrat–Alabama), 1936–40

Sam Rayburn (Democrat–Texas), 1940–47

Joseph W. Martin (Republican–Massachusetts), 1947–48

Sam Rayburn (Democrat–Texas), 1949–52

Joseph W. Martin (Republican–Massachusetts), 1953–54

Sam Rayburn (Democrat–Texas), 1955–61

John W. McCormack (Democrat–Massachusetts), 1962–71

Carl Albert (Democrat–Oklahoma), 1971–77

Thomas P. ("Tip") O'Neill, Jr. (Democrat–Massachusetts), 1977–87

Jim Wright (Democrat–Texas), 1987–89

Thomas S. Foley (Democrat–Washington), 1989–

House parliamentarian, refers all bills to committee and also appoints the chairs of the committee of the whole (a device by which the House suspends its rules to meet as a committee, to limit debate and amendments). A combination of administrative, legislative, protocol, and political responsibilities makes the Speaker, in the words of Thomas B. Reed, "the embodiment of the House, its power and dignity."

SEE ALSO
Blaine, James G.; Cannon, Joseph G.; Clark, James Beauchamp ("Champ"); Clay, Henry; Committee of the whole; Foley, Thomas S.; Garner, John Nance; Longworth, Nicholas; Muhlenberg, Frederick Augustus; Officers of the House and Senate; Rayburn, Sam; Reed, Thomas B.; Rules committees; Wright, Jim

FURTHER READING
Peters, Ronald M., Jr. *The American Speakership: The Office in Historical Perspective.* Baltimore, Md.: Johns Hopkins University Press, 1990.

Special orders

WHILE WATCHING the proceedings of the House of Representatives on television, viewers are sometimes surprised to see the cameras show an entirely empty chamber, except for the person speaking. When this occurs, the House is likely to be operating under special orders. In regular session, the House places strict limits on the amount of time that members may speak. But when no legislative business is planned, members may reserve the chamber under special orders, to speak at length on any topic that concerns them. Even though the House is not in regular session, remarks made during special orders are carried on C-SPAN's television network and are recorded in the next day's *Congressional Record.* However, to alert viewers that the speaker is addressing an empty cham-

ber, and that opponents are not present to rebut the speaker, the television cameras regularly pan the vacant seats.

The Senate has a different form of "special orders," permitting senators to speak for five minutes each on a variety of topics during the Morning Hour, before debate begins on specific legislation.

SEE ALSO
Morning Hour

Special rules

SEE Rules, House and Senate

Special sessions

IF AN EMERGENCY occurs when Congress is not in session, the Constitution empowers the President to call Congress back into special, or extraordinary, session. Prior to the passage of the 20th Amendment in 1933, Congress met for only a limited number of months each year. Up to that date Presidents called the Senate into special session on 46 occasions, usually to confirm nominations to the cabinet or to deal with important treaties. On 27 other occasions, Presidents called both the House and Senate into special session. These special sessions responded to wars, economic crises, and important legislative proposals. For instance, Abraham Lincoln called Congress into special session on July 4, 1861, to deal with the outbreak of the Civil War. Franklin D. Roosevelt called Congress into special session in March 1933 to pass emergency banking and relief legislation during the Great Depression. This session became known as the "first hundred days of the New Deal."

After the 20th Amendment changed the opening date of Congress to January 3, and after Congress began meeting for most of the year, the need for special sessions diminished. Since 1933 Presidents have called Congress back only four times. Franklin Roosevelt called a special session in October 1937 to enact legislation that would establish minimum wages and maximum hours of work. In September 1939 Roosevelt called Congress into special session when Germany invaded Poland and triggered World War II. During the 80th Congress, when Republicans held the majority in Congress, Democratic President Harry S. Truman called Congress back in October 1947 and July 1948 to deal with unfinished domestic legislation. President Truman planned to campaign for reelection against the "Do-Nothing 80th Congress," so he called these sessions to embarrass the Republican majorities by accusing them of not acting on important social matters.

In recent years when Congress has adjourned, it has also authorized the leaders of the Senate and House to call the Congress back in case of emergency.

Sponsoring and cosponsoring legislation

THE SPONSORS of a bill are its principal authors. Bills often take their sponsors' names, such as the Gramm-Rudman-Hollings Act, known for its three Senate sponsors, or the Humphrey-Hawkins Act, known for its chief sponsors in the Senate and House. To demonstrate the popularity of a bill and to gather further support, sponsors will send out "Dear Colleague" letters, circulating the bill among other members and urging them to cosponsor it. The names of sponsors and cosponsors are printed at the top of each bill and in the *Congressional Record*.

SEE ALSO
"Dear Colleague" letters

Staff

CONGRESS RELIES on a large staff to get its work done. By the 1990s the House was hiring some 11,000 staff members and the Senate another 6,000. Counting the additional support staff of the Architect of the Capitol, Capitol Police, Library of Congress (including the Congressional Research Service), General Accounting Office, Congressional Budget Office, and Office of Technology Assessment, the total number of legislative branch employees topped 30,000. Still, this is a smaller staff than that of

Humorist Mark Twain (center) in 1868, while he served as secretary to Senator William Stewart of Nevada.

some cabinet departments. Critics have called the congressional staff an anonymous bureaucracy of "unelected representatives." Senator Herman Talmadge (Democrat–Georgia) complained:

> We have got a lot of bright-eyed, idealistic young people right out of law school, seeking new worlds to conquer. They spend virtually all of their time writing speeches for Senators, and developing brand new spending programs for Senators to introduce . . . and if you double the staff you double the amendments and double the costly new programs.

But was the increased staff the cause of the congressional work load or the result of it? In the 19th century clerks were hired only for the months that Congress was in session. Only a few committees, such as the Ways and Means, Finance, Printing, and Claims Committees, had enough work to hire a year-round staff. The first committee clerks handled the mail and supervised the printing of committee reports, hearing transcripts, and other official documents. By 1900 there were still fewer than 300 congressional employees. These staff members got their jobs mostly through patronage—that is, congressional sponsors hired them to reward them for their political activities and party loyalty.

The construction of Senate and House office buildings gave every member of Congress an office and the ability to employ a small personal staff, consisting of a secretary and one or two assistants. When they drafted complex legislation, members of Congress often had to rely on the executive branch agencies to provide the language for the bills, prepare reports, and even ghostwrite their speeches. Lobbyists from corporate law firms also provided assistance in drafting legislation to help their clients.

Legislative Reorganization Acts

After World War II Congress sought to modernize its proceedings and gain independent expertise. The Legislative Reorganization Act of 1946 provided a professional, nonpartisan staff for every committee, authorized the creation and government funding of Republican and Democratic policy committees, and expanded members' personal staffs by creating the post of administrative assistant. The Reorganization Act also expanded the Legislative Reference Service, later renamed the Congressional Research Service, to provide nonpartisan expertise on almost every issue with which Congress deals. At the same time, cold war global responsibilities and the growth of government services at home pressured Congress into remaining in session for more months each year to handle an ever-increasing work load. Between the 1940s and 1970s the staff expanded steadily to match this demand on members' time.

Further reorganization in the 1970s provided every committee member with his or her own staff person on that committee and also established a separate staff to serve the minority party's interests on that committee. The combined

Staff members working in the office of Representative Eugene Johnston.

effect of these reforms was to lessen Congress's dependence on executive agencies, lobbyists, and other outside sources for gathering information and preparing legislation. The reforms also lessened the dependence of minority party members on staffs that previously had been appointed by committee chairmen from the majority party. Even junior members of the majority party gained more independence by having their own staff members participate in the committees' work.

Women and minorities on the staff

In 1970 women staff members examined the range of jobs and salaries on Capitol Hill. They protested that women were not employed in the highest posts and were paid less than men doing comparable work. During the next two decades, salaries became more equal and women held more high-level positions, including the elected posts of secretary of the Senate and sergeant at arms. Congress had also exempted itself from civil rights legislation and other bills that provided for fair employment practices. These bills were enforced by the executive branch through the Justice Department, which could not hold jurisdiction over the legislature. Although members of Congress pledged to comply voluntarily with these laws, the hiring of minorities continued to lag.

Congressional staff turnover

Members of the congressional staff are not protected by civil service laws. They serve at the pleasure of the member who employed them or the majority party of their house. When the legislative majority switches from one party to the other, many staff members are replaced by people from the incoming majority party. Even without a change in party, there is regular turnover in the staff. Those who work for individual members tend to be relatively young, often fresh out of college. They work long hours at relatively low pay. Energetic and eager, they seek the opportunity to influence government policy and to advance their own careers after they leave Capitol Hill. Committee staff tend to be older, hold postgraduate degrees, and stay longer in their jobs.

Some staff members are "legislative technicians" who draft amendments and prepare analyses of bills for the members. Others handle political functions, answer mail, keep the files, deal with press relations, coordinate members' schedules, provide computer services, operate home-district offices, conduct research, monitor the work of executive agencies and federal funding, and handle innumerable other tasks to enable Congress to function effectively.

SEE ALSO

Legislative Reorganization Acts (1946 and 1970); Patronage

FURTHER READING

Fox, Harrison W., and Susan Webb Hammond. *Congressional Staffs: The Invisible Force in American Lawmaking.* New York: Free Press, 1979.
Malbin, Michael J. *Unelected Representatives: Congressional Staff and the Future of Representative Government.* New York: Basic Books, 1980.

State legislatures

JUST AS many state capitol buildings are modeled after the U.S. Capitol, most state legislatures resemble the U.S. Congress. The state legislatures are mostly bicameral (they have two chambers), with a House and Senate; do most of their work through committees; control appropriations; and oversee the state governors and executive agencies. However, there are also significant differences. Using a device called the line-item veto, for example, most governors can reject a single item in a large appropriation bill, whereas the President must sign or reject an entire bill.

Initially, state legislatures had a close relationship with Congress. Until the ratification of the 17th Amendment to the Constitution in 1913, state legislatures elected U.S. senators, and many members of the House and Senate had previously served in their state legislature. During the early Congresses, some state legislatures also tried to "instruct" their senators on how to vote. But senators showed no inclination to follow their instructions.

In the federal system, the states have also served as "laboratories" of legislation, notably in social matters. State legislatures pioneered in the development of railroad regulations, restrictions against child labor, health and unemployment insurance, and other issues well in advance of the national Congress. At other times, Congress has prompted state legislatures to act by promising to give or withhold federal funds unless the state legislatures complied with federal rules (such as setting a minimum drinking age and maximum speed limits to receive federal highway money).

State of the Union message

EVERY YEAR, as required by the Constitution, the President addresses the Congress on the State of the Union. Presidents traditionally deliver their State of the Union message at the beginning of each session of Congress and use the occasion to outline their legislative program for that session.

In writing or in person

Presidents George Washington and John Adams gave their State of the Union messages in person. But to President Thomas Jefferson the practice too closely resembled the British monarch's annual address to the houses of Parliament and was therefore too regal for his tastes. Jefferson also lisped and disliked

President John F. Kennedy delivering his State of the Union message to a joint session of Congress in January 1963.

public speaking. So he sent his message in writing to be read aloud to Congress by a clerk. This practice continued for the rest of the 19th century and had the effect of diminishing the President's role in setting the legislative agenda. In 1893 a journalist observed that although the President's annual message was "regularly and respectfully submitted to the proper committees for consideration, it is very rare that any suggestion made by the Executive has any practical result."

Then in 1913 President Woodrow Wilson dramatically went to Congress to deliver his State of the Union message in person. This act symbolized Wilson's belief that Presidents should take a more active role in proposing and promoting legislation. Since then, most Presidents have followed Wilson's example.

A ceremonial occasion

Much ceremony accompanies the State of the Union message. Members of the Senate march in procession the length of the Capitol from the Senate to the larger House chamber. Members of the cabinet and the Supreme Court take seats in the front rows of the chamber, and honored guests fill the galleries. The House doorkeeper loudly announces: "Mr. Speaker, the President of the United States," and members rise for a standing ovation. Unlike the British Parliament, which listens in respectful silence to their monarch's annual address, members of Congress punctuate a President's message with applause. Members from the President's party heartily cheer his proposals, while members of the opposition party remain quietly restrained. In 1923 President Calvin Coolidge's State of the Union message was broadcast on the radio, and in 1947 television carried President Harry S. Truman's message. Since then, Presidents have taken the opportunity to talk beyond Congress, to address the nation

as a whole as a means of stimulating public support for their programs in the legislative battles that lie ahead.

Stevens, Thaddeus

☆ *Born: Apr. 4, 1792, Danville, Va.*
☆ *Political party: Republican*
☆ *Representative from Pennsylvania: 1849–53, 1859–68*
☆ *Died: Aug. 11, 1868, Washington, D.C.*

A LAME, old man with a weak heart, so feeble that he had to be carried into the House chamber on a chair, Representative Thaddeus Stevens remained influential and powerful enough to win the impeachment of President Andrew Johnson by the House. As chairman of the Ways and Means Committee, Stevens was the leader of the radical Republicans in the House during the Reconstruction era. He used his powers to block the President from readmitting the former Confederate states into the Union until they had pledged full equality for the freedmen, including the right to vote. Southerners detested Stevens as the symbol of what they saw as a fanatical and vindictive Reconstruction, a man who supported voting rights for African Americans only to maintain the Republican party in office. The freedmen, and many Northerners, revered Stevens as a defender of the ideals of the Declaration of Independence, that all people are created equal and endowed with inalienable rights.

Representative Thaddeus Stevens being carried to the House chamber in 1868.

S E E   A L S O
Impeachment of Andrew Johnson (1868); Reconstruction, congressional

F U R T H E R   R E A D I N G
Brodie, Fawn. *Thaddeus Stevens: Scourge of the South*. New York: Norton, 1959.

Subcommittees

HOUSE AND Senate committees distribute their work among various subcommittees to handle specific areas of the committee's jurisdiction. Subcommittees have smaller memberships, their own chair and ranking members, and their own staff. Subcommittees hold hearings, take testimony, and prepare the initial draft of legislation before submitting the bill for approval, revision, or rejection by the full committee. In recent years, both the House and Senate have adopted rules changes to make sure that senior members do not monopolize the chairmanships of subcommittees, as they did in the past. In the Senate, every member of the majority party chairs a subcommittee, and every member of the minority serves as the ranking member of a subcommittee. In the House, junior members also stand a better chance to chair a subcommittee relatively early in their legislative careers. In an effort to streamline business, at the start of the 103rd Congress the House agreed to limit all major committees to no more than six subcommittees and nonmajor committees to no more than five subcommittees.

SEE ALSO
Committees

A congressional subcommittee investigated the sinking of the Titanic in 1912.

Subpoena power

CONGRESS CAN subpoena witnesses, or force them to testify under oath, before its committees. This authority comes from the Constitution's grant to Congress of "all legislative powers" (Article 1, Section 1). Witnesses are subpoenaed to provide information that will assist committees in preparing legislation. In the case of *McGrain v. Daugherty* (1927), the Supreme Court recognized that Congress could subpoena even private citizens to testify. The Court noted that since not everyone would volunteer needed information, "some means of compulsion are essential to obtain what is needed." Witnesses who refuse to respond to a congressional subpoena, or refuse to give information (unless they invoke their 5th Amendment protection

THE SENATE SUBCOMMITTEE IN SESSION INVESTIGATING THE TITANIC DISASTER.

against self-incrimination) may be found in contempt of Congress and sent to prison.

The most famous use of the congressional subpoena occurred in 1973, when the Senate Select Committee on Presidential Campaign Activities (popularly known as the Watergate Committee) subpoenaed the tape recordings that President Richard M. Nixon had secretly made of White House conversations. This was the first time that Congress had ever subpoenaed a President. Nixon tried to withhold the tapes, claiming executive privilege (the right of the President not to release internal documents of the administration to the Congress). The courts ruled that the President could not use executive privilege as blanket protection, but the White House then released only a heavily edited version of the tapes. In June 1974, in *United States v. Nixon,* the Supreme Court ruled that executive privilege was a limited power and that the President must turn over all of the requested tapes to a special prosecutor investigating the Watergate incident. The opening of these tapes led Congress to begin impeachment proceedings against the President, causing Nixon to resign.

SEE ALSO

Contempt of Congress; Executive privilege; Investigations; Watergate investigation (1973)

FURTHER READING

Hamilton, James. *The Power to Probe: A Study of Congressional Investigations.* New York: Vintage, 1976.

Substitute motion

A LEGISLATIVE tactic designed to significantly alter a bill is to offer a substitute motion or a substitute amendment. Such a motion substitutes a different text for part or all of the bill being debated. A majority vote to accept the substitute kills the original version of the bill.

Subways

BECAUSE SENATORS and representatives frequently travel back and forth between their offices and the chambers, and have only 15 minutes from the time the bells first ring in which to cast their vote, the Senate and House operate subways that link the Capitol with the various office buildings. The subway dates back to 1909, when the first Senate office building (later named the Russell Building) opened. At that time, senators rode in two battery-powered buses that shuttled through an underground tunnel. In 1912 the buses were replaced by an electric railway train that ran between the build-

Senator Robert Taft rides the Senate subway. This model was used between 1912 and 1961.

ings at a speed of 20 miles per hour. When the Dirksen and Hart Senate office buildings were constructed, the subway system was extended to connect them with the Capitol. On the House side, only the Rayburn Building, opened in 1965, has subway transportation to the Capitol. However, the Cannon and Longworth buildings are linked to the Capitol by pedestrian walkways. The public may ride on the Senate and House subways except during votes, when the cars are generally reserved for members only.

Sumner, Charles

☆ *Born: Jan. 6, 1811, Boston, Mass.*
☆ *Political party: Free Soil, Republican*
☆ *Senator from Massachusetts: 1851–74*
☆ *Died: Mar. 11, 1874, Washington, D.C.*

OUTSPOKEN ON many issues, Charles Sumner was passionately opposed to the existence and spread of slavery in the United States. In 1856 Sumner delivered a heated speech against allowing slavery into the Kansas territory and denounced several Southern senators by name. Representative Preston Brooks of South Carolina took special offense at Sumner's sharp criticism of his uncle, Senator Andrew Butler (Democrat–South Carolina). "I have read your speech and it is a libel on South Carolina," said Brooks as he brought his cane down repeatedly on the startled Sumner, who sat writing at his desk in the Senate chamber. For the next two years, the badly injured Sumner was absent from the Senate, recuperating from his wounds. His empty desk stood as a powerful symbol of the tensions between North and South. (Later, efforts in the House to censure Brooks failed on a straight party-line vote. Brooks then resigned and won reelection by his con-

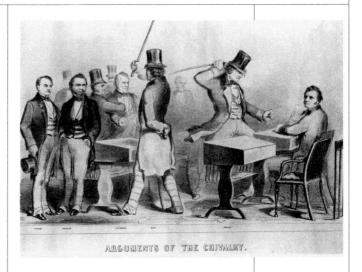

ARGUMENTS OF THE CHIVALRY.

stituents as a show of support.)

Brooks's blows did not end Sumner's controversial career, however. When the Republicans came into the majority, Sumner became an influential committee chairman and a spokesman for civil rights and against racial segregation. In 1875, shortly after his death, Congress passed the major civil rights bill that Sumner had ardently promoted.

SEE ALSO

Civil rights legislation

FURTHER READING

Donald, David. *Charles Sumner and the Coming of the Civil War.* New York: Knopf, 1960.
Donald, David. *Charles Sumner and the Rights of Man.* New York: Knopf, 1970.

"Sunshine" rules

"SUNSHINE" RULES passed by the House in 1973 and the Senate in 1975 required congressional committees to do most of their work in open session. Previously, committees had held most hearings in public, but all executive sessions—dealing with internal committee

Representative Preston Brooks struck Senator Charles Sumner with his cane in the Senate chamber in 1856, in a lithograph by Winslow Homer.

business and markups of a bill (in which the final revisions were made prior to reporting the bill to the full chamber)—were done behind closed doors. Many members felt that they could bargain and reach compromises more easily if they were not under public scrutiny. However, reformers believed that the public's business should be done out in the open, where the press and public could watch.

SEE ALSO
Markup sessions

Suspension of the rules

TO ENABLE the House to move speedily on noncontroversial matters, members will ask for a "suspension of the rules." If two-thirds of the House votes to suspend, then debate is limited to 40 minutes, and no additional amendments to the bill are permitted. The Senate achieves the same result with a unanimous consent agreement (that is, limitations on debate and amendment can be achieved if no member objects).

SEE ALSO
Rules, House and Senate; Unanimous consent agreements

Taft-Hartley Act (1947)

DURING THE 1930s, labor union membership in the United States increased rapidly, aided by the Wagner Act of 1935, which had protected the right of workers to organize and strike. Conservatives cited a coal miners' strike during World War II and a wave of strikes across many industries after the war as evidence that labor unions had become

too powerful and unrestrained. In 1946 Republicans won control of both the House and Senate for the first time since 1930. Senator Robert A. Taft, Sr. (Republican–Ohio), chair of the Senate Labor and Public Welfare Committee, and Representative Fred Hartley, Jr. (Republican–New Jersey), chair of the House Education and Labor Committee, sponsored the Labor-Management Relations Act of 1947 to regulate union activities. Their legislation became known as the Taft-Hartley Act.

Passed over President Harry Truman's veto, the Taft-Hartley Act allowed states to enact "right to work" laws to outlaw closed shops, companies where only union members could be employed. Taft-Hartley also prohibited jurisdictional strikes, in which different unions struck a company to determine which one would represent its workers, and barred communists from serving as union officers. Taft-Hartley gave Presidents the right to seek a federal court injunction to call off strikes for an 80-day "cooling off" period. This would allow work to continue while management and labor negotiated a contract. Although highly controversial, and strongly opposed by labor unions, the Republican-sponsored Taft-Hartley Act has remained largely unchanged by later Democratic majorities in Congress.

SEE ALSO
Taft, Robert A., Sr.; Veto

FURTHER READING
Donovan, Robert J. *Conflict and Crisis: The Presidency of Harry S. Truman, 1945–1948.* New York: Norton, 1977.
Hartmann, Susan M. *Truman and the 80th Congress.* Columbia: University of Missouri Press, 1971.

Congress "rescues" labor with the Taft-Hartley Act.

Taft, Robert A., Sr.

☆ Born: Sept. 8, 1889, Cincinnati, Ohio
☆ Political party: Republican
☆ Senator from Ohio: 1939–53
☆ Senate majority leader: 1953
☆ Died: July 31, 1953, New York, N.Y.

WHEN SENATOR John F. Kennedy published *Profiles in Courage*, he commended Senator Robert Taft as a politician who had stood firm for his principles, no matter how unpopular they were. Although a liberal Democrat, Kennedy admired the conservative Republican Taft. Taft had opposed the

Robert A. Taft and Arthur H. Vandenberg led Senate Republicans in the 1940s.

New Deal's popular social and economic programs and had argued against U.S. participation in World War II. During the cold war, Taft vigorously opposed the increasing military role of the United States, which was seeking to contain communism around the world. He also embroiled himself in the labor unrest of the 1940s by sponsoring the Taft-Hartley Act, which allowed the government to impose "cooling off" periods in nationwide strikes. These controversial stands ruined Taft's repeated attempts to be elected President. But they won praise for Taft from other senators who recognized his unusual degree of honesty, courage, and unwillingness to bend to public pressure.

SEE ALSO
Taft-Hartley Act (1947)

FURTHER READING
Kennedy, John F. *Profiles in Courage.* New York: Harper & Row, 1955.
Patterson, James T. *Mr. Republican: A Biography of Robert A. Taft.* Boston: Houghton Mifflin, 1972.

Tariff of Abominations (1828)

DUTIES ON imports set by the Tariff of 1828 were so high that its opponents denounced it as the Tariff of Abominations. Northern bankers, merchants, and manufacturers favored high duties, or taxes, on imports to protect American goods from foreign competition. Southern planters feared that high tax rates would increase the cost of nearly everything they bought. When Northerners in Congress worked to increase tariff rates, opponents adopted the tactic of adding many excessively high duties to make the whole tariff unattractive enough to defeat. But their strategy backfired, and the highly protective tariff was enacted. The South was so outraged over the Tariff of Abominations that Vice President John C. Calhoun (Democrat–South Carolina) drafted a proposal that states could "nullify," or effectively cancel, offensive federal laws within their own jurisdiction. President Andrew Jackson and his supporters vigorously denied that states had any right of nullification. A constitutional crisis was avoided in 1832, when Congress adopted a new tariff that significantly lowered the rates set by the Tariff of Abominations.

FURTHER READING
Remini, Robert V. *Martin Van Buren and the Making of the Democratic Party.* New York: Norton, 1970.

A bust of Vice President John C. Calhoun stands in the Senate chamber.

Taxation

S E E Revenue bills

Tenure of Office Act (1867)

THE CONSTITUTION gives the President the power to make all nominations of executive branch officials with the advice and consent of the Senate. But the Constitution says nothing about how those officials might be removed, other than by impeachment. After the Civil War, a bitter clash took place between radical Republicans in Congress and President Andrew Johnson over Reconstruction of the South. To prevent Johnson from removing hard-line supporters of Reconstruction from office, Congress passed the Tenure of Office Act in 1867. This act required the President to seek the Senate's consent before removing any cabinet officer or other high-ranking official. Despite its passage over his veto, Johnson insisted that the Tenure of Office Act was unconstitutional. In 1868 he ignored the act and fired Secretary of War Edwin Stanton without consulting the Senate. This was the event that triggered Congress's unsuccessful attempt to remove Johnson from the Presidency. In the 1926 case of *Myers v. United States,* the Supreme Court finally declared the Tenure of Office Act unconstitutional. Since then, Presidents have been free to fire or ask for the resignation of any of their appointees in the executive branch. But this removal power does not extend to the independent regulatory commissions (such as the Federal Trade Commission and the Securities and Exchange Commission), whose members serve limited terms and function independently of both the executive and legislative branches. Nor can Presidents remove Supreme Court justices and other federal judges, who serve lifetime appointments, subject only to impeachment.

FURTHER READING

Benedict, Michael Les. *The Impeachment and Trial of Andrew Johnson.* New York: Norton, 1973.

Term limits

HOW LONG should a member of Congress serve? The Constitution set two years for a House term and six years for a Senate term but put no restriction on how often members could run for reelection. This lack of regulation contrasted sharply with the Congress under the Articles of Confederation (1781–89), where members could serve only three out of every six years. The turnover of membership this limit caused denied the Congress continuity and members with experience in office.

In the 19th century, most members served only briefly in the national legislature before returning to state politics or private life. Even Henry Clay (Whig–Kentucky), who served between 1806 and 1852, actually left Congress and returned several times during those years.

In the 20th century, as advancement in Congress became determined by seniority, continuous service grew more important. As more members aimed to spend their entire career in Congress, it became commonplace for more than 90 percent to win reelection. Although citizens often expressed dissatisfaction with Congress in general, they regularly reelected their own senators and representatives. Turnover occurred more often through voluntary retirement than through election defeats. In 1990, 81

House Speaker John McCormack, who served in Congress for 42 years.

House members had no opponents, and another 168 faced challengers who could not raise enough money to mount a competitive campaign. Out of 435 members of the House, only 15 lost their election.

Opponents of this trend charged that campaign money from political action committees (PACs) heavily favored incumbents (those already holding office) against their challengers. Incumbents also had the benefit of such perks of office as the frank, or free mailing privileges, to keep their names before the voters. Noting that the 22nd Amendment to the Constitution, ratified in 1951, had limited Presidents to no more than two four-year terms, a number of states called for an amendment that would limit representatives to three two-year terms and senators to two six-year terms. The aim would be to rotate more citizens through Congress, so that members would not lose touch with "the real world." Those who opposed term limits warned that such an amendment would replace experienced members with rookies and would deprive voters of the option of reelecting members who had performed well. Instead of a constitutional amendment, they suggested that voters could limit the terms of their senators and representatives simply by voting against them in the next election.

In 1992 voter displeasure over the congressional salary increase, the House bank scandal, and other congressional behavior led to a major turnover of membership. An unusually large number of members voluntarily retired, and 43 members of the House and 5 senators were defeated. The 124 new members entering the 103rd Congress (110 in the House and 14 in the Senate) were the largest new class since 1948. At the same time, voters in 14 states approved ballot initiatives to set congressional term limits.

SEE ALSO
Campaign financing; Incumbents; Perks; Seniority; Terms of office

Terms of office

TO MAKE representatives as responsive as possible to the voters, the Constitution set their term of office at two years. The House should have "an immediate dependence on, and an intimate sympathy with, the people," James Madison wrote in the *Federalist Papers* (a defense of the new Constitution). "Frequent elections are unquestionably the only policy by which this dependence and sympathy can be effectually secured." Senators, by contrast, serve six-year terms, to give them greater distance from the "sudden and violent passions" of public opinion.

Senators are divided into three classes, with one class (or one-third of the Senate) standing for election every two years. When a new state joins the Union, the two new senators will flip a coin to determine which class they will join—meaning who will get the longer or shorter term.

SEE ALSO
Elections; Public opinion

FURTHER READING
Jones, Charles O. *Every Second Year: Congressional Behavior and the Two-Year Term.* Washington, D.C.: Brookings Institution, 1967.

"Treason of the Senate"

SEE Scandals, congressional

Treaties

NO TREATY that the United States negotiates is valid until it receives approval by a two-thirds vote in the Senate. The Constitution's requirement of consent by the Senate (Article 2, Section 2) reflected concerns that treaties reached by the national government might injure the interests of some of the states. In 1786 the Congress under the Articles of Confederation had approved the Jay-Gardoqui Treaty, which conceded American navigation rights on the Mississippi River to Spain. Westerners had seen this treaty as sacrificing their interests in favor of those of New England merchants.

Between 1789 and 1989 the Senate ratified some 1,500 treaties, or about 90 percent of the total it received. It rejected only 20 treaties by formal vote. The other unratified treaties were either withdrawn by the President or never acted upon by the committees. The Senate has also altered treaties by means of amendments (which actually change the language of a treaty), reservations (which indicate a substantial change in the interpretation of treaty provisions), and understandings (which clarify relatively minor aspects of the treaty's implementation).

Sometimes the Senate has amended treaties so severely that it caused the other nation to reject the agreement. In 1824, when the United States signed a treaty with Great Britain to suppress the international slave trade, pro-slavery senators so severely amended the treaty that the British rejected the agreement. At other times, nations have accepted Senate amendments as the price necessary for Senate approval. The Supreme Court upheld the Senate's right to amend a treaty, in the 1869 case of *Haver v. Yaker,* when the Court ruled that "a treaty is something more than a contract, for the Federal Constitution declares it to be the law of the land. If so, before it becomes a law, the Senate . . . must agree to it. But the Senate are not required to adopt or reject it as a whole, but may modify or amend it."

SEE ALSO
Advice and consent

FURTHER READING
Byrd, Robert C. "Treaties." In *The Senate, 1789–1989: Addresses on the History of the United States Senate.* Vol. 2. Washington, D.C.: Government Printing Office, 1991.

A portion of the Louisiana Purchase treaty

Treaty of Versailles

TWICE, IN 1919 and 1920, the Senate rejected the Treaty of Versailles. This treaty set peace terms following World

In a 1920 cartoon, Humanity accuses the U.S. Senate of slaying the Treaty of Versailles.

"irreconcilables" for their extreme opposition to American participation in the League of Nations.

To get the two-thirds vote needed for ratification, supporters of the treaty needed to forge an alliance with those favoring reservations. But Wilson refused to make any compromises. Instead, he took his case directly to the people, confident that public opinion would force the Senate to accept the treaty and the League of Nations. During a national speaking tour in 1919, Wilson suffered a paralyzing stroke from which he never fully recovered. Lacking his leadership, or his approval to compromise, supporters of the treaty failed twice to win its ratification.

SEE ALSO
Advice and consent; Treaties

FURTHER READING
Bailey, Thomas A. *Woodrow Wilson and the Great Betrayal.* Chicago: University of Chicago Press, 1963.

Truman Committee (1941–45)

In 1941, as the United States busily expanded its defense-industry production just before entering World War II, Senator Harry S. Truman (Democrat–Missouri) proposed a special Senate committee to investigate the national defense program. With millions of dollars being spent to mobilize the army and navy, Truman believed that some contractors were misusing government programs for their own profit. The Senate voted unanimously to create the special committee, which Truman was appointed to chair. During the war, the Truman Committee held many hearings to root out corruption and to promote unity among

War I and created a League of Nations to maintain order among nations. These Senate votes were a major defeat for President Woodrow Wilson, who had gone to Paris to personally negotiate the treaty with the Allied leaders and the defeated Germany and Austria and who led the fight for its ratification.

Why did Wilson fail? Facing a Republican majority in the Senate, the President made a tactical error by not inviting to the negotiations the chairman of the Senate Foreign Relations Committee, Henry Cabot Lodge, Sr. (Republican–Massachusetts) or any other Republican legislators. Senator Lodge felt suspicious of Wilson's international ideals and of the political rewards that Democrats might gain from the treaty. Seeking to put a Republican stamp on the treaty, Lodge introduced 14 reservations (changes in interpretation of the treaty) that he insisted were necessary to make the treaty acceptable. However, even these reservations were not enough to satisfy the isolationist wing of the Republican party, known as the

Harry S. Truman (center) presiding over the Truman Committee.

business, labor, and agriculture in support of the war effort. Favorable publicity from the hearings won Senator Truman the nomination to run for Vice President in 1944. The following April, after the death of Franklin Roosevelt, Truman became President.

FURTHER READING

Wilson, Theodore. "The Truman Committee." In *Congress Investigates: A Documented History, 1792–1974,* edited by Arthur M. Schlesinger, Jr., and Roger Bruns. New York: Bowker, 1975.

Unanimous consent agreements

UNANIMOUS CONSENT agreements are motions that the Senate or House adopts as long as no member objects to them. Many unanimous consent requests deal with routine business, such as "Madam President, I ask unanimous consent to dispense with the reading of the journal" or "Mr. Speaker, I ask unanimous consent to revise and extend my remarks in the *Congressional Record.*" To these requests the presiding officer will respond: "Without objection, so ordered."

The Senate also uses unanimous consent agreements, which are worked out in advance by the majority and minority leaders and managers of a bill, to set the details of how it will consider a bill, how long it will debate each amendment, whether all amendments must be germane (relevant) to the bill's subject matter, and when the final vote will be taken. Sometimes whole bills are adopted by unanimous consent, if members are able to agree in advance to all of the bill's provisions. Unanimous consent agreements help the leadership move noncontroversial matters quickly through the Senate. However, a single senator's objection can stop a unanimous consent agreement, giving the minority another chance to stop or delay the majority from acting. The House generally uses special rules to achieve the same results as unanimous consent agreements.

SEE ALSO

Rules, House and Senate

Unlimited debate

SEE Filibuster

"Upper house"

BECAUSE NEITHER the Senate nor the House is superior to the other, there is technically no "upper" or "lower" house. However, the Senate has been called the "upper house" because its members serve longer terms, represent whole states, and—in the smaller body—have more individual influence over legislation than most House members. Many representatives run for the Senate, but only a few former senators have gone on to serve in the House. The term *upper*

house dates back to the 1st Congress, when the smaller Senate met upstairs above the larger House chamber.

Vandenberg, Arthur H.

☆ *Born: Mar. 22, 1884, Grand Rapids, Mich.*
☆ *Political party: Republican*
☆ *Senator from Michigan: 1928–51*
☆ *Died: Apr. 18, 1951, Grand Rapids, Mich.*

SENATOR ARTHUR Vandenberg first won national attention as an isolationist—someone who believed that the United States should defend its own interests and should avoid international organizations and "entangling alliances." But the Japanese attack on Pearl Harbor in December 1941 shattered the illusion that the United States could stand alone, protected on both sides by vast oceans. Vandenberg came to believe that the United States must take a greater role in keeping the peace after World War II ended. On January 10, 1945, he rose in the Senate to deliver what the *Cleveland Plain Dealer* called "a shot heard round the world." In it he abandoned isolationism and embraced international cooperation, urging other senators to follow him. Because Vandenberg was a prominent Republican, his conversion to internationalism made him a leader in building a bipartisan foreign policy under Democratic President Harry S. Truman. As chairman of the Foreign Relations Committee during the 80th Congress, he strongly supported Truman's program for combatting the Soviet Union during the cold war. Vandenberg also introduced the Senate resolution that cleared the way for U.S. participation in NATO (the North Atlantic Treaty Organization). This pact with Canada and 10 Western European nations was the first mutual defense treaty that the United States entered into since its alliance with France during the American Revolution.

SEE ALSO
Bipartisan foreign policy; Vandenberg Resolution (1948)

FURTHER READING
Vandenberg, Arthur H., Jr., ed. *The Private Papers of Senator Vandenberg.* Boston: Houghton Mifflin, 1952.

Vandenberg Resolution (1948)

AS U.S. relations with the Soviet Union worsened during the early years of the cold war, President Harry S. Truman determined that the United States must enter a military alliance to defend Western Europe against a Soviet invasion. However, since George Washington's farewell address warned against entering into "entangling alliances," the United States had steadfastly opposed joining any military alliances. Senator Arthur H. Vandenberg (Republican–Michigan) lobbied strongly for congressional support of Truman's foreign policies. To test whether the Senate would give the two-thirds vote necessary to pass a treaty setting up a military alliance, Vandenberg introduced a resolution in the Senate in June 1948 calling for the United States to pursue "regional and other collective agreements" for defense against communism. The Senate passed the Vandenberg Resolution by a vote of 64 to 4, clearing the way for the North Atlantic Treaty Organization (NATO). NATO included Belgium, Canada, Denmark, France, Great Britain, Iceland, Italy, Luxembourg, the Netherlands, Norway, Portugal, and the United States (Greece, Turkey, West Germany, and Spain later joined, while France withdrew).

SEE ALSO
Treaties; Vandenberg, Arthur H.

Veto

FROM THE Latin for "I forbid," the veto is the device Presidents use to reject legislation that Congress has passed. Article 1, Section 7, of the Constitution provides that the President may return any legislation he disapproves of to Congress with an explanation of his objections. Congress can then vote again on the legislation, but two-thirds of both houses of Congress must vote in favor of it to override the President's veto.

Although British monarchs ceased using their veto power over Parliament in 1707, the American colonies inherited the veto practice. Royal governors were able to veto laws passed by the colonial legislatures. The independent states also gave this power to their governors, and the Constitutional Convention extended it to the President.

President George Washington tried to avoid vetoing bills, using the power only twice. He believed that Presidents should defer to the will of Congress and use this power only as an emergency measure, when they considered legislation unconstitutional. But when Andrew Jackson vetoed the law to recharter the

Andrew Jackson vetoed the Second Bank of the United States, which issued this currency.

Bank of the United States in 1832, he established the precedent that a President could veto bills simply because he did not like them. Not until 1843 was Congress able to muster the necessary two-thirds of both houses to override a veto, in this case a tariff bill vetoed by the unpopular President John Tyler.

Pocket vetoes

Another form of Presidential veto, known as the pocket veto, cannot be overridden by Congress. Using this technique, the President in a sense places a bill in his pocket and refuses to sign it or return it to Congress. If Congress has adjourned or is in recess for more than ten days, the absence of the President's signature kills the bill. When Congress returns to session, it must start all over again if it wishes to revive the bill.

Overriding a veto

Because it is difficult to achieve a two-thirds majority in Congress, very few Presidential vetoes have been overridden. Presidents have vetoed nearly 2,500 bills, about 1,000 of which were pocket vetoes. Of the remaining 1,500, Congress has been able to override just more than 100. Presidents Andrew Johnson, Harry S. Truman, and Gerald R. Ford battled the Congresses of their eras and sustained the largest number of veto overrides. By contrast, Presidents Grover Cleveland and Franklin D. Roosevelt vetoed the largest number of bills and had very few vetoes overridden. Especially in periods when the President's party does not have a majority in Congress, such as the administrations of Ronald Reagan and George Bush, Presidents can make the veto, or even the threat of a veto, an effective weapon in shaping legislation to their liking.

Recent Presidents have also called for the power of a line-item veto, similar to the power exercised by most state

PRESIDENTIAL VETOES OF CONGRESSIONAL LEGISLATION

PRESIDENT	TOTAL VETOES	REGULAR VETOES	POCKET VETOES	OVER-RIDDEN
George Washington	2	2	0	0
John Adams	0	0	0	0
Thomas Jefferson	0	0	0	0
James Madison	7	5	2	0
James Monroe	1	1	0	0
John Quincy Adams	0	0	0	0
Andrew Jackson	12	5	7	0
Martin Van Buren	1	0	1	0
William H. Harrison	0	0	0	0
John Tyler	10	6	4	1
James K. Polk	3	2	1	0
Zachary Taylor	0	0	0	0
Millard Fillmore	0	0	0	0
Franklin Pierce	9	9	0	5
James Buchanan	7	4	3	0
Abraham Lincoln	7	2	5	0
Andrew Johnson	29	21	8	15
Ulysses S. Grant	93	45	48	4
Rutherford B. Hayes	13	12	1	1
James A. Garfield	0	0	0	0
Chester A. Arthur	12	4	8	1
Grover Cleveland	414	304	110	2
Benjamin Harrison	44	19	25	1
Grover Cleveland	170	42	128	5
William McKinley	42	6	36	0
Theodore Roosevelt	82	42	40	1
William H. Taft	39	30	9	1
Woodrow Wilson	44	33	11	6
Warren G. Harding	6	5	1	0
Calvin Coolidge	50	20	30	4
Herbert Hoover	37	21	16	4
Franklin D. Roosevelt	635	372	263	9
Harry S. Truman	250	180	70	12
Dwight D. Eisenhower	181	73	108	2
John F. Kennedy	21	12	9	0
Lyndon B. Johnson	30	16	14	0
Richard M. Nixon	43	26	17	7
Gerald R. Ford	66	48	18	12
Jimmy Carter	31	13	18	2
Ronald Reagan	78	39	39	9
George Bush	45	28	17	1

governors. Used primarily for appropriations bills, the line-item veto would allow a President to disapprove of a single expenditure without vetoing the entire bill. Congress has opposed the line-item veto as an infringement of its "power of the purse."

SEE ALSO

Line-item veto; Presidential relations with Congress

FURTHER READING

Spitzer, Robert J. *The Presidential Veto: Touchstone of the American Presidency.* Albany: State University of New York Press, 1988.

Vice President

WHEN SENATORS address the presiding officer during debates, they say "Mr. President." In this case, the title refers not to the President of the United States but to the president of the Senate, who is the Vice President of the United States. Other than being available to succeed the President in case of death, disability, or impeachment, the Vice President's only constitutional job is to preside over the Senate. The post carries more responsibility than power. The Vice President can vote only to break a tie and may address

Vice President Richard Nixon announces the electoral vote in 1961: he had been defeated for President by John F. Kennedy.

the Senate only with the Senate's permission. The Vice President may also interpret the Senate rules, but his decisions may be—and have been—overruled by a majority vote of the Senate. John Adams, the first Vice President, felt perplexed about the dual nature of his job. "I am Vice President," he told the Senate. "In this I am nothing, but I may be everything. But I am president also of the Senate. When the President comes into the Senate, what shall I be?"

Vice Presidents presided on a regular basis until 1953, when Richard M. Nixon occupied an office near the White House and spent more time on executive than on legislative business. Although Vice Presidents remain on the legislative branch payroll and maintain a staff and office at the Capitol, they have increasingly tended to preside only when their vote might be needed to break a tie or during ceremonial occasions. The Senate elects a president pro tempore to preside in the Vice President's absence. The president pro tem in turn designates junior members of the majority party to take turns, usually for an hour at a time, presiding over the Senate. Today the Senate chamber and surrounding corridors are lined with marble busts of the Vice Presidents, in recognition of their official role as president of the Senate.

FURTHER READING

Young, Donald. *American Roulette: The History and Dilemma of the Vice Presidency.* New York: Viking, 1974.

Voting

MEMBERS OF Congress cast hundreds of votes during each session on a multitude of issues. Some votes, usually on routine or less controversial issues, are cast by voice. The presiding officer or-

The House of Representatives uses an electronic system to cast its votes.

ders, "All in favor say aye, all opposed nay," noting whether the ayes or nays have it. When voting by voice, the votes of individual members are not identified. By contrast, a roll call vote records the names of all who voted for or against the bill as well as those who were absent or who simply answered "present" without voting.

Different percentages of the vote are needed for different functions in Congress. A majority of 51 percent of the votes cast is necessary to pass an amendment, a bill, or a resolution, to set rules and elect officers, to overturn a ruling of the presiding officer, and to confirm nominations. It takes three-fifths of the senators to invoke cloture and cut off debate. Two-thirds of the vote is needed for the Senate to approve a treaty or to remove an impeached official from office. A two-thirds vote of both the House and Senate is also necessary to override a Presidential veto.

The Senate, with 100 members, votes aloud during a roll call vote, with the legislative clerk recording whether a senator voted aye or nay. Votes in the Senate generally take 15 minutes, although the leadership sometimes will stretch the time to accommodate members hurrying to the chamber from a distance. To keep its voting time down, the House, with 435 voting members, has adopted an electronic voting system. Each representative has a card to insert into one of the small boxes on the back of the benches near the entrances to the House chamber. Using the card, a member can vote yes, no, or present. Members' votes are then lit up on a large scoreboard above the press gallery, with a green light indicating a yes vote and a red light indicating a no. Vote tallies are shown electronically on either side of the chamber. Because being absent during a vote can hurt members politically when they run for reelection, they instruct their party leaders to announce the reason, such as illness or a trip out of town, that prevented them from voting. If absent members wish to show how they would have voted, they can arrange in advance to pair their vote with another absent member who would have voted the opposite way. Paired votes are listed in the *Congressional Record*, indicating the members' position on the bill and that their votes would not have changed the eventual outcome.

Any number of reasons affect the way members of Congress cast their votes. In a dissenting opinion in the case of *Edwards v. Aguillard* (1987), Supreme Court Justice Antonin Scalia suggested—somewhat sarcastically—some of the factors that might influence a legislator's vote:

He may have thought the bill would provide jobs for his district, or may have wanted to make amends with a faction of his party he had alienated on another vote, or he may have been a close friend of the bill's sponsor, or he may have been repaying a favor he owed the Majority Leader . . . or he may have been pressured to vote for a bill he disliked by a wealthy contributor or by a flood of constituent mail, or he may have been seeking favorable publicity, or he may have been reluctant to hurt the feelings of a loyal staff member who worked on the bill, or he may have been settling an old score with a legislator who opposed the bill, or he may have been mad at his wife who opposed the bill, or he may have been intoxicated and utterly unmotivated when the vote was called, or he may have accidentally voted "yes" instead of "no," or, of course, he may have had (and very likely did have) a combination of some of the above motives.

SEE ALSO
Pair voting

Wade, Benjamin F.

☆ *Born: Oct. 27, 1800, Springfield, Mass.*
☆ *Political party: Republican*
☆ *Senator from Ohio: 1851–69*
☆ *President pro tempore: 1865–69*
☆ *Died: Mar. 2, 1878, Jefferson, Ohio*

"BLUFF" BEN Wade won the South's hatred for his uncompromising opposition to slavery before the Civil War and his demand for the federal government to protect the rights of the freedmen after the war. Wade entered the Senate during the debate over the Kansas-Nebraska Act of 1854, which he loudly opposed. He declared himself a believer in the sentiments of the Declaration of Independence, that "all men are created equal." Southern senators demanded to know if Wade meant that slaves were the equals of white men. "Yes," replied Wade. "Why not equal? Do they not have their life by Almighty God?" During the war, he sponsored the Wade-Davis Bill, calling for military rule over the defeated South and requiring a majority of voters to take a loyalty oath before their state

Ben Wade (standing) served as president pro tempore of the Senate.

could be readmitted to the Union. President Abraham Lincoln, who wanted a speedier Reconstruction, pocket vetoed the Wade-Davis Bill. Davis broke even more sharply with Lincoln's successor, Andrew Johnson, over Reconstruction. As president pro tempore, Davis would have become President of the United States had the Senate not failed by a single vote to remove Johnson from office.

SEE ALSO
Impeachment of Andrew Johnson (1868); Reconstruction, congressional; Veto; Wade-Davis Bill (1864)

FURTHER READING
Trefousse, Hans L. *Benjamin Franklin Wade: Radical Republican from Ohio.* New York: Twayne, 1963.

Wade-Davis Bill (1864)

AS THE North progressed toward victory in the Civil War, Senator Benjamin F. Wade (Republican–Ohio) and Representative Henry Winter Davis (Unionist–Maryland) introduced a bill to reconstruct the Southern states after the war ended. In harsh language, the Wade-Davis Bill demanded that a majority of voters in the Confederate states must swear an "Ironclad Oath" of allegiance to the Union and that the former slaves must be assured their equality with whites. President Abraham Lincoln had proposed a much more lenient plan of reconstruction that would have required only 10 percent of each state's voters to demonstrate their allegiance to the Union in order for their state to be readmitted. Lincoln pocket vetoed the Wade-Davis Bill, slipping it into his pocket so that Congress would not have the opportunity to override his veto. Wade and Davis angrily accused President Lincoln of acting like a dictator. The Wade-

Davis Bill served as an indication of the even greater battles that would follow between the executive branch and the legislature over reconstruction of the South.

SEE ALSO
Reconstruction, congressional; Veto

FURTHER READING
Foner, Eric. *Reconstruction: America's Unfinished Revolution, 1863–1877.* New York: Harper & Row, 1988.

Wagner, Robert F.

☆ *Born: June 8, 1877, Nastatten, Germany*
☆ *Political party: Democrat*
☆ *Senator from New York: 1927–49*
☆ *Died: May 4, 1953, New York, N.Y.*

SHORT, STOCKY, with a heavy New York accent (saying "woik" for "work"), Robert F. Wagner may have appeared to be a typical machine politician. But he proved to be one of the most effective legislators of the New Deal era. Wagner worked best behind closed committee doors, making his case for legislation, reaching necessary compromises, and rounding up votes before going into debate on the Senate floor. Wagner sponsored a long list of important legislation, but his two greatest achievements occurred in 1935: the Wagner Act, guaranteeing labor's right to organize into unions, and the Social Security Act to provide old-age pensions to most Americans. Milton Handler, a young New Dealer who watched Wagner firsthand, credited Wagner's legislative success to these qualities:

> First, his ingrained, humanitarian, progressive philosophy; second, his uncanny capacity to recruit good men to do the detail work for him; third, his masterful ability to maneuver bills through the

legislative mill; and fourth, and most important of all, his willingness and determination to stick to his basic conviction through thick and thin—in a word, his "guts."

FURTHER READING
Huthmacher, J. Joseph. *Senator Robert F. Wagner and the Rise of Urban Liberalism.* New York: Atheneum, 1968.

Wall Street investigation (1932–34)

IN TERMS of the evidence it uncovered and the legislation it stimulated, one of the most successful congressional investigations was the Senate banking committee's inquiry into the causes of the stock market crash of 1929 and the Great Depression that followed. Ferdinand Pecora, an Italian immigrant who had been an assistant district attorney in New York, served as the committee's counsel and so dominated the hearings that they became known as the Pecora investigation. Pecora subpoenaed the records of major bankers and stockbrokers and called them to testify. J. P. Morgan, Jr., the nation's most prominent banker, was among those whose testimony made national head-

Wall Street banker J. P. Morgan, Jr. (center) listening to testimony before the Senate Banking and Currency Committee, 1933.

lines. (During a break in the hearings, a circus promoter slipped a midget into Morgan's lap, and the next day's news photos used the incident as a symbol of the congressional humbling of a powerful banker.) The Pecora investigation led to major banking and stock market reforms, most notably the creation of the Securities and Exchange Commission to provide federal regulation of the nation's stock exchanges.

SEE ALSO
Investigations; Regulation of commerce

FURTHER READING
Ritchie, Donald A. "The Wall Street Exposé." In *Congress Investigates: A Documented History, 1792–1974,* edited by Arthur M. Schlesinger, Jr., and Roger Bruns. Vol. 4. New York: Bowker, 1975.

War hawks

A GROUP of zealous young Southern and Western representatives known as the "war hawks" seized the initiative from President James Madison in 1812 and prodded the nation into war with Great Britain. The war hawks were expansionists who wanted the United States to add both Canada and Florida to its territory. They also wanted the United States to take tougher military action against American Indians. And they wanted the country to stand firm and defend its national honor against the British policy of seizing former British sailors off of American ships (called "impressment" of sailors). When the 11th Congress met in December 1811, the war hawks elected the charismatic Henry Clay to be Speaker on his first day in the House. President James Madison reluctantly supported the congressional demands for war with Great Britain. In most respects, the War of 1812 proved a disaster for the United States. While Clay was in Belgium, negotiating a peace treaty to end the war, British troops overran Washington and burned the Capitol building and White House. The peace treaty achieved none of the gains that the war hawks had originally sought. Only General Andrew Jackson's victory over the British at New Orleans (after the peace treaty had been signed) saved the national pride after this misadventure.

SEE ALSO
Clay, Henry

FURTHER READING
Remini, Robert V. *Henry Clay: Statesman for the Union.* New York: Norton, 1991.

War powers

ONLY CONGRESS has the constitutional power to declare war (Article 1, Section 8). Yet U.S. troops have fought in many conflicts without a formal declaration of war. Congress is empowered to raise and fund the armed services, but the President serves as commander in chief. The Constitution therefore separates the war powers but also allows them to be shared—an ambiguity that has caused much disagreement and friction between the executive and legislative branches.

Thomas Jefferson believed that giving Congress the power to declare war was "an effectual check to the Dog of war by transferring the power of letting him loose from the Executive to the legislative, from those who are to spend to those who are to pay." Congress must appropriate all money necessary to raise and equip American armed forces and to send them into battle.

Twice in the 19th century, Congress pressed reluctant Presidents into war. In 1812 congressional "war hawks" favored war with Great Britain, despite President James Madison's reservations, and in 1898 Congress pushed a dubious President William McKinley into war with Spain. A more divided Congress endorsed President James K. Polk's call for war with Mexico in 1846. After a long and difficult period of neutrality, Congress supported Woodrow Wilson's call for the United States to enter World War I. It took the Japanese bombing of Pearl Harbor on December 7, 1941, for Congress to declare war on Japan and Germany during World War II. Since 1941 there have been no formal declarations of war, despite U.S. participation in a "police action" in Korea from 1950 to 1953, in a long war in Vietnam from 1965 to 1973, and in many smaller conflicts around the globe.

President as commander in chief

The cold war—a military and ideological struggle between the United States and the Soviet Union and allies of both nations, which lasted from the 1940s through the 1980s—vastly increased Presidential power and reduced congressional influence over foreign policy. Presidents expanded their role as commander in chief of the armed services to assume more independent decision-making authority. Presidents asserted that they needed to be able to act quickly, in the face of a possible nuclear attack, without prior consultation with Congress. They argued that they were better equipped to make decisions about war and peace than the "535 secretaries of state" on Capitol Hill. In the 1940s Congress embraced a bipartisan foreign policy, in which the two parties came together to support the national interest, and generally deferred to the President in foreign and military affairs. Lyndon B. Johnson (Democrat–Texas) felt that as Senate majority leader he had deferred to

U.S. troops advance against German lines in 1918. Congress officially declared war after President Wilson called for participation in World War I.

President Dwight D. Eisenhower. So when Johnson became President, he expected Congress to follow his lead. In 1964 Johnson asked Congress to enact the Gulf of Tonkin Resolution, permitting him to use American armed forces in retaliation for North Vietnam's alleged assaults on U.S. ships. With only two senators dissenting, Congress adopted the Gulf of Tonkin Resolution, which Johnson considered a declaration of war. Congressional and public dissatisfaction with the course of the Vietnam War disrupted the bipartisan foreign policy and strained relations between the executive and legislative branches.

War Powers Act

In 1973 Congress passed the War Powers Act over President Richard M. Nixon's veto. This joint resolution requires the President to notify Congress within 48 hours of sending American troops into hostile action. It also requires that those troops must be withdrawn after 60 to 90 days if Congress does not vote to support the action. It encourages Presidents, "in every possible instance," to consult with Congress before sending troops into hostilities. Since 1973 Presidents have questioned whether the War

Powers Act is constitutional, and they have not always complied with it. Congress has been similarly reluctant to apply the War Powers Act, which might force them to endorse the sending of troops into a hostile situation. In 1991 President George Bush sent U.S. forces into battle against Iraq, which had invaded neighboring Kuwait. Instead of invoking the War Powers Resolution, Congress voted to support military action to enforce a United Nations demand that Iraq withdraw from Kuwait.

Despite the steady shift of war powers from Congress to the Presidency, Congress as a representative body still serves as an extension of public opinion. Recalling the lessons of the unpopular Vietnam War, Presidents seek to achieve national unity by winning congressional support for their foreign and military policies.

SEE ALSO

Gulf of Tonkin Resolution (1964); Persian Gulf debate (1991); Separation of powers

FURTHER READING

Fisher, Louis. *Constitutional Conflicts between Congress and the President.* Princeton, N.J.: Princeton University Press, 1985.
Schlesinger, Arthur M., Jr. *The Imperial Presidency.* Boston: Houghton Mifflin, 1973.

Senator Howard Baker (left) and chairman Sam Ervin conducted the Senate Watergate investigation.

Watergate investigation (1973)

AT 2:00 A.M. on June 17, 1972, five men were arrested while breaking into the Democratic National Committee offices at the Watergate buildings in Washington, D.C. Although these men had connections with the Committee to Re-Elect the President (CREEP), President Richard M. Nixon insisted that the "White House had no involvement whatsoever" in this "third-rate burglary." The Watergate incident did not prevent the President's landslide reelection in November. But persistent stories in the *Washington Post* and other newspapers linked administration officials to the break-in, wiretapping, illegal use of campaign contributions, forged documents to embarrass rival candidates, and other political "dirty tricks." The Senate appointed a Select Committee on Presidential Campaign Activities, chaired by

Sam Ervin (Democrat–North Carolina), a folksy "country lawyer" and a specialist in civil liberties.

In May 1973 the Watergate committee began nationally televised hearings that captured public attention for the next three months. Former White House counsel John Dean testified that the President had taken part in an elaborate cover-up of improper activities. Committee staff members also uncovered evidence that the President had secretly tape-recorded conversations in his White House offices. When both the committee and a special prosecutor subpoenaed these tapes, President Nixon stonewalled them. He cited executive privilege (the protection of confidential executive branch materials from legislative scrutiny, under the separation of powers) as justification for his refusal to turn over the tapes. The Supreme Court ruled in June 1974 that executive privilege did not protect documents needed for criminal prosecution. The released tapes exposed the President's involvement in the cover-up, and the House Judiciary Committee voted to recommend his impeachment. With almost no support left in Congress, President Nixon resigned from office in August 1974.

The Watergate scandal symbolized a dangerous imbalance in the federal system of checks and balances. It was the product of an excessive growth of Presidential power and of Presidential efforts to circumvent the legislative branch. The Senate investigation helped Congress restore its public image and regain some of its lost authority.

S E E A L S O

Ervin, Samuel J., Jr.; Executive privilege; Investigations; Nixon, Richard M.

F U R T H E R R E A D I N G

Kurland, Philip B. "The Watergate Inquiry, 1973." In *Congress Investigates: A Documented History, 1792–1974*, edited by Arthur M. Schlesinger, Jr., and Roger Bruns. Vol. 5. New York: Bowker, 1975.
Kutler, Stanley. *The Wars of Watergate*. New York: Knopf, 1990.

Ways and Means Committee

ONE OF the oldest and most important committees of the House, the Ways and Means Committee originates all revenue (tax and tariff) bills. As the name implies, the committee is responsible for finding the ways and means of financing the operations of the federal government. (The equivalent committee in the Senate is the Finance Committee.) Because the Constitution (Article 1, Section 7) assigns the origination of revenue bills to the House, the House created the Ways and Means Committee first as a select committee in 1789 and then converted it to a standing committee in 1802. In the 19th century, chairmen of the Ways and Means Committee often functioned as floor leaders

of the House, and 21 Speakers served on the committee.

S E E A L S O

Revenue bills

F U R T H E R R E A D I N G

Kennon, Donald R., and Rebecca M. Rogers. *The Committee on Ways and Means: A Bicentennial History, 1789–1989.* Washington, D.C.: Government Printing Office, 1989.

Webster, Daniel

☆ *Born: January 18, 1782, Salisbury, N.H.*
☆ *Political party: Federalist, Whig*
☆ *Representative from New Hampshire: 1813–17*
☆ *Representative from Massachusetts: 1823–27*
☆ *Senator from Massachusetts: 1833–41, 1845–50*
☆ *Died: October 24, 1852, Marshfield, Mass.*

DURING HIS long career in Congress, Daniel Webster won fame as an orator and as the chief spokesman for New England's interests. He most notably promoted protective tariffs (taxes on foreign imports that would make it easier for American industry to develop) and national banking policies (the creation of a government-sponsored national bank to control the supply of money). Webster also devoted his debating skills to defending the Union against those who talked of secession, most notably in his famous reply to South Carolina senator Robert Y. Hayne in 1830. When Hayne promoted the idea that states could nullify, or overrule, federal laws, Webster responded that the United States was not a government of states but a "popular Government, erected by the people." Warning of the possibility of civil war, Webster denounced as foolish the notion of "Lib-

A bronze statue of Daniel Webster in the Capitol

erty first and Union afterwards." He declared instead for "Liberty *and* Union, now and forever, one and inseparable."

At the end of his career Webster risked his entire reputation with a memorable speech in favor of the Compromise of 1850. Seeking to organize the Western territories in a way that would appease both pro-slavery opinion in the South and antislavery sentiment in the North, Henry Clay (Whig–Kentucky) put together an omnibus bill with something for all sides. For New England, the bill's most controversial feature was its fugitive slave provision, which would permit slave owners to reclaim their slaves who had fled to freedom in the North. To win New England's support, Clay persuaded Webster to throw his prestige behind the compromise. On March 7, 1850, Webster rose in the Senate and said: "Mr. President—I wish to speak today not as a Massachusetts man, not as a Northern man, but as an American, and a member of the Senate of the United States." Abolitionists and free-soil advocates, who opposed the spread of slavery into the territories, denounced Webster's March 7 speech as a betrayal. People in Massachusetts formed vigilance committees to protect runaway slaves. Webster's public standing plunged, and his Presidential aspirations were destroyed as a result of his efforts to hold the Union together through compromise.

SEE ALSO

Compromise of 1850; Oratory

FURTHER READING

Bartlett, Irving H. *Daniel Webster*. New York: Norton, 1978.
Current, Richard N. *Daniel Webster and the Rise of National Conservatism*. Boston: Little, Brown, 1955.

Whip

EACH PARTY in the Senate and House elects assistant leaders known as whips, who help the floor leaders count heads and round up party members for quorum calls and votes. The title comes from a fox-hunting expression for the person, called the "whipper-in," who kept the dogs from straying during the chase. A part of the British Parliament as early as 1621, whips did not become official positions in Congress until the 20th century. In 1899 House Republicans established the first whips in Congress to help keep their majority in line. In 1971 Carl Albert (Democrat–Oklahoma) became the first party whip to rise to Speaker of the House (Albert also served as House majority leader). In the Senate James Hamilton Lewis (Democrat–Illinois) became the first party whip in 1913; the Republicans selected their own whip two years later. As Lewis described his post, "The duties of the Senate whip demand his presence on the floor as constantly as possible. Sometimes the long hours test his physical capacity, but generally he is

Outgoing Senate Republican whip Hugh Scott (left) passed a symbol of his office to his successor, Robert Griffin, in 1969.

devoted to 'watchful waiting.' " Whips sometimes stand in for the majority or minority leaders in their absence. They have issued "whip notices" to other members of their party, notifying them of scheduled debates and votes. "The whip's job is not to create policy," House Speaker Thomas P. ("Tip") O' Neill, Jr. (Democrat–Massachusetts) has explained, "but to determine whether the votes are there for the policy that has already been determined."

SEE ALSO
Leadership

FURTHER READING
Byrd, Robert C. "Party Whips." In *The Senate, 1789–1989: Addresses on the History of the United States Senate.* Vol. 2. Washington, D.C.: Government Printing Office, 1991.

Wilmot Proviso

ANTISLAVERY ADVOCATES devised the Wilmot Proviso as a legislative tactic to stop the spread of slavery into the vast Southwestern territories that the United States had acquired from its war with Mexico between 1846 and 1848. This proviso (an amendment that sets a provision or requirement) stipulated that no federal funds could be spent to acquire any territory that permitted slavery. Seeking someone to sponsor the bill who had the best chance of winning recognition to speak in the House, the antislavery group chose David Wilmot (Democrat/Republican–Pennsylvania), who had not been unfriendly to Southern interests. The amendment, which became known as the Wilmot Proviso, was attached repeatedly to many bills. Although it passed the House, the Wilmot Proviso was never enacted by the Senate. Even without passage, the Wilmot Pro-

viso became a rallying point for the new Republican party and equally an object of scorn by defenders of slavery.

FURTHER READING
Potter, David M. *The Impending Crisis, 1848–1861.* New York: Harper & Row, 1976.

Woman suffrage

THE CONSTITUTION left the question of who should have the right to vote to the states. Initially, women who owned property could vote in New Jersey, but by 1808 this right had disappeared even there, and throughout the 19th century women could not vote. In 1848 delegates to the Women's Rights Convention in Seneca Falls, New York, demanded that women have the right to vote. After the Civil War, the woman suffrage campaign spread, led by Susan B. Anthony. Woman suffragists held conventions in Washington, lobbied members of Congress, and testified before congressional committees. In 1913 women paraded down Pennsylvania Avenue and militant protestors began picketing the White House, even chaining themselves to its fence, to draw attention to their campaign. When President Woodrow Wilson delivered his State of the Union message to Congress in December 1916, women in the galleries unfurled a large banner that read, "Mr. President, What Will You Do For Woman Suffrage?" (Ever since that incident, visitors have been prohibited from leaning over the railings of the galleries.) Several states, mostly in the West, individually gave women the right to vote in both state and national elections, and in 1916 Montana elected suffrage leader Jeannette Rankin to the House of Representatives. World War I, fought to "make the world safe

Women protestors in the galleries of the House chamber unfurled this banner during President Wilson's address in 1916.

224

★ WOMEN IN CONGRESS ★

Speaker Frederick Gillette (seated) signed the Woman Suffrage Amendment when it passed the House in 1919.

for democracy," finally spurred Congress to pass the 19th Amendment to the Constitution, granting women the vote, in 1919, and the states ratified it in 1920.

SEE ALSO

Women in Congress

FURTHER READING

Flexner, Eleanor. *Century of Struggle: The Woman's Rights Movement in the United States.* Cambridge: Harvard University Press, 1975.

Women in Congress

REGARDLESS OF their party or political philosophy, women have always found themselves a minority within the "old boy" Congress. When Catherine May (Republican–Washington) entered the House in 1959, she requested assignment to the Joint Atomic Energy Committee, only to be told that the committee's ranking Republican "just can't see a woman on that committee." It took four terms before Representative May got on the committee. Other women members faced the same institutional obstacles and banded together in the Congressional Caucus for Women's Issues to defend their interests and to promote their legislative agenda.

The 19th Amendment gave women nationwide the right to vote in 1920, but a woman had already entered Congress four years earlier. Jeannette Rankin (Republican–Montana) won election after successfully leading the woman suffrage movement in her state. She lost a race for the Senate in 1918. The first woman senator, Rebecca Felton (Democrat–Georgia), was appointed to a vacancy in 1922 and served for only a single day. Women were often appointed to fill out unexpired Senate terms, especially widows who succeeded their husbands. Hattie Carraway (Democrat–Arkansas) was appointed to take her late husband's Senate seat in 1931 and was expected to hold it only until the next election. In-

Equal Rights

VOL. XVIII, No. 20
FIVE CENTS

SATURDAY
JUNE 18, 1932

A Woman Makes Senate History

Hattie W. Caraway, Senator from Arkansas, wrote a new chapter in Senate history when she presided over the sessions of that body May 9. She was the first woman ever to rule over the deliberations of the Senate, and is shown occupying the Vice-President's chair. She recently announced her candidacy in the forthcoming Senatorial election in her State.

Senator Hattie Carraway presided over the Senate in 1932.

stead she enlisted the help of Senator Huey P. Long (Democrat–Louisiana), who campaigned with her and helped her win election in 1932. Six years later Carraway was reelected. Margaret Chase Smith (Republican–Maine) won election to her late husband's House seat in 1940 and then was elected senator in 1948. Smith served 24 years in the Senate and became an influential member of the Armed Services Committee. In 1968 Representative Shirley Chisholm (Democrat–New York) became the first African-American woman to serve in Congress. And in 1973 Yvonne Brathwaite Burke (Democrat–California) became the first member of Congress to be granted maternity leave.

More women have served in the House, where they are called "gentlewomen" in debate. Representative Rose DeLauro (Democrat–Connecticut) described the House as "a very competitive place," where it is important to build

coalitions. Because all women in Congress do not think alike, they do not always vote together. As DeLauro explained, "You build coalitions among women and you build coalitions among men."

In 1991 the Senate Judiciary Committee conducted hearings on the nomination of Clarence Thomas to be a Supreme Court justice and heard allegations that he had sexually harassed a female employee. Watching the televised hearings, many women became angry when they realized that no women served on the Judiciary Committee. Pointing out that women constituted only 2 percent of the U.S. Senate, more women ran for Congress in the next election. Frequently called the Year of the Woman, 1992 saw 24 new women members elected to the House and 4 new women senators. These included Barbara Boxer and Dianne Feinstein, elected to the Senate as Democrats from California, and the first black woman senator, Carol Moseley-Braun (Democrat–Illinois).

For a century the sign on the swinging doors just outside the Senate chamber read "Senators Only." It was a men's rest room. Although women had served in the Senate since 1922, not until after the 1992 election was a nearby room hastily converted into a women's rest room. It was a small symbol of a major change in American politics.

Representative Clare Boothe Luce (Republican–Connecticut)

SEE ALSO

Chisholm, Shirley; Felton, Rebecca Latimer; Rankin, Jeannette; Smith, Margaret Chase

FURTHER READING

Chamberlin, Hope. *A Minority of Members: Women in the United States Congress.* New York: Praeger, 1973.

Office of the Historian, U.S. House of Representatives. *Women in Congress, 1917–1990.* Washington, D.C.: Government Printing Office, 1991.

Work load

THE WORK load of Congress can be measured in the number of bills and resolutions introduced, referred to committee, discussed in hearings, amended, marked up, debated, and enacted or rejected. After World War II Congress's work load increased dramatically. In the 1940s, 10,000 bills and resolutions, on average, were introduced in each Congress. By the mid-1960s that number had doubled to 20,000. Later the numbers declined because rules changes permitted several members to cosponsor the same bill, eliminating the need for each of them to introduce their own version of the bill. The number of bills passed also declined because of the elimination of the need for many private bills (to assist specific individuals) and the combining of small pieces of legislation into larger, more complex bills. As a sign of this complexity, the number of pages in the average bill has grown considerably. Both houses have also seen a marked increase in the number of roll call votes, in which members must go to the chambers to have their yeas and nays recorded.

Congress now meets throughout the year because members prefer to spend long weekends and week-long recesses back in their district or state, rather than to adjourn earlier in the year and spend more consecutive months at home. Although members may spend fewer days each week in Washington, they spend longer hours in session each day. The workday has grown from about five hours a day after World War II to about eight hours a day during the 1990s.

Senators and representatives actually spend less of their time on the floor than in committee meetings. The amount of time devoted to committee and subcommittee meetings increased dramatically, reaching a peak in the mid-1970s, when reorganization of the committee structure reduced the number of committees and subcommittees. Individual offices have also recorded an increase in the amount of mail received and sent, telephone calls, and visitors, all of which represent part of the congressional work load.

SEE ALSO

Bills; Committees; Legislative Reorganization Acts (1946 and 1970); Resolutions

FURTHER READING

Ornstein, Norman J., Thomas E. Mann, and Michael J. Malbin. *Vital Statistics on Congress.* Washington, D.C.: American Enterprise Institute, 1991.

Wright, Jim

☆ Born: December 22, 1922, Fort Worth, Tex.
☆ Political party: Democrat
☆ Representative from Texas: 1955–89
☆ House majority leader: 1977–87
☆ Speaker of the House: 1987–89

JIM WRIGHT once noted that Congress could "rise to heights of sparkling statesmanship, and it can sink to levels of crass mediocrity." Although never mediocre, Wright's own career as a representative, majority leader, and Speaker had its spectacular highs and lows. As Speaker, Wright pursued an activist legislative program in opposition to Republican Ronald Reagan in the White House. Together with the restored Democratic majority in the Senate, he pushed for increased social programs and stronger civil rights laws. Wright opposed the Reagan administration's support for the Nicaraguan Contras (the armed opposition to the communist-leaning Sandinista government) and drafted a peace plan that would let Central

America solve its own problems. In pursuit of his goals, Wright was never afraid to twist arms, to stretch the rules, and to otherwise use the powers of his office to their fullest. This approach earned him many opponents who resented his aggressive style.

In 1988 Representative Newt Gingrich (Republican–Georgia) raised questions about Wright's ethics, citing the royalties the Speaker had received from his book, *Reflections of a Public Man,* as a cover to evade House restrictions on outside income. The next year, after the House ethics committee investigated the charges and found merit behind them, Wright tearfully resigned as Speaker and as a member of the House.

SEE ALSO
Speaker of the House

FURTHER READING
Barry, John M. *The Ambition and the Power.* New York: Viking Penguin, 1989.
Wright, Jim. *Reflections of a Public Man.* Fort Worth, Tex.: Madison, 1984.

Yielding

ANY MEMBER of Congress who has been recognized by the presiding officer and is speaking may yield the floor to another speaker—or refuse to yield. If other members wish to interrupt the speaker, they will address the chair and ask, "Will the gentleman [or gentlewoman] from [the speaker's state] yield?" This device enables two members to engage in a colloquy, or back-and-forth debate, over a particular point. If the speaker wishes to continue his remarks after such an interruption, the speaker will stipulate that by yielding for a question, he is not giving up the right to regain the floor. Speakers also yield as a courtesy to other members who may have an amendment to introduce or a short statement to make and do not wish to remain for long in the chamber.

APPENDIX 1

TABLE OF CONGRESSES

(Senate listed above, House listed below in italics)

CONGRESS	YEARS & PRESIDENT(S)	MAJORITY PARTY	MINORITY PARTY	OTHERS	TOTAL
1st	1789–91	Pro-Administration–18	Anti-Administration–8		26
	Washington	*Pro-Administration–37*	*Anti-Administration–28*		*65*
2nd	1791–93	Federalist–16	Anti-Federalist–13	1 vacant	30
	Washington	*Federalist–39*	*Anti-Federalist–30*		*69*
3rd	1793–95	Federalist–16	Anti-Federalist–14		30
	Washington	*Federalist–54*	*Anti-Federalist–51*		*105*
4th	1795–97	Federalist–21	Democratic-Republican–11		32
	Washington	*Democratic-Republican–59*	*Federalist–47*		*106*
5th	1797–99	Federalist–22	Democratic-Republican–10		32
	J. Adams	*Federalist–57*	*Democratic-Republican–49*		*106*
6th	1799–1801	Federalist–22	Democratic-Republican–10		32
	J. Adams	*Federalist–60*	*Democratic-Republican–46*		*106*
7th	1801–03	Democratic-Republican–17	Federalist–15	2 vacant	34
	Jefferson	*Democratic-Republican–68*	*Federalist–38*	*1 vacant*	*107*
8th	1803–05	Democratic-Republican–25	Federalist–9		34
	Jefferson	*Democratic-Republican–103*	*Federalist–39*		*142*
9th	1805–07	Democratic-Republican–27	Federalist–7		34
	Jefferson	*Democratic-Republican–114*	*Federalist–28*		*142*
10th	1807–09	Democratic-Republican–28	Federalist–6		34
	Jefferson	*Democratic-Republican–116*	*Federalist–26*		*142*
11th	1809–11	Democratic-Republican–27	Federalist–7		34
	Madison	*Democratic-Republican–92*	*Federalist–50*		*142*
12th	1811–13	Democratic-Republican–30	Federalist–6		36
	Madison	*Democratic-Republican–107*	*Federalist–36*		*143*
13th	1813–15	Democratic-Republican–28	Federalist–8		36
	Madison	*Democratic-Republican–114*	*Federalist–68*		*182*
14th	1815–17	Democratic-Republican–26	Federalist–12		38
	Madison	*Democratic-Republican–119*	*Federalist–64*		*183*
15th	1817–19	Democratic-Republican–30	Federalist–12		42
	Monroe	*Democratic-Republican–146*	*Federalist–39*		*185*
16th	1819–21	Democratic-Republican–37	Federalist–9		46
	Monroe	*Democratic-Republican–160*	*Federalist–26*		*186*
17th	1821–23	Democratic-Republican–44	Federalist–4		48
	Monroe	*Democratic-Republican–155*	*Federalist–32*		*187*

CONGRESS	YEARS & PRESIDENT(S)	MAJORITY PARTY	MINORITY PARTY	OTHERS	TOTAL
18th	1823–25 Monroe	Democratic-Republican–43 *Democratic-Republican–189*	Federalist–5 *Federalist–24*		48 213
19th	1825–27 J. Q. Adams	Jacksonian–26 *Adams–109*	Adams–22 *Jacksonian–104*		48 213
20th	1827–29 J. Q. Adams	Jacksonian–27 *Jacksonian–113*	Adams–21 *Adams–100*		48 213
21st	1829–31 Jackson	Democrat–25 *Democrat–136*	National Republican–23 *National Republican–72*	5	48 213
22nd	1831–33 Jackson	Democrat–24 *Democrat–126*	National Republican–22 *National Republican–66*	2 21	48 213
23rd	1833–35 Jackson	National Republican–26 *Democrat–143*	Democrat–20 *National Republican–63*	2 34	48 240
24th	1835–37 Jackson	Democrat–26 *Democrat–143*	National Republican–24 *National Republican–75*	2 24	52 242
25th	1837–39 Van Buren	Democrat–35 *Democrat–128*	Whig–17 *Whig–100*	14	52 242
26th	1839–41 Van Buren	Democrat–30 *Democrat–125*	Whig–22 *Whig–109*	8	52 242
27th	1841–43 W. H. Harrison Tyler	Whig–29 *Whig–142*	Democrat–22 *Democrat–98*	1 vacant 2	52 242
28th	1843–45 Tyler	Whig–29 *Democrat–147*	Democrat–23 *Whig–72*	3	52 223
29th	1845–47 Polk	Democrat–34 *Democrat–142*	Whig–22 *Whig–79*	2 vacant *6 (1 vacant)*	58 228
30th	1847–49 Polk	Democrat–38 *Whig–116*	Whig–21 *Democrat–110*	1 4	60 230
31st	1849–51 Taylor Fillmore	Democrat–35 *Democrat–113*	Whig–25 *Whig–108*	2 *11 (1 vacant)*	62 233
32nd	1851–53 Fillmore	Democrat–36 *Democrat–127*	Whig–23 *Whig–85*	3 21	62 234
33rd	1853–55 Pierce	Democrat–38 *Democrat–157*	Whig–22 *Whig–71*	2 6	62 234
34th	1855–57 Pierce	Democrat–39 *Whig/Republican–100*	Whig/Republican–22 *Democrat–83*	1 51	62 234
35th	1857–59 Buchanan	Democrat–41 *Democrat–132*	Republican–20 *Republican–90*	5 15	66 237

CONGRESS	YEARS & PRESIDENT(S)	MAJORITY PARTY	MINORITY PARTY	OTHERS	TOTAL
36th	1859–61 Buchanan	Democrat–38 *Republican–116*	Republican–26 *Democrat–83*	2 (2 vacant) *39*	68 *238*
37th	1861–63 Lincoln	Republican–31 *Republican–108*	Democrat–15 *Democrat–44*	3 (1 vacant) *31*	50 *183*
38th	1863–65 Lincoln	Republican–33 *Republican–85*	Democrat–10 *Democrat–72*	9 *27*	52 *184*
39th	1865–67 Lincoln A. Johnson	Republican–39 *Republican–136*	Democrat–11 *Democrat–38*	4 *19*	54 *193*
40th	1867–69 A. Johnson	Republican–57 *Republican–173*	Democrat–9 *Democrat–47*	2 vacant *4 (2 vacant)*	68 *226*
41st	1869–71 Grant	Republican–62 *Republican–171*	Democrat–12 *Democrat–67*	*5*	74 *243*
42nd	1871–73 Grant	Republican–56 *Republican–136*	Democrat–17 *Democrat–104*	1 *3*	74 *143*
43rd	1873–75 Grant	Republican–47 *Republican–199*	Democrat–19 *Democrat–88*	7 (1 vacant) *5*	74 *292*
44th	1875–77 Grant	Republican–46 *Democrat–182*	Democrat–28 *Republican–103*	1 (1 vacant) *8*	76 *293*
45th	1877–79 Hayes	Republican–40 *Democrat–155*	Democrat–35 *Republican–136*	1 *2*	76 *293*
46th	1879–81 Hayes	Democrat–42 *Democrat–141*	Republican–33 *Republican–132*	1 *20*	76 *293*
47th	1881–83 Garfield Arthur	Republican–37 *Republican–151*	Democrat–37 *Democrat–128*	2 *14*	76 *293*
48th	1883–85 Arthur	Republican–38 *Democrat–196*	Democrat–36 *Republican–117*	2 *12*	76 *325*
49th	1885–87 Cleveland	Republican–42 *Democrat–182*	Democrat–34 *Republican–141*	*2*	76 *325*
50th	1887–89 Cleveland	Republican–39 *Democrat–167*	Democrat–37 *Republican–152*	*6*	76 *325*
51st	1889–91 B. Harrison	Republican–51 *Republican–179*	Democrat–37 *Democrat–152*	*1*	88 *332*
52nd	1891–93 B. Harrison	Republican–47 *Democrat–238*	Democrat–39 *Republican–86*	2 *8*	88 *332*
53rd	1893–95 Cleveland	Democrat–44 *Democrat–218*	Republican–40 *Republican–124*	4 *14*	88 *356*

★ A P P E N D I X 1 ★

CONGRESS	YEARS & PRESIDENT(S)	MAJORITY PARTY	MINORITY PARTY	OTHERS	TOTAL
54th	1895–97 Cleveland	Republican–44 *Republican–254*	Democrat–40 *Democrat–93*	6 *10*	90 *356*
55th	1897–99 McKinley	Republican–44 *Republican–206*	Democrat–34 *Democrat–124*	12 *27*	90 *357*
56th	1899–1901 McKinley	Republican–53 *Republican–187*	Democrat–26 *Democrat–161*	10 (1 vacant) *9*	90 *357*
57th	1901–03 McKinley T. Roosevelt	Republican–56 *Republican–200*	Democrat–32 *Democrat–151*	2 *6*	90 *357*
58th	1903–05 T. Roosevelt	Republican–57 *Republican–297*	Democrat–33 *Democrat–176*	*8*	90 *386*
59th	1905–07 T. Roosevelt	Republican–58 *Republican–215*	Democrat–32 *Democrat–135*		90 *386*
60th	1907–09 T. Roosevelt	Republican–61 *Republican–223*	Democrat–31 *Democrat–167*	*1*	92 *391*
61st	1909–11 Taft	Republican–60 *Republican–219*	Democrat–32 *Democrat–172*		92 *391*
62nd	1911–13 Taft	Republican–52 *Democrat–230*	Democrat–44 *Republican–162*	*2*	96 *394*
63rd	1913–15 Wilson	Democrat–51 *Democrat–291*	Republican–44 *Republican–134*	1 *10*	96 *435*
64th	1915–17 Wilson	Democrat–56 *Democrat–230*	Republican–40 *Republican–196*	*9*	96 *435*
65th	1917–19 Wilson	Democrat–54 *Republican–215*	Republican–42 *Democrat–214*	*6*	96 *435*
66th	1919–21 Wilson	Republican–49 *Republican–240*	Democrat–47 *Democrat–192*	*2 (1 vacant)*	96 *435*
67th	1921–23 Harding	Republican–59 *Republican–302*	Democrat–37 *Democrat–131*	*2*	96 *435*
68th	1923–25 Harding Coolidge	Republican–53 *Republican–225*	Democrat–42 *Democrat–207*	1 *3*	96 *435*
69th	1925–27 Coolidge	Republican–54 *Republican–247*	Democrat–41 *Democrat–183*	1 *5*	96 *435*
70th	1927–29 Coolidge	Republican–48 *Republican–238*	Democrat–46 *Democrat–194*	1 (1 vacant) *3*	96 *435*
71st	1929–31 Hoover	Republican–56 *Republican–270*	Democrat–39 *Democrat–164*	1 *1*	96 *435*

CONGRESS	YEARS & PRESIDENT(S)	MAJORITY PARTY	MINORITY PARTY	OTHERS	TOTAL
72nd	1931–33 Hoover	Republican–48 *Democrat–217*	Democrat–47 *Republican–217*	1 *1*	96 *435*
73rd	1933–35 F. Roosevelt	Democrat–59 *Democrat–313*	Republican–36 *Republican–117*	1 *5*	96 *435*
74th	1935–37 F. Roosevelt	Democrat–69 *Democrat–322*	Republican–25 *Republican–103*	2 *10*	96 *435*
75th	1937–39 F. Roosevelt	Democrat–76 *Democrat–334*	Republican–16 *Republican–88*	4 *13*	96 *435*
76th	1939–41 F. Roosevelt	Democrat–69 *Democrat–262*	Republican–23 *Republican–169*	4 *4*	96 *435*
77th	1941–43 F. Roosevelt	Democrat–66 *Democrat–267*	Republican–28 *Republican–162*	2 *3*	96 *435*
78th	1943–45 F. Roosevelt	Democrat–57 *Democrat–222*	Republican–38 *Republican–209*	1 *2*	96 *435*
79th	1945–47 F. Roosevelt Truman	Democrat–57 *Democrat–242*	Republican–38 *Republican–191*	1 *2*	96 *435*
80th	1947–49 Truman	Republican–51 *Republican–246*	Democrat–45 *Democrat–188*	*1*	96 *435*
81st	1949–51 Truman	Democrat–54 *Democrat–263*	Republican–42 *Republican–171*	*1*	96 *435*
82nd	1951–53 Truman	Democrat–49 *Democrat–235*	Republican–47 *Republican–199*	*1*	96 *435*
83rd	1953–55 Eisenhower	Republican–48 *Republican–221*	Democrat–47 *Democrat–213*	1 *1*	96 *435*
84th	1955–57 Eisenhower	Democrat–47 *Democrat–232*	Republican–47 *Republican–203*	2	96 *435*
85th	1957–59 Eisenhower	Democrat–49 *Democrat–234*	Republican–47 *Republican–201*	*1*	96 *435*
86th	1959–61 Eisenhower	Democrat–65 *Democrat–283*	Republican–35 *Republican–153*	*1*	100 *437*
87th	1961–63 Kennedy	Democrat–64 *Democrat–263*	Republican–36 *Republican–174*		100 *437*
88th	1963–65 Kennedy L. Johnson	Democrat–66 *Democrat–259*	Republican–34 *Republican–176*		100 *435*
89th	1965–67 L. Johnson	Democrat–68 *Democrat–295*	Republican–32 *Republican–140*		100 *435*

☆ A P P E N D I X 1 ☆

CONGRESS	YEARS & PRESIDENT(S)	MAJORITY PARTY	MINORITY PARTY	OTHERS	TOTAL
90th	1967–69 L. Johnson	Democrat–64 *Democrat–247*	Republican–36 *Republican–189*	*1 vacant*	100 *435*
91st	1969–71 Nixon	Democrat–57 *Democrat–243*	Republican–43 *Republican–192*		100 *435*
92nd	1971–73 Nixon	Democrat–54 *Democrat–255*	Republican–44 *Republican–180*	2	100 *435*
93rd	1973–75 Nixon Ford	Democrat–56 *Democrat–242*	Republican–42 *Republican–192*	2 *1*	100 *435*
94th	1975–77 Ford	Democrat–60 *Democrat–291*	Republican–38 *Republican–144*	2	100 *435*
95th	1977–79 Carter	Democrat–61 *Democrat–292*	Republican–38 *Republican–143*	1	100 *435*
96th	1979–81 Carter	Democrat–58 *Democrat–277*	Republican–41 *Republican–158*	1	100 *435*
97th	1981–83 Reagan	Republican–53 *Democrat–242*	Democrat–46 *Republican–192*	1	100 *435*
98th	1983–85 Reagan	Republican–54 *Democrat–269*	Democrat–46 *Republican–166*		100 *435*
99th	1985–87 Reagan	Republican–53 *Democrat–253*	Democrat–47 *Republican–182*		100 *435*
100th	1987–89 Reagan	Democrat–55 *Democrat–258*	Republican–45 *Republican–177*		100 *435*
101st	1989–91 Bush	Democrat–55 *Democrat–260*	Republican–45 *Republican–174*	*1 vacant*	100 *435*
102nd	1991–93 Bush	Democrat–56 *Democrat–267*	Republican–44 *Republican–167*	*1*	100 *435*
103rd	1993–95 Clinton	Democrat–57 *Democrat–258*	Republican–43 *Republican–176*	*1*	100 *435*

Source: Martis, Kenneth C. *The Historical Atlas of Political Parties in the United States Congress, 1789–89.* New York: Macmillan, 1989.

APPENDIX 2

VISITING CONGRESS

Although you can follow the debates of the House and Senate on television, there is much more of Congress to see during a visit to Capitol Hill. Free public tours of the Capitol are available without appointment during the day, and the galleries are open as long as the House and Senate are in session. (From outside the Capitol you can tell which house is meeting because a flag will fly over the House or Senate wing whenever that chamber is in session.) To obtain gallery passes, go to the offices of your senator or representative in the Senate and House office buildings. Subways and tunnels link these office buildings to the Capitol.

Because Congress does the largest share of its work in committee, you should visit one of the many committee hearings in addition to the floor debates. Each morning the Washington newspapers publish lists of open committee meetings, the subjects of the testimony, and the rooms where these committees will meet (in one of the House or Senate office buildings). Seats are usually available, but those hearings that draw the most media attention will also draw the largest audience, and visitors sometimes must wait in line for available space.

Spend some time on the Capitol grounds as well, to view the Mall from the terraces on the West Front, explore the grotto designed by Frederick Law Olmsted, survey the variety of trees (which are labeled by species), and visit the Botanical Gardens at the base of Capitol Hill. Surrounding the Capitol's East Front plaza, every building that you see represents some function that once took place within the Capitol, including the Supreme Court (which left the Capitol for its own building in 1935) and the

Library of Congress (which moved into the first of its three main buildings in 1897). Like the Capitol and congressional office buildings, the Supreme Court and Library of Congress are open and have public exhibition areas.

The Capitol grounds are regularly the scene of much activity: the motorcade of a visiting dignitary, the television cameras set up on the lawn for news broadcasts, school bands performing on the Capitol steps, demonstrators promoting a cause, or the National Symphony Orchestra entertaining in honor of a national holiday. As a citizen, you are a constituent of Congress and a welcomed guest. Make the most of your visit.

A horse-drawn trolley at the East Front of the Capitol, around 1900.

DOING RESEARCH ON CONGRESS: FURTHER READING

Many of the entries in this volume contain references to books dealing with that specific subject. The following volumes will be useful for further study.

Overviews of Congress in General

Bernstein, Richard B., and Jerome Agel. *Into the Third Century: The Congress*. New York: Walker, 1989.

Biographical Directory of the United States Congress, 1774–1989. Washington D.C.: Government Printing Office, 1989.

Congressional Quarterly. *Guide to Congress*. Washington, D.C.: Congressional Quarterly, 1991.

Davidson, Roger H., and Richard C. Sachs, eds. *Understanding Congress: Research Perspectives*. Washington, D.C.: Government Printing Office, 1991.

Josephy, Alvin. *On the Hill: A History of the United States Congress*. New York: Simon & Schuster, 1979.

Oleszek, Walter J. *Congressional Procedures and the Policy Process*. Washington, D.C.: Congressional Quarterly, 1989.

The House of Representatives

Cheney, Richard B., and Lynne V. Cheney. *Kings of the Hill: Power and Personality in the House of Representatives*. New York: Continuum, 1983.

Currie, James. *The United States House of Representatives*. Malabar, Fla.: Krieger, 1987.

Galloway, George B., and Sidney Wise. *History of the House of Representatives*. New York: Crowell, 1976.

McNeil, Neil. *Forge of Democracy: The House of Representatives*. New York: McKay, 1963.

Ragsdale, Bruce A. *The House of Representatives*. New York: Chelsea House, 1989.

White, William S. *Home Place: The Story of the U.S. House of Representatives*. Boston: Houghton Mifflin, 1965.

The Senate

Baker, Richard A. *The Senate: A Bicentennial History*. Malabar, Fla.: Krieger, 1987.

Baker, Richard A., and Roger H. Davidson, eds. *First among Equals: Outstanding Senate Leaders of the Twentieth Century*. Washington, D.C.: Congressional Quarterly, 1991.

Byrd, Robert C. *The Senate, 1789–1989: Addresses on the History of the United States Senate*. 2 vols. Washington, D.C.: Government Printing Office, 1989–1991.

Hess, Stephen. *The Ultimate Insiders: U.S. Senators in the National Media*. Washington, D.C.: Brookings Institution, 1986.

Reedy, George E. *The U.S. Senate: Paralysis or a Search for Consensus?* New York: Crown, 1986.

Ritchie, Donald A. *The Senate*. New York: Chelsea House, 1988.

White, William S. *Citadel: The Story of the U.S. Senate*. New York: Harper, 1956.

Using Congressional Documents

Congress publishes extensive documentation on its activities. These published documents date back to the 1st Congress in 1789 but have multiplied over time as the work load of Congress has increased. The starting place for most research on Congress is the *Congressional Record*, which is a record of most everything spoken and done on the floor of the House and Senate. The index to the *Record* identifies each member's speeches, together with bills and resolutions introduced and the subjects that Congress debated. The *Congressional Record* covers all debates since 1873. For earlier debates, the *Annals of Congress* covers 1789 to 1824; the *Register of Debates* covers 1825 to 1837; and the *Congressional Globe* covers 1833 to 1873. In addition, both the House and Senate publish journals that provide summaries of all floor activities, including bills introduced, referred to committee, amended, voted upon, and signed into law. These journals do not include members' speeches. The Senate also publishes an executive journal containing all nominations and treaties.

Congress does a great deal of its work in committee and publishes the transcripts of most of the hearings it holds in public. The Congressional Information Service (CIS) publishes *CIS U.S. Congressional Hearing Index,* which lists each of these hearings by committee, by subject, and by witness. CIS has also produced similar guides to the previously unpublished hearings of the House and Senate (*CIS Index to Unpublished U.S. Senate Committee Hearings* and *CIS Index to Unpublished U.S. House of Representatives Committee Hearings*). In addition to hearing transcripts, Congress publishes many reports to furnish background material in support of bills, to record members' experiences during foreign travel, and to cover a wide range of other legislative interests. These reports can be located through the *CIS Serial Set Index.* The *Congressional Record,* hearings, reports, and CIS indexes and microfiche editions of congressional documents can be found in the government documents section of most large public libraries and university libraries.

Congressional Quarterly Inc. (CQ) also produces a variety of helpful tools for research on Congress, including a weekly magazine and an annual almanac for each session of Congress since 1945. CQ's *Guide to Congress* and *Congress A to Z* are handy one-volume encyclopedias on congressional history, practices, and procedures. CQ's multivolume *Congress and the Nation* series summarizes the wide range of legislation Congress has dealt with since 1945. In addition, CQ publishes a variety of books about specific congressional and political issues that are available at most larger libraries.

The old Congressional Library in the Capitol, 1897.

INDEX

Donald A. Ritchie is associate historian of the U.S. Senate. He is the author of *Press Gallery: Congress and the Washington Correspondents* (which won the Richard Leopold Prize of the Organization of American Historians), *A Necessary Fence—The Senate's First Century, The Senate, The U.S. Constitution,* and *James M. Landis: Dean of the Regulators.* He is coauthor of a high school textbook, *History of a Free Nation,* and a curriculum package entitled *American History and National Security.* Dr. Ritchie has contributed articles to many reference works on the Congress and in 1990 he won the James Madison prize for the best article on the history of the federal government, presented by the Society for History in the Federal Government. Dr. Ritchie has served on the editorial boards of *The Public Historian* and the National Council on Public History, was editor of *The Maryland Historian,* and is series editor of the Twayne oral history series. A member of the council of the Organization of American Historians and a former president of the Oral History Association, he has taught at the University of Maryland, George Mason University, and the Cornell in Washington program.